Beatrix Campbell was born in Carlisle in 1947. Her parents met in Holland during the Second World War, and both are active communists. When Beatrix Campbell was fourteen she joined the CND Aldermaston march and also became a communist. After leaving school she sought her fortune in London. She worked for ten years on the *Morning Star* and from 1979 was a news reporter on the London magazine *Time Out*, leaving at the end of a long occupation and strike in 1981 to defend equal pay for all and workers' right to consultation over investment. She then joined the majority of the *Time Out* staff in setting up the successful, co-operatively owned magazine *City Limits*, where she still works, as a reporter. Her work has also appeared in the *Guardian*, the *New Statesman* and on television. Women's liberation became from 1970 one of the organising principles of her life. During the last fifteen years she has worked for socialist-feminism, writing and speaking about sexual politics and a feminist approach to trade unionism and economic strategy. She was a founder member of the women's liberation journal *Red Rag*, set up in 1971, and has contributed to several feminist and socialist anthologies. With Anna Coote, she co-authored the bestselling book *Sweet Freedom*. Virago published her highly acclaimed *Wigan Pier Revisited*, a brilliant exposé of poverty and politics in Britain, in 1984. She lives in London.

THE IRON LADIES
Why Do Women Vote Tory?

BEATRIX CAMPBELL

To Margaret Bluman
with love

Published by VIRAGO PRESS Limited 1987
41 William IV Street, London WC2N 4DB

Copyright © Beatrix Campbell 1987

British Library Cataloguing in Publication Data

Campbell, Beatrix
   The iron ladies: why do women vote Tory.
   1. Conservative party   2. Women in politics
   – Great Britain
   I. Title
   324.24104   JN1129.C7

ISBN 0-86068-689-2

Typeset by Rowland Phototypesetting Limited
Bury St Edmunds, Suffolk
Printed in Great Britain by
Cox and Wyman Limited, Reading, Berkshire

CONTENTS

ACKNOWLEDGEMENTS

For all their clues, comments and contacts thanks to Margaret Bluman, who helped work it all out, my sister Tina Webb, Sally Alexander, Catherine Hall, Ruth Lister, Freda Tallantyre, Raphael Samuel, Andrew Gamble, Lewis Minkin, Cynthia Cockburn, Rosalind Delmar, Anna Davin, Zoë Fairbairns, Sara Maitland, Richard Johnson, Bill Schwarz, Stephen Hayward, Angela John, Donald Stewart, Jessica Sacret, Jenny Hurstfield, June Statham, Dr Sarah Street and Helen Langley of the Bodleian Library, Cath Farrell at the Equal Opportunities Commission, Sarah Matthews at MORI, my parents Catherina and Jim Barnes, and last but never least my brother Jimmy Barnes for lots of cups of coffee and lots of laughs. Thanks to Ursula Owen and the Virago workers for nursing the idea, and to Ruthie Petrie and Jane Parkin for heroic editorial work.

Over fifty women were interviewed for the book, from three areas, London, the Borders and Birmingham, ranging from voters, party activists and officials, to councillors and senior politicians in the House of Lords and the Commons: I'm grateful for their time and for their trust. Thanks, too, for the co-operation of Emma Nicholson and librarian Joan West at Conservative Central Office.

INTRODUCTION

The first thing to say about the Tory woman is that we all think we know what she is, and yet she is a remarkably unstudied political animal. We take her for granted, and we don't take her seriously.

She has been the backbone of the Conservative Party organisation and her vote has guaranteed its electoral successes – but she has been treated as a bit of a joke.

The right depend on her but don't take her seriously, for sexist reasons, and the left can't stand her and don't take her seriously, for equally sexist reasons. What about feminism though? Certainly, within the Women's Liberation Movement there could be no endorsement of snidey sexism, but perhaps we have not known *how* to take her seriously: did we want to find common ground, or did we hesitate to discover that there might be any? Was the problem that old tension between the feminine and the feminist? Tory women, socialists and feminists all get twitchy in the middle of that tension.

In Britain, women's politics are strongly aligned to the traditions of the right and the left: the politics of femininity are most fervently endorsed by the anti-egalitarian right, and feminism tends to belong to liberal or socialist politics; that doesn't put it straightforwardly on the left because feminism has a dialectical relationship to the left – it is in it and against it. But so strong are those alignments that women's politics have often been defined by them.

If there has been an indifference among women of the left to women of the right, that may have been because we've had other things on our mind – we have been busy creating our own politics and recovering our own history. But the endurance of a formidable phalanx of Tory women demands serious scrutiny. This book is part of growing attention among feminists to the question: How does

Conservatism enable women to make sense of themselves and their world?

An obvious question, too, is why a political tradition so little associated with the emancipation of women should be so strongly rooted among women. If the Tory Party had been forced to rely on the vote that Labour secures from women it would not have survived electorally, nor would it be able to represent itself, as it does, as the 'national party'.

To answer the question with anything other than 'These women have been duped' or 'They're suffering from false consciousness' makes it necessary to jettison the notion that only the movements of the left which formally claim to emancipate women actually appear to women to advance their interests. Women's support for the right cannot be explained solely by reference to their class interests, religious beliefs or biology – there is nothing inherently conservative about women.

There has been a tendency on both the right and the left to make an assumption – one which now more than ever seems no more than an excuse – that women's conservatism lies in their absence from wage labour. This is a self-fulfilling prophecy, given the long history of, at best, indifference and at worst exclusion of women from the ranks and rewards of workers. There has to be another approach, however, one that searches for the ways in which Conservatism appears to women to help them make sense of themselves and the world around them, and helps them find a way of being in a world they don't control.

This approach is most useful if we go back to the beginning and work from the extraordinary development of a mass Tory base among women 100 years ago. It was, in fact, the remarkable achievement of an auxiliary to the Conservative Party, the Primrose League, that drew thousands of women into the political sphere. It enabled women to become social beings before their claims for citizenship were finally and fully realised in the twentieth century. It was the Primrose League, above all, which constituted the base for the Conservative Party as a modern mass party and it was the Primrose League which put women in there at the beginning. Women, in other words, were active in the modernisation of the Conservative Party from a cliquey élite to a mass party.

The modern Conservative Party continued to hold on to that tradition, which placed women at the centre of its ideology of separate spheres for men and women, and designated the 'domestic' organisation of the Tory Party as women's special sphere. The Labour Party, in contrast, came into existence to represent the labour movement in the political and state institutions. It was designed to represent *organised* labour, which by the twentieth century had defeated women's demands for equal access to work and wages. Ironically, then, the formally egalitarian political party had its roots in a masculinised political tradition, while the anti-egalitarian party assigned to women a special place. Both traditions were patriarchal: for Labourism to deliver *for* women it has to be transformed *by* women; but the Conservative Party created a culture that embraced women, that celebrated their subordination.

So, Conservative women have been strong and yet subordinate, idealistic about the power of women and yet pessimistic about the power of politics to improve their lot. This fatalism provided an important element of emotional and political survival: it rested on an affirmation of sexual difference, and it profiled personal responsibility in a chaotic world. Women sought safety in their own survival skills, in religion, in their separate sphere, and among women.

After the Second World War, the Conservative Party undertook a new phase of modernisation, faced with the irreversible challenge of the mass working-class vote. The Conservative Party rapidly re-grouped and placed women at the centre of its attack on Labour and post-war austerity: the Tories promised to 'liberate' the house-wife. Labour held on to its following among women but failed to reach beyond its loyal base, not least because of its repudiation of labour movement women's demands for economic equality at the moment of women's most visible economic contribution to a crisis-torn economy – the war. The all-party repudiation of a feminist programme for women left the Tories with the 'feminine' political initiative.

Even before the war, however, there were signs of a 'women's agenda' within the party, which erupted in the late 1950s and 1960s to challenge the party's powers-that-be and which associated women with the embryonic emergence of the new right, an anti-modernist axis which became Thatcherism. This agenda was almost entirely expressed in the language of law and order and moral authoritarian-ism. The law and order debates which punctuated Conservative women's conferences from the late 1930s were remarkably sexualised. It was *women's fear* which provided the emotional ignition for the law and order debates, and which seemed to induce bewildered silence, or worse, in the enlightened 'reformism' of the party leadership.

Although women's insubordination in the party encouraged the rise of Thatcherism, Thatcherism did not represent a triumph for women. The evidence since 1979 suggests that Thatcherism appealed strongly to both *men and women*, though often for different reasons. But something is happening to Britain's gender gap. Historically, more men than women supported the Labour Party and more women than men supported the Tory Party. But there is another feature to the gender gap: on social issues ranging from unemployment and sexual reform, to nuclear power and nuclear weapons, women tend to be the more progressive sex. There is evidence that women's alignment to the right has been destabilising. Women have tended to move away from the right, while men have been moving towards it.

Throughout the history of the modern Conservative Party women have been in its mind. But does that tell us enough about what has been in the minds of Conservative women? No, because the party's representation of women has tended to imagine a homogenous group with fixed ideas and aspirations and a unified way of life. Looking in more detail at themes like the family and sex, equality, peace and power, it becomes evident that there is no stereotype of the Conservative woman. She is not epitomised by Mary Whitehouse or Victoria Gillick or Margaret Thatcher, the three populist heroines of the right. You never can tell, she may admire – or abhor – all or none of them.

But what also became apparent talking to the fifty or so Conservative women I interviewed for this book was a profound pessimism about *all* political parties. They didn't seem to think *any* were much good for women. If I were Margaret Thatcher I'd be very worried about that.

This book takes Conservative women seriously. Although it does not share their perspective, it looks for what they see as well as what I see.

THE PRIMROSE LEAGUE

The story of the Primrose League is in part the story of the Tory Party's creation as a modern, mass party in the very moment which threatened its demise – the era of democracy.

In the 1880s, the party was faced with a dramatic contradiction: its failure to create a rank and file movement after the 1867 Reform Act jeopardised its ability to capitalise on its great triumph – imperial domination of the world. According to Janet Robb, whose book *The Primrose League 1883–1906*[1] long stood as the only history of this extraordinary movement, the Tories themselves were oblivious to the need for a new social base. There was 'no attempt to make the rank and file themselves participants in the new glories of the Disraeli regime in realising the magnificent dream of empire,' she writes. 'Here was the opportunity for the Tories to find the urban equivalent for the old manorial fidelity and they missed it completely. The Tory rank and file was expected to cheer and vote, while the Liberal rank and file were soldiers in the thick of the battle.'

The survival of the Tories amidst the new electorate created during the Disraeli era, which ended in 1880, was by no means certain then. Could they find a gladiator strong enough to challenge Gladstone, the Liberal leader, at the hustings? Were they equipped to challenge the Liberals' innovations in the cities, or rather the popularity of a new mode of political organisation particularly associated with Joseph Chamberlain, the great municipal reformer. His Liberal Party apparatus in Birmingham became the model of the modern political party. Known as the Birmingham caucus, Chamberlain's party stitched up the city with an elaborate network of hundreds of rank and file activists structured around a form of democratic centralism. The Tories, who thought this was cheating, had nothing with which to challenge the Liberals among the two million new urban electors.

According to the Conservative Party historian Robert Blake, Disraeli's great achievement was to promote patriotism, which fitted more easily with his notion of 'one nation' than issues of social reform, and which also represented the repudiation of class war. One of the great Disraelian themes was the equation between conservatism and 'the inchoate, half-romantic, half-predatory emotions and ideas inspired by the idea of empire during the last quarter of the nineteenth century. While these ideas remained vague and almost mystical they had an appeal to the imagination, which constituted one of the party's great assets.'[2]

But the mystique of imperialism needed the Primrose League, the first empire loyalists, to succeed where Disraeli had failed – to share the success among the masses!

But we are running ahead of our story. Disraeli was too old to recreate the party on his ideological foundations. His successors, the young lions like Randolph Churchill, while never quite fulfilling their promise, were nevertheless the bridgehead between the party of the past and the mass party which the Tories became. If nothing else they created the Primrose League, and inadvertently brought thousands of women into politics for the first time. Women of course could not vote, but if they could not engage in politics on their own account, as Primrose Leaguers they were to engineer an impeccable electoral machine for the Conservative Party. And it was the Primrose League which was 'among other things the great, the greatest promoter of the "socialisation" of politics'.[3] The significance of this achievement becomes apparent when compared to the Tories' sloth in squaring up to the new facts of political life – the creation of a new electorate after the 1867 and 1885 Reform Acts, which enfranchised a majority of working men in the boroughs.

The modernisation of Conservatism had already begun with the creation of the National Union of Conservative and Constitutional Associations in 1867. Until then political organisation had been orchestrated by the London clubs – the Carlton was and is a Tory citadel – but the party leadership was neither attentive to the need to organise the new voters, nor was it well disposed towards the incipient political challenge of the National Union. The need to create a mass popular base was recognised by a young barrister called John Gorst, a great believer in working-class conservatism and the first leader of the National Union to take on board the new electorate.[4] His base was in the constituencies while the power remained – then as now – in the hands of Central Office and the party leaders. His problem was to 'satisfy and harness a party which still remained predominantly landed and whose funds still derived from the purses of the great territorial magnates'.[5]

The urban Party leaders were still excluded from the social circuit of the country houses and London society 'where party affairs were still settled over port'. According to Blake, the notion of Tory democracy meant more middle-class control over the party machine and policies designed to appeal to working-class voters; it did not mean direct participation in policy-making by the working class or, indeed, the urban middle class. It was 'about party organisation just as much as sanitary legislation for the lower orders'. But by 1880 Gorst had failed to transform the relationship between the leadership and the National Union; a new national infrastructure to register and canvass voters had still not been created. The Tories lost the 1880 general election, which was 'conducted amidst the maximum of incoherence and confusion'.[6] In the early 1880s the National Union secured some symbolic concessions from the party leadership, but it remained subordinate and 'went quietly to sleep until 1903'.[7]

A clue to the state of the party is provided by a special conference called in 1886 to consider two vital issues: party organisation and Home Rule for Ireland. It was chaired by Ellis Ashmead Bartlett, MP who was reported as saying that the party had 'clearly fallen behind the exigencies of the times'. In the wake of the 1867 and 1885 Reform Acts 'it has been felt that a new and wider and more perfect organisation is required. Especially was it felt that our organisation needed broadening and popularising – (Hear Hear) – in view of the greatly increased power which has been given to what are termed the working classes.'

Enter what was known as the Fourth Party, the boisterous Parliamentary faction around Randolph Churchill, which challenged the party leadership not so much for its politics as for its style of leadership.

Churchill wore the mantle of Disraeli, talking the language of Tory democracy. It mattered less that Churchill's politics could not be differentiated from the leadership, and more that the pressure of the young oppositionists shifted the leadership towards a recognition that the working-class voter had to be addressed. Most important of all, the leadership of the party was never hijacked from the aristocrats – Churchill himself was part of that class. The triumph of the new Toryism lay in the creation of an alliance between the aristocracy and the urban working class, rather than in the defeat of the aristocracy by the constituency-based National Union.

Why not start a Primrose League?

In 1883, Churchill and his Fourth Party buddies conceived the idea of a memorial to Disraeli – the Primrose League. A great Victorian hostess, Lady Dorothy Nevill, recalls its birth:

> [The League] in a way originated at my luncheon-table, at which on Sundays many leading lights of the more militant section of the Conservative Party used to assemble, and here it was that Sir Henry Drummond Wolff, Lord Randolph Churchill and Sir Algernon Borthwick (now Lord Glenesk) first conceived the idea of moulding into a compact body the more active and energetic partisans of the newer and more dramatic school of conservatism.[8]

Jennie (Lady Randolph) Churchill remembered that at the time 'the Fourth Party was in a kind of limbo', and that while sitting in Parliament wearing a primrose on the anniversary of Disraeli's death, came up with an idea: why not start a primrose league? ' "Let's go off and do it at once,"' Randolph answered.[9] And they did – the men became the Grand Council of the Primrose League.

At first, according to Lady Dorothy Nevill, it was only to be another club of

> young and enterprising conservatives, which, whilst requiring adherence to the main principles of the party, would yet be of such a broad-minded nature as to enlist the sympathies of many who had hitherto looked upon conservative associations as close corporations of landlords and parsons.[10]

The men's Grand Council gathered their wives, mothers, cousins, some of them already stalwarts of the social and political circuit, into their own Ladies Grand Council. Perhaps the Primrose League institutionalised the rites of the great Tory hostesses, women who exercised political power by proxy, as personified by Lady Firebrace in Disraeli's novel *Sybil*. Confidante and conspirator among the most powerful of men, she was a woman from whom nothing was a secret, not even 'the inmost mind of the sovereign; there was not a royal prejudice that was not mapped in her secret inventory; the cabinets of the whigs and the clubs of the tories, she had the "open sesame" to all of them'.[11] But little did the men know then what these Primrose League Dames would become.

The first meeting of the Ladies Grand Council, which included Lady Dorothy and her daughter Meresia, who later became its treasurer, took place at Lady Borthwick's home. Jennie Churchill was an enthusiast from the start, and after the League's statutes had been drawn up, Sir Henry Drummond Wolff arrived at Blenheim Palace, where she was staying at the time, 'to initiate us. All the female members of the family who happened to be there enrolled as Dames, and were given badges and a numbered diploma. Mine was No. 11. The Duchess of Marlborough [Randolph's mother] was made president of the Ladies' Grand Council.' Although in its first year membership of the League and the wearing of its badges 'exposed one to much chaff, not to say ridicule', Jennie decided that 'as a "Dame" I was determined to do all I could to further its aims'. Her faith was rewarded, and in retrospect she reckoned that the League had 'materially helped to keep the Conservative Party in power 20 years'.[12]

One of the ways in which the League, and the Ladies in particular, did this was in providing the Tories with the machinery of a modern mass party. The electioneering Ladies could 'mobilise the great body of vaguely conservative and definitely traditional sentiment which the old party organisation of the Tories had failed to galvanise into action'.

The general electoral imperatives facing the Tories were the Reform Acts which created a new electorate, prior to which 'parties had hardly existed outside the walls of Parliament'. And the particular ignition was the regulation of elections by the 1883 Corrupt Practices Act, which attempted to curb intimidation, control bribery and make it easier and cheaper to enter Parliament. It was this Act which compelled the Conservative Party to become a modern political party, an assembly of voluntary activists constantly working for the cause. No longer could candidates employ hordes – sometimes thousands – of canvassers to register the voters, buy their votes and distribute party propaganda. 'The voluntary worker in the constituency, organised by a body like the Primrose League, and the party headquarters, with their large financial resources and supply of posters and leaflets, became for the first time the key to electioneering.'

Although the League's principles were large they were vague – God, England's institutions and Empire – but not so vague as to blur the clarity of their allegiance: they were anti-Radical. And although the League quickly dropped 'Tory' from its title, it was never other than a blindly Tory activist auxiliary. As early as 1883 it was the women who became the party's election corps. In June, the League asked Central Office

> to supply the Ladies' committee with the names of the residents of East St Pancras in order that the request of the political secretary for the aid of the Ladies Branch in the canvass of this constituency be carried out.

The scale of the problem was laid before the Ladies Grand Council's inaugural meeting in 1885 when a Fourth Party man and future Tory Party leader, Arthur Balfour, described the pressure on the party created by a vast new electorate in the countryside 'totally devoid of political principles and political knowledge' and yet the Conservatives were 'too much disposed to inaction'. It was vital, he said, to 'shake off the torpor' which had for too long afflicted Tories. Even the party leader, Sir Stafford Northcote, known as the Goat, recognised the potential of the League in organising during elections. Only a year earlier, however, the Parliamentary gentlemen had refused to amend the 1884 Reform Bill so that 'words importing to the male gender' might be interpreted as including women too. Some Tory leaders by then acknowledged that selective woman suffrage, at least, was inevitable. But not yet awhile, even if they were to come to depend on women to win their elections for them.

Lord Hamilton told the Ladies that they were not expected to take part 'in the rough and tumble of the contest' but that is exactly what they did. In 1884 a Radical candidate entered the lists in South Kensington five days before the election, facing the Tories with a terrific problem in mobilising and distributing voting papers. According to the *Primrose League Gazette* of 15 October 1887, 'At once some 80 or 100 ladies enrolled themselves, and so admirably, so steadfastly, so efficiently did they work that in less than 24 hours, 10,000 voting cards were written, directed, stamped and posted.'

There was no escaping us

The year 1885 was perhaps the most memorable. That was the year in which the League's electoral prowess became visible, and that was the year when the League's women stole the show. The star was Jennie Churchill. She already

> knew the stimulation and fascination of politics for women
> eager to escape the routine of running a household and to move
> away from personal problems into the realm of the unexpected,
> of association with people of all classes and kinds, of
> commitment to a cause.[13]

She was already regarded as 'the fifth member of the Fourth Party' and was used to accompanying her husband around the country, spending hours 'talking platitudes to the wives and daughters who have been invited to meet her'.

In 1885 Lord Randolph was promoted into the government and had to seek re-election in his Woodstock constituency. But he couldn't be bothered to campaign: 'He had neither the time nor the energy to work for votes, even though it was a key election and the Liberals went out to defeat him.' Since Churchill had decided to stay away, Jennie ran the election for him, assisted by her friend Lady Georgiana Curzon, who proved particularly useful because of the terrain. 'The distances to cover were great and motors were not yet in existence', so Lady Georgiana brought her tandem

> and we scoured the countryside with our smart turnout, the
> horses gaily decorated with ribbons of pink and brown,
> Randolph's racing colours. Sometimes we would drive into the
> fields, and, getting down, climb the hayricks, falling on our
> unwary prey at his work. There was no escaping us.[14]

She put up at Woodstock's Bear Hotel, the election headquarters, and

> there we had daily confabulations with the friends and
> Members of Parliament who had come to help. Revelling in the

hustle and bustle of the committee rooms, marshalling our
forces and hearing the hourly reports of how the campaign
was progressing, I felt like a general holding a council of war
with his staff in the heat of battle.[15]

The campaign was as grand as it was dedicated to detail, and
individual voters were meticulously targeted, like the man whose

wife, a wicked abominable Radical, was trying to influence her
husband, who we thought secure, to vote the wrong way. At once
they must be visited and our arsenal of arguments brought to
bear upon them.

Her speeches were so similar to Randolph's in style that some
observers began to wonder who the real politician in the family
might be. As effective as long speeches on Churchill's politics or
Gladstone's scandalous anti-imperialism were her pleas: 'Oh please
vote for my husband; I shall be so unhappy if he does not get
in . . .'[16]

Jennie's Woodstock campaign was without the benefit of the
Primrose League – there hardly was one in the constituency then.
The family didn't help either; a dispute over the family treasures
at Blenheim kept Churchill's mother – and mentor – and the
Marlboroughs away. But the election was the first in which the
League's badges were worn.

It was a ferocious election and the campaign team were often
pursued by jeering opponents or treated to jingles:

But just as I was talking
With neighbour Brown and walking
To take a mug of beer at the Unicorn and Lion
(For somehow there's a connection
Between free beer and an election)
Who should come but Lady Churchill with a turnout that was
   fine
And before she stopped her horses
As she marshalled all her forces
And before I knew what happened I had promised her my vote.

She won. 'I surpassed the fondest hopes of the suffragettes, and thought I was duly elected, and I certainly experienced all the pleasure and gratification of being a successful candidate.' It was to be another couple of generations before women were to enjoy the pleasure and gratification of becoming Parliamentary candidates in their own right, and even then they were only a handful.

This election was revolutionary. Never had women canvassed in this way before, and never had there been so stunning a surrogate MP. The Woodstock election established women's presence in elections for a generation, a perverse pleasure for the suffragettes perhaps, not least because of Jennie herself, the pin-up of the ruling class and the Primrose League (which used to distribute cheap portraits of her to the members). This was no respectable election, and her presence added eroticism to the political frisson. Sir Henry James wrote to Jennie congratulating her after the election and suggestively mooted a new Corrupt Practices Act which required that 'tandems be put down, and certainly some alteration – a correspondent informs me – must be made in the means of ascent and descent therefrom . . .'[17]

In 1885 there was a second election for Jennie Churchill to fight because the old Woodstock constituency had been abolished. This time Churchill stood against the popular Radical John Bright in Birmingham, the fortress of the Liberal Party organisation. By now, the family quarrels had subsided and Churchill's mother, the Dowager Duchess of Marlborough, descended on Birmingham with Jennie. This was 'the first time that women had ever indulged in any personal canvassing in Birmingham and we did it thoroughly. Every house in the constituency was visited. The Duchess would go in one direction and I would go in another.' It was a big constituency and a well-informed electorate – the Liberals had worked it well. The ladies found the men argumentative, presumably less intimidated than the agricultural labourers of Oxfordshire by the ruling class in person, and 'the wives of the Radicals were also admirably informed, and on more than one occasion routed me completely'. In those days, women with no vote were taken seriously by these canvassers as a force for their husbands to reckon with. And the urban voters' pride in the recent privacy of their vote was affronted when Jennie bustled through the factory gates and asked men for their votes. 'On one occasion I was received in utter silence, when I inquired why, one, speaking for the rest, said they did not like being asked for their vote.'[18]

Bright held his seat, albeit with a reduced majority. But this election was followed by a third in South Paddington, in which Jennie again campaigned.

By mid-1885, the Primrose League was primed to the participation of women in elections and decided to ask every candidate in the general election 'to communicate with the executive committee of the Dames Grand Council for any assistance that can be rendered to him'. Jennie's Woodstock triumph prompted Wigan Operative Conservative Association to write to the League expressing 'a desire to see other ladies displaying the same amount of courage in furthering the cause of conservative and patriotic principles'. Certainly, the Ladies were willing. A pamphlet published by the League in August 1885, when it was enrolling 1,000 new members a week and 400 new habitations (branches) had opened within a couple of months, explained how to set up a local organisation and how to reach the voters. A preface by Jennie Churchill made a virtue of necessity.

> The fact that women have no vote should help largely to contribute to their influence in canvassing, as proving their disinterestedness, and should lend weight to those powers of argument, which they are well known to possess, and in which they can infuse all the persuasive gentleness characteristic of their sex.

Although the subordination of women was taken for granted, Churchill insisted that the League was the 'first political association to recognise the influence which ladies can exercise over all classes of voters'. The Dames believed that they could do more than simply affirm Conservative principles. Jennie imputes some independence to the Ladies' Grand Council 'which by putting itself in direct communication with Central Office, has already been able to do much valuable work for the Conservative Party; and which may be destined to exercise no inconsiderable influence on political contests throughout the empire.'

The ordinary work of electioneering, rather than the oratory, was increasingly seen by Tory leaders to determine the party's fate. Earl Stanhope told the Ladies Grand Council's 1888 annual meeting:

> It is all very well to make speeches, but they are not well

attended to, and moreover, the mass of electors is so enormous that any number of speeches cannot reach them all (Hear Hear). Therefore, it is to the ladies, and especially the ladies of the Primrose League, that we must look for the political education of the people.

Even the Liberal woman-suffrage campaigner Mrs Millicent Fawcett conceded, with some generosity, that

> it is an undeniable fact that the Primrose League has done more to give women the position which has been so long and so rigidly withheld than any other organisation in this or in any period of the world's history. The originators of this movement showed their judgement and their discrimination when they included women in their ranks . . . it is admitted by friend and foe, that the Primrose League . . . has rendered the organisational help of women in such a way as no help has ever been given before at Parliamentary or municipal elections. It has been the frank and universal admission of successful Conservative candidates that they have been lifted into Parliament by the Primrose League.

The first Women's Liberal Association was formed in 1870 by the Misses Priestman, relatives of John Bright; by 1886 there were fifteen associations and in 1887 the Women's Liberal Federation was launched, co-ordinating the activities of 6,000 women. Like the Primrose League women, who were not yet admitted to the Tory Party, Liberal women had to form their own organisation because their exclusion from the franchise excluded them from the Liberal Party. Unlike the Primrose League, the Liberal women were passionately committed to campaigning for women's suffrage.

Ostrogorski, the acerbic historian of the development of modern democratic politics, concludes that no party wishing to think of itself as such was able to 'dispense with the aid of the women. Excluded by the constitution from all participation in political affairs, kept at a distance from the forum by tradition and natural manners, they are now entreated on all sides to descend into the lists.' Only the 'fury of the parties was required to drive men to this extremity'.[19]

What were the conditions that created the space for this extraordinary intrusion into men's political territory? The first was the limited nature of the franchise. The absence of universal suffrage on the one hand and drastic demographic change on the other made registration central to triumph or defeat in an election. It meant, in other words, keeping track of the voters and then keeping them on the electoral registers. The second was women's relationship to the community and how they adapted from the philanthropic tradition to a political tradition. As the 'insiders' in the community, used to finding their way around its nooks and crannies and to knowing its business, upper- and middle-class women with time on their hands and resources at their disposal became the pioneer corps, who reconnoitred the voters and then canvassed them.

Registration

Between the Tory defeat in 1880 and their triumph in 1885 the two most important new factors were the Corrupt Practices Act, which reformed the conduct of elections, and the Primrose League. The first made the second necessary. Nevertheless, the secret ballot was not always a guarantee of a secret vote and the hierarchical nature of the League's habitations, presided over locally by the gentry or the most 'influential' member of local society, perpetuated their dominance among the local electorate, particularly in the counties where the Conservatives remained strong. The creation of political associations like the Primrose League 'with the squire or parson as president and the estate agent as organiser and collector of subscriptions, was indeed not very different from the old informal arrangements'.[20] The established tradition was that when the electoral register appeared, both the Liberals and the Tories would challenge it, the main target being the registration of lodgers, who needed a twelve-month residential qualification – something which many did not possess or could not prove.

The professional party agents, who became expert in all this, would have responsibility for ensuring that the party's supporters appeared in the list, which would be promptly challenged by the opposition party, which was obliged to object, for the sake of it, to the names of known supporters of the opposition. 'Such work could make all the difference to the lodgers' vote since they had to make a fresh application every year.'[21] They would be sniffed out if they or the householder happened to move house. The importance of running to earth the party's potential voters is shown in the number of challenges to the register. In Newcastle between 1888 and 1891,

9,500 names were challenged. And in neighbouring Gateshead, despite a 16 per cent increase in the population, the electorate actually decreased: 'The party that neglected registration work for a year or two suffered badly.'[22] Pugh argues that 'the parties, as much as the law, determined the franchise before 1891'.

Ironically, the very party which found democracy distasteful was the one which rose to the challenge presented by the expansion of the electorate and the mammoth task of running voters to earth. It wasn't its own superior organisation, for the party leaders' distaste for popular mobilisation and its concern to keep the constituency-based National Union strictly under control led to under-development of the National Union. It was the Primrose League which took responsibility for the role of registrations and for updating the annual lists of voters, and thus became 'a key political institution curiously neglected by historians of the Conservative Party'.[23]

The labour of monitoring the register fell to the women. They were the sleuths. Describing the skills women could bring to Primrose politics, Lady Lechmere argued that the contribution of the 'gentler sex' lay in propagating Conservative principles, securing Tory success at the polls and registering voters. Her experience in Birmingham was that as 'each new register is issued the ladies of each association might meet and divide their parishes into districts, one or more ladies being responsible for each district'. And while they toured the constituency, continually updating the register, 'pamphlets and leaflets might be left, and a word or two added'. Proud of their successes in Birmingham, Lady Sawyer claimed that the districts were thoroughly canvassed every few months. 'A few men help occasionally, but it is found that the lady visitors do more good.'

Canvassing remained the focus for the League's electoral work: 'It suited the men of the party that the women should involve themselves so constructively without pressing for power or for their enfranchisement.' Indeed the Primrose ladies were among the first people in modern party politics to design systems of canvassing by monitoring the register, updating the party's data on its supporters and distributing propaganda *between* rather than only *during* elections. The situation was summed up in a report to the second inaugural meeting of the Ladies Grand Council in 1886:

it has been generally found that where well-organised

habitations composed of all classes exist the registration of voters has been well-attended to, the conveyance of electors to the poll has been made easy, and an efficient canvass secured.

In the previous election, 'many thousands of canvassers were furnished by the Primrose League'.

However, the League's ladies were often accused of going beyond the proprieties of the new electoral legislation. They were advised to stop their drawing-room meetings during elections in case they might be misinterpreted or, rather, correctly interpreted. Habitations got into the habit of formally dissolving during elections so that their services to the party became, officially at least, invisible. The very traditions of womanly contact with the community also gave them considerable powers of intimidation. The League's ladies protested against the embarrassing appearance of an advertisement in the *Gazette* suggesting that habitations give preference to local businesses supporting the League, which confirmed a widespread suspicion that the League went in for boycotts of local tradespeople – an illicit form of pressure. The League rather enjoyed this kind of notoriety as an index of its social power, although it regularly repudiated the allegations. 'Day by day illustrations are forthcoming of the marvellous power' of the League, crowed the *Gazette* in October 1887, including 'the negative testimony supplied in the bitter criticism, unscrupulous denunciations and glaring misrepresentations of Radical speeches and writing'. The *Gazette* then challenged the Northampton *Mercury*'s account of an alleged boycott: the local headmaster had banned the boys from his school from shopping at Mrs Eliza Sealy's confectionery shop – clearly a disaster for her trade. Boycotting, said the *Mercury*, was one of the League's 'cherished weapons', and it had been applied to Eliza Sealy because she had refused to join. The *Gazette* then claimed that Mrs Sealy's letter of protest had, in fact, been written by the local non-conformist minister. That proved a plot, as far as the League was concerned, locked in combat as it was with the non-conformist campaign to secularise state education.

Sir Henry James, who had earlier congratulated Jennie Churchill for her Woodstock campaign, was reported at an annual meeting of the Ladies Grand Council to have complained about 'the interference of ladies in elections', which prompted Lord Harris to reply that in the context of this invocation of the Corrupt Practices Act, 'he did not suppose that he would suggest that the sex for whom it was necessary to draw up the Corrupt Practices Act had any reason to throw stones at the sex for whom the act was not drawn up'. But the mud did stick. Gladstone had described the League as a 'curious compound of duchesses and maids of all work' and 'a great instrument to the Tory party for bribery and corruption ... All the unscrupulous women of England are members of the Primrose League,' he complained. 'In the country districts they threaten; in the towns they cajole; in both town and country their armouries are overflowing with thousands of yards of flannel and countless sacks of coal.'[24] At least as far as the opposition was concerned, the canvassers used all their resources!

The very networks which gave them their social strength were also the source, then, of the allegations of 'undue influence'. Their denials seem a bit disingenuous. The League 'had a local monopoly of social prestige, but also commanded the services of many active women workers constituting a large number of influential local consumers'.[25] They were often also important local employers. The assumption that the secret ballot changed all this is challenged by the evidence of intimidation of this type. The secret ballot made least difference in the countryside because 'it was accompanied by no change in the relations of landlord and tenant'.[26] A former Primrose League Dame, Lady Wimborne, of Dorset, was the subject of a notorious electoral corruption trial in 1910. She'd become a Liberal and made her agent, Mr Easby, also formerly a Primrose Leaguer, ensure that her tenants voted according to her current persuasion. Mr Justice Lawrence thought that Mr Easby had also had the duty 'possibly to take a penny book and to see whether the Primrose Leaguers had given their vote properly, for years'. Suddenly the unfortunate Mr Easby was 'called upon to turn around like a weather cock from north to south in a moment and say "Now you go and do the same for the Liberals as you did for the Conservatives."' The judge concluded that even the benign Mr Easby, 'as the representative of those who sent him, might be an influence for evil'. So, despite electoral reform, the political complexion of the counties 'was decided almost entirely by its landlords, the recognised leaders of social, administrative and judicial life'.[27]

The ladies who were landlords in their own right, or who were the wives of the local gentry, would be likely, if they were Tories, to belong to the Primrose League. And at the moment when the expanded franchise, particularly to include agricultural labourers, threatened to loosen the bonds of their history, the Primrose League revitalised them. Not that the League directly went in for philanthropy. Indeed, its whole tone is not so much about appealing to the poor or policing the poor, but welding a social alliance with the newly enfranchised, waged, working class. This gave rise to accusations of bribery: in Hackney Wick, a Radical fortress in the 1880s, for example, 'The ladies of the League had found themselves an interesting occupation in collecting subscriptions for cheap dinners to the poor children of the neighbourhood.' The women, about seventy of them, were accused by the Radicals of trying to get round the poor. The Dames of the League were no doubt involved in local charities, but the League consistently avoided any charitable work, as such. It thus escaped the equation between philanthropy and policing which characterised some of the good works of their Liberal sisters. Certainly, it was believed that Primrose Leaguers had the leisure for politics when their Liberal counterparts were immersed in philanthropic works or social reform. The radical presence in the school boards and among the Poor Law Guardians incited the Primrose Leaguers to make a bid for local government in the early twentieth century, although they were never so successful as in their great general election triumphs.

A formidable Tory militia

The League played on power for all it was worth as it drew all classes into its orbit. Its structures were hierarchical and ceremonial, and its style placed it in some imagined continuum of tradition: leadership came 'naturally' to the rich who bought their way into its mediaeval court and had the titles 'Dame' and 'Knight' conferred upon them. Ordinary people were only associates. But they had access through the League to the great and the good. Every Dame was expected to be affiliated to a local habitation and local dignitaries were to be seen amidst political activity and Primrose entertainments. Jennie Churchill, for example, was the president of many local habitations and threw herself into entertaining them – on one occasion playing the piano at Hackney habitation.

But lest anyone thought the Dames should be confined to the parochial, the Countess of Jersey reported to an annual general meeting of the Ladies Grand Council in May 1890 that its members had 'what I may call a national work also. (Hear Hear)'. Apart from raising money and promoting the arts of propaganda, 'these ladies have enrolled themselves into what I may call a headquarters staff, which is in communication with English ladies in all parts of the country'.

The *Primrose League Gazette* advertised meetings for ladies of the gentry in one another's homes, and relied on the elaborate social life of 'society' and 'the season' to enclose the women of that class. The annual meeting of the Ladies Grand Council in 1887 heard its executive report that to extend the League into the hinterland of Britain (one of its greatest strongholds was in Scotland), and to ensure that everywhere women were represented, had been the LGC's objective. They had been staggeringly successful – in that year there were 1,724 habitations and 565,961 Knights, Dames and associate members, all in less than five years. Between 1885, when the presence of women was first felt in an election, and 1891, total membership rose from 11,366 to more than one million.

One of the key devices had been to draw on existing social networks and make them work for the League:

> Hundreds of ladies, coming from all parts of the country and collected temporarily in London for the season, were induced to join it, and through personal influence and action many more ladies resident in the country were also recruited.

The importance of the ladies' very presence was endlessly re-affirmed in the *Gazette*'s regular round-ups of news from the habitations, which read like society columns, without the gossip, from a national newspaper. Four hundred people turned up at Lindow habitation in Cleator Moor, deep in the heart of Cumberland, for a meeting in the market hall, presided over by the local squire, Jonas Lindow, Esq., with his daughter Miss Lindow on the platform. Eight hundred people gathered in the same year, 1887, for a Primrose League garden party held by Julia, Lady Jersey, at Middleton Park, where they were joined by 'the élite of the aristocracy of the district'. By the end of the decade the pressure on these top ladies to perform, or only 'to show' themselves, was so intense that the League tried to reach further into the hinterland. It was hoped that a county structure for the League would 'induce local ladies of position and influence to keep up the necessary animation' and take the pressure off ladies like the Dowager Duchess of Marlborough.

The women's effectiveness in canvassing was partly explained by the circumstances of these leisured women who were free 'for party hack work and day to day social contacts'. Particularly in the rural constituencies, they trafficked in the inner-life of the community. 'Political work, and especially house to house canvassing came naturally to many women accustomed to church visiting and volunteer charity work.'[28] It was this tradition and the Primrose League's adaptation of it which, Ostrogorski believed, gave women freedom of movement within their own communities to engage in political work, which contradicts the popular historical legacy of women's social isolation. While they may have been barred from power, they also had access to ordinary citizens. One of the ladies' strengths, according to Lady Lechmere, was that they above all 'assist in visiting the working class in their homes'. That was their great forte, particularly in the countryside where the League truly triumphed, generating a whole world of modern entertainments in the villages, as well as weaving afresh the web binding the classes together:

> It was in the rural districts where the relationship between visitor and visited was most personal, that church visiting provided the most valuable education and experience for the feminine propagandist.[29]

Assimilating the church's own vocabulary, Northcote's successor as party leader, Lord Salisbury, described the Primrose Leaguers as 'general missionaries of the principles which you profess'. Women were

> especially valuable to the service of information, which often requires dexterity and lightness of hand. Having more leisure time than the men and taking advantage of the privilege of their sex, which enables them to circulate among the population with more freedom, that is to say without drawing attention to their capacity as political emissaries, the dames quietly work their constituency in a continuous fashion.

For Ostrogorski, it was the women who made the League what it was:

The women carried the men with them and in a short time the ramifications of the League extended into the four corners of the kingdom, forming in less than ten years a formidable Tory militia of more than a million, which surpasses the regular army of the Tory party not only in numbers, but also in fighting strength.[30]

A sentimental alliance

The League's relationship to the 'lower orders' is described in their commitment to an alliance between classes. League functions were occasions in which the classes could come together, for play as well as politicking. 'Apparently the corps d'élite deemed it more effective to enroll the proletariat in the advancing army than to march against them.'[31] The social purpose of the League was to establish 'a sentimental alliance between the masses and Toryism, by means of a league founded outside the orthodox organisation of the party and appealing frankly to popular aspirations and emotions'.[32] The masses didn't start flocking in, however, until the women got their hands on the League. It was the Ladies Grand Council which promoted the notion of pleasure in politics in the face of the Grand Council's hesitation. Smoking concerts were very popular, and teas, and although the party had initiated a national league of Conservative clubs to attract working men, the Primrose League established a greater hegemony among the working-class Tories because it embraced women and children. Indeed, the League established its own children's section – the Buds. Among its great achievements was bringing popular and modern entertainments to the masses, particularly in the socially barren countryside. At St Hilda's habitation, Whitby, for example, the 'West Cliff Saloon was filled to the utmost, scores turned away for the entertainment', which were *tableaux vivants* and moving waxworks, 'vanishing lady' tricks and a local and much-loved entertainer.

The League had its own choir and always called upon popular singers for its events, and the *Gazette* regularly published advertisements from magicians and ventriloquists for its parties and socials:

A rich profusion of punchinellos, pierrots, jugglers and ventriloquists vied for favour on habitation programmes with oriental illusions, waxworks, conjuring tricks, marionettes and exhibitions of microscopic objects or of Egyptian antiquities.[33]

The entertainments were generally viewed to be more important than the speeches. MPs were given clear instructions about their time and were left under no illusions as to what constituted the serious business of the League's gatherings. The Tory MP Radcliffe Cook recalled how, sandwiched inside a League programme of entertainments,

> I abandon all my high hopes of swaying by winged words the destinies of our empire, and deliver a scratch speech . . . to an audience dying to hear Melville Jones in his celebrated song, 'The Man Who Went to Bed in His Boots'.[34]

The important thing was that the League integrated itself into the popular culture, indeed promoted it. Not only had it courted the working class, but it had brought a large number into membership – the majority were reckoned to be working people – and provided a social life which was integrated with its political life. 'The league is among other things the great, the greatest promoter of the "socialisation" of politics.'[35]

It wasn't just popular, it was vulgar. Jennie Churchill recalls how Lady Salisbury rebuked a member who thought perhaps some of the entertainments, though attractive to the masses, might be thought slightly vulgar. 'Vulgar? Of course it's vulgar,' exclaimed the president, 'but that is why we have got on so well.'[36]

It was in its social endeavours that the League promoted its most important theme: imperialism. Besieged by the Home Rulers on the one hand and the rising trade unions on the other, the League sensed that strong as it was, it was fighting for a way of life.

The realignment of the British ruling class, occasioned by the Liberal Unionists' breakaway from Gladstone's support for Home Rule for Ireland in the 1880s, was a crucial moment. For the Unionists, Home Rule was the beginning of the end of the empire. The League was inherently unionist, because it was inherently imperialist, and it threw itself into the movement against Irish nationalism. It brought lady Unionists over from Ireland to the mainland of Britain, billeted them and helped them put their case to the women. Simultaneously it was showing to hundreds of habitations the glories of the greatest empire on earth.

Magic messages

Before cinema and celluloid, the League brought the latest communications technology to its modernist political project. New media of communication with the masses, from the safety bicycle to the magic lantern, were audaciously deployed. The magic lantern enjoyed its boom during the heyday of the Primrose League in the 1890s, 'an integral part of English social life until it was displaced by moving pictures'. It was, above all, the medium for the imperialist message: 'On the retina of the British public, the magic lanterns stamped scenes of the flag flying at some outpost of the empire, of the fleet in battle formation off Spithead, of the death of Nelson on the deck of the Victory, or of the Queen enthroned as Empress of India.'[37] Gordon's fate at Khartoum was a particular favourite.

But the Empire was not only important to the Tories as an idea and as a market; its aura within the League was also important in constituting the Primrose League woman as at least an extra in the biggest show on earth. With no rights, no vote of her own, 'she is at once lifted out of her individuality as a unit and translated into part of a huge force'.

The Ladies Grand Council, more than the men, perceived the need for mass propaganda, as well as the great utility of the magic lantern. In 1891–92 they had to fight the men's Grand Council over the despatch of a horse and carriage, plus magic lantern and driver/lecturer into the barren villages of England. Ultimately they won and sent a plasterer called Mr Crabbe into the villages of East Dorset where he 'gave 70–80 lectures, with the aid of his lantern and was enjoyed well enough by agricultural labourers'.

The women's zeal was multiplied by the popularity of the 'safety' bicycle – without a crossbar – in the 1890s. The League organised its own cycling corps, some of which performed formation cycling spectacles at League fêtes, but the bicycle boom was most important for canvassing. 'England of the '90s teemed with women on wheels', and this doubled their value as 'mobile skirmishers'.[38]

But the League was primarily associated with the grand style of four rather than two wheels. Dames were reported to have descended in their purple and gold landaus from the West End to Stepney to deliver election leaflets. And Tories were on these occasions still

regarded as the harbingers of not only manifestos but also a good
time.

> London districts were invaded by a human type quite foreign
> to them in normal times. Perfect ladies, very 'hatty' and
> affable, called upon our parents (if they had a vote), kissed the
> children and made themselves at home in the kitchen.[39]

The Liberals, on the other hand, were associated with a more
abstemious approach. While the Tories were regarded as the patrons
of festivals and 'providers of cakes and ale', the Liberals 'were
looked upon as kill-joys, sour misanthropes who were in a secret
conspiracy to close all the pubs'.

'We don't wish to govern the country'

The electoral success of the Primrose League occupies a curious
place in the positioning of Tory women: it marked a break with
women's traditional 'separate sphere' and yet it became women's
'separate sphere' within Conservative politics.

Initially, electioneering was regarded as scandalous, and went far
beyond what the Knights had anticipated when they first welcomed
the ladies into the League. At the inaugural meeting of the Ladies
Grand Council in June 1885, Lord John Manners prescribed what
the Knights really had in mind:

> It might be asked did the League expect that ladies were to
> turn themselves into electioneering agents and go about
> canvassing in the streets and the villages of the country, perhaps
> making impassioned addresses to these new electors. Nothing
> of the kind. There was no wish on the part of the League that
> the Ladies who joined it should take this active and overt
> part, but at the same time it held that the Ladies would not be
> going beyond their proper province if they canvassed for
> members to join the League and endeavoured to establish
> Habitations throughout the country.

As 'wives and mothers' they 'might be pardoned if they wished to
exercise in a proper and subordinate manner the influence they
possessed'. This influence was not to exercise itself over the politics
of the nation, but only the concerns deemed suitable for their sex:

religion in schools, a major Tory campaign against Chamberlain
and the non-conformists, and the maintenance of the institutions
which would secure that. Their labours should be subordinated to
the direction of the party and its election agents.

At the second inaugural meeting in 1886, Lord Frederick Hamilton suggested that although the League had invited women to
canvass, 'it was considered best' that all the wardens (officials)
should be men. But where the men had not created an appropriate
political network themselves, the women, according to an important
speech by Lady Jersey in 1890, were to take the initiative. The vital
work of registering voters was normally to be in the hands of the
League's wardens, but where it was not, 'it becomes the duty of the
ladies of the Primrose League, if they find that any conservative
elector is not on the register, to give the registration agent due
notice'. As we have seen, the women of the Primrose League were
to take elections into their own hands. But the women were to
remain subordinate to the men.

The Dames of the Primrose League defended their excursions into
politics in a language later deployed on both sides of the suffrage
argument by some of the same protagonists. Lady Montagu told the
annual meeting of the Ladies Grand Council in May 1888 that the
answer to the question 'Why should women care for politics?' was
simply 'Why not. It is natural for women to take an interest in the
government of their country.' But the redoubtable Lady Jersey dis-
tinguished between *politics* and *parties* in a speech to the 1890 Ladies
Grand Council annual meeting. It was an exciting challenge to the
opponents of women in politics, and yet it was an apparently contradictory assertion both of women's power and women's powerlessness.

Lady Jersey further specified the distinct role of women, which
observers could have been forgiven for misunderstanding and which
aspiring activists might unwittingly usurp. Her speech to the May
1890 annual meeting of the LGC was an exacting challenge to the
opponents of women's participation in politics and at the same time
a stringent assertion both of women's power and their proper
powerlessness. In contesting Radical complaints about women en-
gaging in party politics, she argued that women eschew *party* politics
but are the upholders and promoters of political principles. The
Primrose League, she said, saw itself as defender of a way of life,
against the 'division of the people of the country into factions with
the sole object of undermining and thwarting the efforts that are

made by any other party in the country'. The League would 'have nothing to do with anything of the kind'. She insisted on a distinction between party politics and 'the science of the state', and gave to women the right to concern themselves in general with 'all that concerns the welfare of the state'. It is that distinction which enabled her to imagine women's participation in politics without being 'in the least desirous of trenching on any department which does not belong to us; we don't wish to govern the country . . . we want to assist in placing men in government . . .'

These distinctions were vital. They reassured the opposition to women's participation in politics that they represented no challenge and yet mapped out the terrain upon which women should operate. In practice, however, the distinctions may have done more to soothe men than to constrain women: we have seen how Jennie Churchill, its president, scored spectacular successes in running elections in the earliest days of the League's existence. The Dames struggled with the men's Grand Council over the limits of their powers and over the priorities of the organisation. Women's politics, as such, were off the agenda.

A Tory feminist well known for her journalism and public-speaking, Frances Power Cobbe, recalls writing to the League after delivering a series of speeches on 'The Duties of Women' in the early 1880s:

> when the Primrose League was in full activity I wrote at the request of the committee of the Women's Suffrage Association a circular letter to the 'Dames' (of whom I am one) begging them to endeavour to make the granting of votes to women a 'plank' in their platform. I received many friendly letters in reply – but the men who influenced the League, apparently finding that they could make the Dames do their work for them *without votes*, discouraged all movement in the desired direction, and I do not suppose that anything was gained by my attempt.[40]

And Lady Montagu argued in 1888:

> Into the vexed question of the franchise I will not enter; we are not called upon to discuss it now . . . our political work . . . ought to be kept scrupulously clear of all such debatable ground.

The Ladies Grand Council confirms that it spurned an invitation by the National Society for Women's Suffrage. 'The executive committee of the Ladies Grand Council cannot enter into questions of contentious politics.' Of course that was never true. The League pitched into the contentious issue of religion in schools – indeed it was Chamberlain and the non-conformists' campaign for secular state education which was part of their *raison d'être*, and it fought against Home Rule. The fact was that suffrage was a contentious issue among the men on the Grand Council, not to mention many of the women themselves – they were split. Lady Randolph became a suffragist; Lady Jersey was implacably opposed, and later organised the Anti-Suffrage League together with Lord Cromer and Lord Curzon. Abstention from the suffrage issue remained one of the League's principles throughout. That abstention was significant, because it enabled the League, a mass movement *of* women, to avoid having to take a stand *for* women.

the Dames evolved forms of political organising which affirmed the accepted norms of femininity and which necessarily distanced them from the woman suffrage activists. They did this with breathtaking confidence – it was they, after all, who had put women and womanliness into politics.

> Until the establishment of the Primrose League, the few women whose names were at all publicly brought forward in connection with political movements belonged to a school of thought which repelled rather than attracted the great mass of their sex . . . aroused alarm and disgust amongst those who valued beyond any political success the preservation of the refinement and dignity of womanhood. These women claimed to be . . . emancipated from the common superstitions and prejudices of their sex . . . It is not by attacking the sanctity and stability of family life that the life of the state can be purified and strengthened . . . The Primrose League has changed all this, and now the awakening political influence and capacity of women have found a just and fitting political outlet.[41]

But the League's isolation from women's politics is also indicated in its response to an invitation from the advisory council of the World's Congress of Representative Women to send a delegate in

1892. The 4 November minutes of the Ladies Grand Council show that it decided it was unable to discuss the invitation and sought the help of the Grand Council. And at the next executive of the LGC on 18 November they decided against sending a representative, on the interesting grounds that as it was 'not a women's association it was unable to do so'.

It is one of the most surprising features of the League that it managed throughout its life to dodge the main issues confronting the women of its time. It 'negatived unanimously' repeated appeals to contribute funds to the unemployed. It refused to support a Primrose League Co-operative Supply Association (an index of the spread of co-operative ideology in British society – even into the Primrose League). And in May 1888 it refused an appeal for support from the Association for Opposing Any Change in the Marriage Laws. This did not concern the League, it said. The trouble was that there were two conflicting centres of power: the Grand Council was the ruling body and composed of men. The Ladies Grand Council had been the inspiration for the League's breathless rise, and yet women were strictly subordinate to the Grand Council.

The power struggle

From the very beginning, it was the growth of the women's power base in the habitations which raised the problem of the Ladies Grand Council's sphere of influence. Was it directly responsible to the habitations, or were its powers and responsibilities to be mediated through the Grand Council? After the LGC's first wonderful year, the treasurer, Lady Gwendolen Cecil, was pressing the League to review its structures – the women were straining at the leash.

By February 1886, the men of the Grand Council conceded the need for reform, but change remained their gift, for it was they, after all, who had made the rules and it was at their own invitation that the women had been allowed to take part in the first place. The quarrel persisted. In April 1886, the Grand Council reminded the ladies about the purposes of their funds – because the women wanted to send funds to poorer habitations, especially in the counties, 'to encourage social political gatherings'. However, this 'did not commend itself to the Grand Council'. Dissatisfied, the ladies argued for a special scheme to support poor habitations. At its next meeting the Grand Council conceded.

One of the most significant differences occurred over propaganda and popularisation of the League's principles. Both were the key to the League's influence and both were the province of the ladies. It was as if the Grand Council continually tried to contain the women by wresting control of propaganda from them without fully appreciating the impact of this public work. The conflict began over pamphlets and leaflets. The LGC was forbidden to publish anything without the Grand Council's approval. In April 1886 the Ladies Grand Council agreed to abandon its Ladies' Literature Committee, which was an early – and autonomous – propaganda committee, although it proposed a compromise: if the Grand Council were to set up a Joint Literature Committee, the women would participate in it. The Grand Council agreed and then built in its own majority: the committee was to have four ladies and five gentlemen. But if the men controlled the literature committee, it was the women, primarily, who funded it. The accounts for 1889 showed that the joint committee received £500 from the Ladies Grand Council and only £100 from the Grand Council, and it spent more than £700 on the printing of leaflets, pamphlets and song sheets.

By the end of 1886 the Ladies Grand Council was still challenging the Grand Council over its status, its right to support local habitations and over 'what are and are not the legitimate objectives of the Primrose League'. It wanted a conference with the Grand Council to discuss the latter, but the Grand Council irrascibly replied that 'no good could possibly come from any such conference, as the objects of the League are already sufficiently defined'.

In the 1890s the League was becoming more ambitious in its methods of propaganda, and again the LGC entered into delicate dispute with the Grand Council over expenditure and priorities. The 3 July meeting of the Ladies' executive had a long discussion on the efficacy of mobile magic lanterns. Already the Radicals had sent out vans – a horse and carriage – into the cities with party propaganda. Lady Marlborough objected to the idea because the Radicals had already thought of it. But since the League had established its strength in the countryside, Lady Salisbury believed that 'there were members of small villages and outlying hamlets in the country that it was impossible for lecturers to visit, owing to the want of accommodation'. But since agricultural labourers had the vote 'it was most important that so large a proportion of voters should not be neglected by our speakers' and the only way to reach them was 'by having vans and making the speakers independent'. It was settled that the Grand Council would send out speakers without vans, although the expenses were to be reported to the ladies, while the Ladies Grand Council would sponsor a van together with a speaker and a magic lantern. Since there was an election coming up in East Dorset, where the terrain was tricky, the LGC van would go there to give lectures and leaflets.

Finally, there was the matter of the ladies' right to direct representation on the Grand Council. This was raised sharply over the 1887 election to the Grand Council. Membership came in two categories: election and co-option. Ladies were not up for election, but a group including the well-connected Lady Randolph Churchill, Lady Gwendolen Cecil, Viscountess Folkestone, the Duchess of Marlborough, the Marchioness of Salisbury and the Countess of Jersey was on the proposed list of co-opted members. We might wonder what discussions took place in the Folkestones' household in the wake of Lord Folkestone's argument that 'the ladies executive did not represent the ladies of the League, and though they might wish to be on the Grand Council yet we must not infer that this is the opinion of the ladies in general'. Lord Limerick 'strongly objected to any members of the ladies executive committee being co-opted as such' although he believed that not only Dames, but rank and file women should be eligible. There was a feeling that the nomination of ladies was a problematic innovation to be avoided, and Lord Folkestone and the Rt Hon Henry Chaplin, a popular member of the Grand Council opposed to woman suffrage, proposed motions either to defer the issue or to restrict the number of co-opted members so that, presumably, the women would be excluded. This dispute over the women's rights to power, and the men's reluctance to share power, coincided with the attempts by the Ladies Grand Council and Lady Gwendolen Cecil in particular to clarify their status.

Before settling the question of co-option, the Grand Council ruled that the Ladies Grand Council had 'no power to intervene between the Grand Council and the Habitations' and furthermore that 'the Ladies Grand Council is by the ordinances subordinate to the Grand Council'. Nevertheless, the Grand Council recognised that precedents had already been set; the ladies had already, as it were, set their own customs and practices. 'Certain powers having by custom been exercised by the Ladies Grand Council, the restriction of which, by ordinance, has produced friction in the management of some habitations.' And so 'some form of consultation' had to be established between the two.

The Grand Council heard that the ladies, for the time being, did not wish to serve on the Grand Council. The struggle for power was resolved, almost before it had been waged. According to Robb, the women were impotent but financially useful. Far from being impotent, however, it could be argued that these women retained a certain power by bowing to the constraints. They succeeded only insofar as they did not challenge and did not invite defeat.

The Primrose League symbolised the modernisation of the Tory Party, and the incorporation of women to its cause secured a place for women in the political firmament. But independence was the price of that incorporation. Like the National Union, the Primrose League was never more than the party leadership's pioneer corps and its formal autonomy from the party simply secured its subordination. The League's function was to organise women for the Conservative cause; it was *not* to organise for the cause of women. Thus it isolated Conservative women as a social force from one of the issues which dominated British politics in the late nineteenth and early twentieth century – women's suffrage. If anything, the league de-mobilised the incipient suffragism of Conservative women. Unlike the Primrose League, which safeguarded its support in the party hierarchy by abstaining on the suffrage, the National Union risked the opprobrium of the party hierarchy in passing a pro-women's suffrage motion in 1887. Women were already allowed to participate in local elections and so the National Union resolved that 'the time has now arrived when the Parliamentary franchise may with perfect safety be extended to women householders'. Moving the motion, Mr H. Wainwright from Blackpool pre-empted the complaint that the National Union might be usurping the prerogatives of the leadership:

> It has been said that in moving a resolution of this kind and if the conference carries it, we shall be dictating to the leaders of the Conservative Party. I deny that altogether. We do not meet here for the purposes of dictation but for the purpose of discussion, and I also feel that as this question is not a party

question and as a large number on both sides are agreed
upon the main principle, the government would be glad to
know the opinion of such a vast and important conference
of Conservative delegates upon it.

Mr Wainwright's argument was that women householders should
share the same rights as male householders:

I have had a little experience in the county of Lancashire in
connection with elections and I am bound to say that women
who vote at municipal elections and the elections of Boards of
Guardians and School Boards take a very great interest in
the elections, and take the same interest as the male population
in recording their votes. We can always get a definite answer
from the ladies (cheers) on one side or the other, and I am
pleased to say that so far as my own county is concerned the
vast majority of the ladies are in favour of the Conservative
Party.

Reassuring opponents who abhorred the idea of women in the
House of Commons, he declared: 'It has been said that if Parliament
would pass a Bill in favour of women having the suffrage in a very
short time women would be allowed to sit in the House of Commons
(cries of "No"). I deny that altogether (hear hear).'

His seconder, Mr Fullager, from Lytham, warned that the matter
could not be put off for much longer, 'I must say why should this
conference neglect the opportunity of bringing it forward and getting
the Conservative Party to carry it through Parliament?' Tory MP
Radcliffe Cook opposed it because 'there is really no public demand on the subject (cries of "yes" "yes")'. He prophesied that
since women acted from sentiment and not from reason, the first
woman who was to sit in Parliament would 'commence the end of
the unity and greatness of the British empire (laughter and cheers)'.
Poor Radcliffe Cook was in a minority. The resolution was carried,
according to the conference report 'amid cheers'. Although the
National Union passed successive motions supporting the suffrage
before the century was out, it mattered not. Enough powerful people
within the hierarchy opposed it, and the party conference had no
power to dictate.

A couple of years later, in 1889, the Conservative novelist Mrs

Humphry Ward organised a protest petition made up of some of the great and the good against women's suffrage and it was published in the periodical *Nineteenth Century*. It was animated by the fear that the Liberal leader Gladstone's opposition to women's suffrage might provoke a Conservative government to support women's inclusion in a reform bill out of 'self-interest'.[1] Mrs Humphry Ward went on to form the National Women's Anti-Suffrage League in 1908, which amalgamated with its brother league for men in 1910, led by the Tory lords, Cromer and Curzon. The men's league seemed to be the Primrose League by another name – although in 1909, its Grand Council had declared that the suffrage was 'a matter of opinion not principle'. Members could have their own views, but they must not oppose Unionist candidates who opposed the suffrage.[2] Nevertheless, prominent figures in the Primrose League presided over the Antis – the Countess Lady Jersey, a formidable political hostess and Primrose League Dame, was President of the women's league. Constance Rover comments that it was 'typical of the attitude of the women anti-suffragists that the Countess of Jersey gave way to the presidency of the Earl of Cromer' after amalgamation with the men's league and became his deputy in 1911.[3]

That the women buckled to the 'Cromer-Curzon combination' was perhaps more an acknowledgement by the women of the realpolitik operating within Conservative circles on the one hand and, on the other, a typical manoeuvre by the 'combination' to protect the habitual domination enjoyed by the men in the other spheres that men and women inhabited.

The men had always ruled the Primrose League; Lord Cromer succeeded Balfour as its Grand Master in 1912. Curzon was a consummate fund-raiser and the amalgamation brought the men's money – and power – to the women's numbers and organisational flair. 'A joint organisation would also have the virtue of demonstrating the Antis' ideal of collaboration between the sexes.'[4] The same principle infused the Primrose League and the women were warned against the 'fallacy' that it was a women's organisation by the *Gazette* in July 1912. They must not cut themselves off from 'men's sympathies' by keeping themselves aloof. If the League offered women social space, then there had to be space, too, for men to be together. 'Let every ruling councillor be a man with men,' editorialised the *Gazette*:

The Primrose League – as distinct from women's associations –
is composed of men and women. It needs men, for without
them it loses proportionately its manly element and its work
and manly character. Splendid as the influences and activities
of women are – and we shall not be far wrong in asserting that
it is women who are largely responsible for the League's
success – it is certain that if men do not lend their presence
and support to the League . . . its character as a political
society must be destroyed.

Lord Cromer admitted as much about the men's and women's
anti-suffrage organisations. Before they amalgamated in 1910–11,
he said, the men's organisation was 'a perfectly useless body, and
did very little work, much less than that of the women'.[5] The
anti-suffrage ideology theorised in the concept of 'separate spheres'
was articulated with the Conservative principle of the necessary
unity of classes, sexes and nations. It was – and is – a theory of
organic unity founded not on equality but difference, a unity which
organised difference within a pre-ordained hierarchy. 'Separate
spheres' contained different ideological meanings for men and
women: for women it was a source both of strength and subordination, it was never only one or the other. For men it was a source
of power, a power that could no longer be safeguarded by exiling
women from their society. United were to be the social strengths of
women and the political power of men.

But within the anti-suffrage amalgamation the women did not
bend easily and the men's power was wrought at some cost to
Cromer's self-esteem. He admitted to Curzon that he had made 'a
serious mistake, of which I am much ashamed' in not securing
sufficient concessions from the women before dissolving the men's
organisation during the wrangles over amalgamation.[6] The Countess was no slouch, she wanted the women to have 'at least equal
place' with the men, and if Cromer were to be president then a
woman should take the chair.[7] Her anti-suffrage sisters were just
as determined: Violet Markham, who was later to be prominent in
'public service', declared in 1910 that she regarded women as
superior to men and therefore 'I do not like to see them trying to
become men's equals'.[8] And there was more than a little decorous
fear of the backlash in the warning in the *Anti-Suffrage Review* that
if woman invaded man's political province 'then his latent jealousy,

his latent resentment, will burst into flame, and everywhere there will be a great revolt from female ascendancy, actual or threatened'.[9] Violet Markham and Mrs Ward dissociated themselves from the sentiments expressed in an 'odious' epistle to *The Times* in 1912 by the misogynist Sir Almroth Wright, calling the suffragettes hysterics.

In the first decades of the twentieth century the relationship of women to the party underwent a second phase of transformation: if the first, the ascendancy of the Primrose League, represented the incorporation of women into the party's social orbit, the second could not escape the full assimilation of women as political subjects. The very existence of the Primrose League might have appeared to undermine residual resistance to women's suffrage – the women had, after all, proved their loyalty and their utility to the Conservative cause. Anti-suffragism seemed to mean not so much a clear, lived separation between public and private, but rather an ideological distinction between public and political. This was, however, already blurred by the very success of Conservatism's army of auxiliaries.

Women, for Conservatism, *embodied* the link between private and public: for Conservative women, the home was never fully separated from 'the world', it was always the altar of Conservatism's moral values. The home and the family were the crucible and the cause of capital accumulation. For the relatively leisured Conservative woman, the home was also the centre of her social networks and her location within her community. Her charitable endeavours in the nineteenth century became institutionalised in the twentieth: the municipalisation of the ladies' roles as community police, pedagogue and philanthropist was still seen as a natural extension of her feminine function, a function which was not confined within the four walls of her own home.

It would be a mistake, argues Constance Rover, 'to assume that most women in the ranks of the Antis had come to a considered conclusion that it was to their advantage to keep to the traditional role of their sex'.[10] Many of their most prominent protagonists were themselves 'new women'. And in any case, the Primrose League had already hoist the party on its own petard; the distinction between private and public was already all but meaningless. 'Politics are not only heard in street corners but they have for some time past invaded the drawing room,' said Primrose Leaguer Page Croft. 'There was a time when the term "political lady" was a term of opprobrium.

Nowadays all ladies belonging to the Primrose League are political ladies.'[11]

If it had any meaning at all, the Antis' definition of separate spheres did not turn on the distinction between the 'private', the 'public' and the 'political' because the rise of the municipalities and growing state intervention in education and social insurance had, in any case, expanded the reach of the political sphere. Rather it represented an attempt to regulate a political division of labour and this in turn expressed the enforcement of sexual difference: 'The sphere of women's action is moral, whereas that of men is material,' declared Lord Cromer.[12] To women was assigned the local, to men the national and super-national. But as their opponents pointed out, the limits of the local were imposed not so much on themselves, but on other women.[13] It was a *class* opposition to suffrage. The political hostess of the ruling class 'enjoyed extensive influence without the vote: indeed, women's suffrage would merely raise up rivals to her influence and she had no reason to support it. For her class loyalty was far more important than loyalty to sex.'[14]

For men like Cromer, however, anti-suffragism was animated not only by misogynist revulsion against this uppity sex, but by its promised impact on the national political agenda. His was a panicky but prescient resistance to the extension of statism. Universal suffrage was a Trojan horse for social democracy. Cromer wasn't wrong. His premonition was to become a reality that dominated British politics in the era of universal suffrage. He was alert to the simultaneous rise of the suffrage movement and socialism and expressed the fear 'that women's sympathy and emotion might lead her to move forward from philanthropy into a sentimental socialism which would offend against all the laws of political economy and greatly extend state influence'. The prominent male Antis 'were wary of legislation on old age pensions' and they were 'alarmed by the suffragist claim that the vote would enable Parliament to regulate wages in women's favour'.[15] That was another story, however.

Tory suffragists

The Primrose League remained militantly agnostic on votes for women. Its agnosticism was not only an accommodation to the powerful opponents of women's suffrage in the party and the League, but a characteristic abstention from women's politics as such. It did not quite mean non-alignment; rather it described the propriety of women's subordination within Conservatism.

Of the two main political parties, it fell to the Liberal women to come out and campaign for the suffrage, but at some cost to inner-party unity. The Women's Liberal Federation had been formed in response to the rise of the Primrose League and in the 1890s a minority began to challenge the federation itself as well as Gladstone and the rest of the Liberal leadership over votes for women. Rosalind Howarth, the radical Countess of Carlisle, reckoned that at the time the

> Liberal headquarters approved the enrolment of Liberal women up to a point. They were quite ready to welcome the help of women in distributing literature, canvassing and what, under a most faulty registration law of the period, was the blessed work of hunting up removals. They were to be the auxiliaries loyally adopting the party line. Mrs Gladstone was the first president of the Women's Liberal Federation. It was perhaps the idea that the Federation should be to the party what Mrs Gladstone was to her husband.[16]

This was of course the relationship between the Primrose League and the Tories, too.

Gladstone had urged that women's suffrage be deferred until Irish Home Rule had been settled – a familiar invitation to feminism to self-destruct within political parties across history. The women's federation answered by adopting women's suffrage after a long wrangle in 1892. The suffragists had triumphed but the struggle split Liberal woman from woman. The Women's Liberal Federation foregrounded the suffrage, but the party loyalists seceded and formed a breakaway Women's National Liberal Federation. At that time there were 16,000 members of the Women's Liberal Federation; after more than a decade of passionate campaigning for the vote for women they reached 100,000. Lady Carlisle was one of the pioneers of the pro-suffrage caucus, although she was later to mourn the divorce: 'We failed to make haste slowly. It was a horrible, hateful chasm which yawned beneath our feet, when we acted in ignorance of all that would follow. We ought to have achieved the same and without the loss of that most expensive victory.'[17] The sisters were not re-united until 1919, after limited women's suffrage was conceded by Parliament.

Constituency women and individuals were at liberty to support Liberal candidates opposed to the suffrage, but the federation would work only for those who supported the cause, a cause which in the years before the First World War was to become what George Dangerfield has called in *The Strange Death of Liberal England* 'above all things a movement from darkness into light, and from death into life'.[18] The federation had no doubt where the blame lay for the wreckage wrought within the party by divisions over votes for women. 'There can be no real peace or concord in the Liberal ranks until the women's suffrage question is settled righteously.'[19] Nor was there – the suffragettes called the Liberal government's bluff and exposed the 'caprice of a fading Liberalism'.[20] It near enough killed the Liberals and 'the old respectability'.

From all that passion the Primrose League abstained. Agnostic it might have been, but that didn't make its habitations anti-suffrage. The men's Grand Council felt moved to speak out:

> The Grand Council has reason to believe that various circulars requesting habitations to take up the question of the suffrage have reached Ruling Councillors, Dame Presidents, and Honorary Secretaries of Habitations and desire to take this opportunity of reminding all officials that the question of women's suffrage is outside the province of the League, and that, therefore, Habitations as a body should take no part in the controversy.[21]

The Grand Council hastened to add that a letter by Lord Beaconsfield in 1878, which was being used to endorse the suffragists, 'applied only to the property qualification and not universal suffrage'. The tone suggested where the Grand Council's sympathies lay. The following year the Grand Council ruled that members might have their own views but must not oppose Unionist candidates in elections.[22]

Despite reassurances to the Conservative suffragists by party leader and Primrose League President Arthur Balfour that all candidates were free to support the suffrage, the heavyweights who *actively* intervened in suffrage politics were Antis. Balfour's predecessor, Lord Salisbury, supported a suffrage Bill in 1884 when the Liberals were in power, although he opposed it during a Tory administration. Balfour supported women's suffrage, too, but neither felt it was a priority.[23]

Some Primrose League Dames (including Jennie Churchill) were also suffragists and when the Antis set up men's and women's committees to campaign against votes for women in 1908 one of them, the Countess of Selborne, formed the Conservative and Unionist Women's Suffrage Association in the same year. She was joined by Betty Balfour, a relative of the Balfour dynasty, who quit as Dame President of her Woking Primrose League Habitation in 1910 because her local Tory MP had voted against the suffrage. This she took to

> imply assent to the anti-suffrage doctrine that to enfranchise women would be an act dangerous to the constitution and the Empire. In my view any Member recording such a vote should consistently with it be averse to women actively working in politics. To continue to work for such a member seems to me an absurdity.[24]

Betty Balfour and her association were pledged not to oppose Unionist candidates in elections, but 'also not to work for anyone who is against the principle of woman suffrage'.

Among its inner circle were the Countess of Ancaster, a Primrose League Dame, and the Viscountess of Castlereagh, Edith Vane-Tempest, whose father was the Tory socialite Henry Chaplin, a Primrose League veteran and anti-suffragist, and whose husband was also a Tory MP. She described herself as an 'ardent supporter of the suffragist Millicent Fawcett. Her mother-in-law was Lady Londonderry, a Primrose League Dame, who 'looked on my ideas with suspicion'.[25] Nonetheless, she believed that the older woman, who was a 'power in the land', held her own secret desires:

> in her subconscious mind she had reserved to herself alone, should victory be won, the right to sit and speak in the House of Commons – a proposition I always thought unnecessary, and at that period impossible.[26]

The Viscountess joined the calumny over a diatribe against votes for women in *The Times* by Sir Almroth Wright and had her own letter published. 'Judge then of my mother-in-law's feelings when she espied a long letter in the centre page of *The Times* in April 1912.' Her letter proposed that the great pathology professor's own sex

> was not immune from mental attacks. How else could we account for sensational headings in the daily press, 'Husband murders wife and family' . . . not to mention sensational murders by men calling themselves the lovers of their victims.[27]

Her commitment was a *cause célèbre* within the dynasty. During a luncheon with her mother-in-law in August 1914, after her husband had been called to war,

> my recent 'goings-on' as they were called, were challenged by the editor of a famous newspaper. He said to me that he would like to make a bet with me. I asked him the purport. 'Well, Lady Castlereagh,' he said, 'it is this, I will bet you five pounds that at the end of the war there will be no suffragettes. War will teach women the impossibility of their demands and the absurdity of their claims.' I immediately accepted the bet.[28]

Lady Castlereagh was a founder of the Women's Legion and a great believer in the women's forces movement during the war. She felt she had won the bet – 'By the end of the war, 80 per cent of the labour in this country was carried on by women' – and she later recalled that the moves to expel women from the workforce left her 'burning with indignation at the injustice of much of this agitation'. By 1918 the franchise was conceded to women over thirty. Even her father softened up on the suffrage. He'd gone to stay at one of the depots where members of the Women's Royal Air Force learned to strap and ride horses.

> He never could resist a horse, and when he saw these attractive amazons in their neat Jodhpur breeches doing all the work in the stables, under the management of a stud groom, his admiration knew no bounds. He had always been opposed

to women's suffrage but seeing these girls he said to me that he had completely changed his idea.[29]

The Selborne group set about lobbying Tory MPs, and adopted tactics rather more sedate than those of their sisters in the suffrage societies and of the Antis. Many of their targets were, of course, also their friends. Arthur Steel-Maitland, a Primrose Leaguer, wrote to Lady Selborne from Central Office in November 1912, disclosing his conservative dilemma: 'I think it is weak not to vote, so until I am convinced of the need for change I vote against it. But I have never been satisfied that I have "found" truth either way.'[30]

Conservative suffragists concentrated their efforts on dogged but discreet lobbying which, given the small and select circles which characterised the ruling class, often meant that the women were lobbying the men in their very households. Edith Castlereagh wrote to Maud Selborne on 23 December 1912: 'Charles says he will vote on any amendment that will upset the government!! Most immoral.' Having promised to support a forthcoming amendment, Edith Castlereagh promised 'to see that he learns it up ... in fact I fear he only supports us as he thinks it is expedient'.[31]

When the suffragist societies decided to combine their resources to lobby MPs on the forthcoming Conciliation Bill, a compromise which would have granted suffrage to women householders only, the Conservative and Unionist Women's Franchise Association were happy to collaborate – but in their own decorous way, and rather protective of their MPs' sensibilities. 'We would be glad to join the suggested Joint Board of Representatives,' wrote Louise Gilbert Samuel, for the association:

It would, of course, be a great help to us, but I think I ought to tell you straight away that although we should be of great use in writing to Conservative Members, and in interviewing them privately, and so on, I don't think we could possibly do any lobbying in the House itself.[32]

Enclosing a list of Unionist MPs who were pledged to support the Conciliation Bill, she reported that:

Lady Selborne and I think that as we are going to remind them of their promises from this office three days before the opening of Parliament, it might be advisable that they should not be bothered from your office also, as we have their promises, and we think it is better that they should not be worried by more than one society.[33]

During the campaign for the Conciliation Bill, when 4,000 pro-suffrage meetings were organised throughout the country,[34] the Conservative suffragette, Lady Constance Lytton, tried in vain to bolster the commitment of Arthur Balfour, who agreed to meet her with Annie Kenney in 1911. 'He listened to the two suffragettes with great courtesy and forbearance, and promised nothing at all.'[35] The confinement of the suffrage to men had 'torpedoed' the Conciliation Bill and furthermore split the cross-party alliance among pro-suffrage women.[36]

After the Conciliation Bill was defeated the suffrage movement went on to the offensive with militant direct action, and although the Conservative suffragists were moderate both in their political practice and in their limited objectives, which stopped short of full adult suffrage, Lady Lytton was prominent among the militants. After meeting Mary Neal, secretary of a North London working girls' club, and sharing a seaside holiday with the girls in 1908, she had met Annie Kenney, the working-class suffragette, and in 1909 joined the Women's Social and Political Union (WSPU). She got herself arrested and encountered the traumas of working-class poverty among prisoners she met in Holloway prison. Thereafter, according to Betty Balfour, 'she immersed herself in the lives of those she befriended, rather than trying to "save" them'.[37] The shift into militant direct action in the years between the demise of the Conciliation Bill and the First World War prompted Lady Selborne to stand aside and wait for the militants 'to break a certain amount of crockery. We can only stand by and be ready to pick up the pieces afterwards.'[38] However, Constance Lytton told Lady Selborne that she believed that

but for militancy the government have nothing to lose by constantly deferring women's suffrage, and according to their view, they run some risks by going ahead with it. It has been our object to reverse that order of their well-being.[39]

Only after limited women's suffrage was conceded after the war did the differences over the appropriate spheres of women's influence appear to dissolve. Prominent Antis and suffrage supporters found themselves together in promoting women and the same Conservative cause. Edith Castlereagh sat with Mrs Humphry Ward on the committee formed to appoint women Justices of the Peace. Edith Castlereagh herself was appointed as the first woman JP. The Duchess of Atholl, an active Anti, became one of the first Conservative woman MPs, following Lady Astor, into the House.

The Liberal Violet Markham, who stood for Parliament unsuccessfully in the 1918 general election, reflected rather regretfully on her past association with the Antis, particularly since the pro-suffrage campaigner Eleanor Rathbone generously offered her support during Markham's election campaign in Mansfield. 'Few men or women would have been capable of such magnanimity, for my conversion was of recent date and she might well have regarded my views with suspicion.'[40] She confessed that she had 'little pleasure' in looking back on her anti-suffrage days, but explained that she had 'real reverence' for Lord Cromer and that 'if I erred, I erred in good company'.[41] Nevertheless, she had suffered qualms: 'I had now and again an uncomfortable feeling that I had stumbled into a hotbed of reactionaries.'[42] Markham shared with Mrs Humphry Ward a desire to 'set on foot constructive proposals for promoting women's public work, especially in the local government field', but she suggests that Lord Cromer refused to be budged even on this. He was simply anti-suffrage, and did not endorse the women's attempts to use the Anti-Suffrage League as an instrument to promote women in local government – in 1912 there were only twenty-one women members of town councils, three members of county councils and 232 women on Boards of Guardians.[43] She became a convert to women's suffrage when it dawned on her that the 'denial of political rights to women involved a spiritual as well as a political principle. It meant, in effect, the stabilisation of a status of permanent inferiority.'[44] And that was not what she had believed at all.

From auxiliaries to members

In the first decades of the twentieth century, Conservative women began the process of transition from auxiliaries to full members of the party. Despite the undoubted and spectacular success of the Primrose League ladies in working for the Tory cause, there had always been redoubts of resistance among some of the male party functionaries, particularly unsympathetic agents. By the early years of the twentieth century, women were beginning to join the party, a prospect which struck fear into the heart of the Primrose League – and for good reason. It lanced its *raison d'être*.

George Lane-Fox, a veteran of the Primrose League, complained in 1906 that the re-organisation of the National Union

> seems to mean in several places simply the formation of 'Women's Conservative Associations' to *work against the Primrose League*, which is not likely to benefit the Party and is causing friction in places and any man who gets women fighting against women will do more harm than all the Radical associations ever did.[45]

Whatever his fears, however, he and the League could not be seen to oppose the women's associations:

> Of course we give the strictest orders to our provincial secretaries and speakers i.e. not to say a word against the new women's associations, hope that the whole blame for the mess that may result, must fall solely upon the Conservative agents, who are starting them on their own responsibility entirely, as the National Union people tell me, *they* have not helped and have *not* suggested this dodge, but there are still men among the agents who oppose and hate the Primrose League as much as they did 20 years ago.[46]

The League had opened up the political space to women. It was only a matter of time before the Conservative associations would have to open their doors, too. To some of them there was apparently no fate worse than the ladies of the Primrose League. Commenting on the confusion about the difference between the Primrose League and the Conservative associations, a Primrose League loyalist, Miss Wilkinson, suggested:

> they know the difference consists in the fact that women's right to know and women's work are recognised in the League, while Conservative Associations are spared (mercifully, as they think!) any interference from women.[47]

The establishment of women's branches within the Tory Party ultimately doomed the Primrose League, which had in any case peaked, and during the 1920s, although the League shared the paranoid anti-socialist preoccupations of the party women's associations, it watched their growth with the gimlet eye of a fading genius. Nevertheless, it remained a formidable social force in Britain throughout the 1920s and 1930s. Norman Lewis notes a piquant encounter with one of the League's squires, Enfield's Tory MP, Col. Sir Henry Ferryman Bowles of Forty Hall, in his autobiography *Jackdaw Cake*. The manor was 'a phenomenon of English rural life hardly changed since the invention of the open field system of agriculture'. The colonel 'wielded huge and uncontested power, paid the lowest wages in the county, and was understood to possess a harem of three young, gracious and well-bred girls'. Lewis met the colonel when he went to ask permission to go birdnesting. The colonel 'glanced down at his watch and said regretfully that he would have come with me but for the fact that he had to chair a meeting of the Primrose League, an association of toilers for the Conservative cause'.[48]

The League was unnerved by the competition and even the threat of being subsumed by the women's associations within the party and in 1924 the Grand Council complained of 'further attempts to stifle Primrose League activity, or to absorb our organisation on the part of newly-formed organisations'. But the process was inexorable. After the vote was conceded to some women in the 1918 Representation of the People Act, the Women's Unionist Organisation was formed, and by its 1921 conference had more than 1,300 branches. In many areas women's Parliamentary committees were set up to link MPs' wives with the party women's network – wives were women's conduit to the ear of their MP. The expanded electorate created a fresh imperative to draw new constituencies and classes into the Conservative orbit, and the Tories' defeat in the 1922 general election prompted a review of inner-party organisation which also assimilated women into the party's infrastructure to a degree unrivalled by their protagonists on the left.

'Women are not natural revolutionaries'

Home and Politics was a party paper the very title of which demonstrated the Conservatives' commitment to the link between the private and the public, and in which regular features on organisation identified both the 'working woman' and the domestic woman as potential activists. Putney women's branch had Lady Moyers as its honorary secretary, and she hinted at the residual resistance to women when she wrote in *Home and Politics* that when she formed the women's branch 'I found I had many prejudices to combat and at first progress was slow.'[49] She established a network of ward committees staffed by women 'who had already given proof of their interest in public work'. She then targeted working women:

> My next step was to hold Working Women's meetings. I think this is the most vital part of our work, because the mind of nearly every working woman is politically virgin soil, and will yield a crop according to the nature of the seed that is sown. Women are not natural revolutionaries. They are loyal and law abiding, and want above all the preservation of their religion and their homes. Convince them that the principles of the Unionist Cause stand for an England true to its traditions of justice and fair play, and their staunch adherence is secured.

The traditions to which the new women's associations appealed had already been well established by the Primrose League.

This was, however, a newly democratised world in which women were seen as virgin citizens to be chaperoned across its threshold by their socially superior sisters. More than that, it was a world riven by revolution, and *Home and Politics* felt obliged to caution its readers not simply to sit and knit while their treasured traditions were ransacked. Some 'educated women' were likened to 'the aristocrats of France before the French Revolution, who refused to listen to the muttering of the storm until it broke over their heads, bringing about their utter annihilation'. As in the formative years of the Primrose League, the Conservative Party seemed to be fighting for its life. Mrs H. J. W. Fosbery pursued the same theme: 'Our opponents are not leaving things to chance, for it is known that the Socialists are straining every nerve to capture constituencies. We must therefore be on our guard.'[50] It was not just a matter of canvassing or electioneering, but of creating a culture and cross-class alliances within the community. She proposed small networks across about twenty households, with meetings attended by 'a lady who is popular and likely to bring her friends', together with all influential Unionist women (representative of all classes), the local Unionist agent and speakers from party headquarters.

Early in Neville Chamberlain's tenure of the Ladywood division, his wife undertook the mobilisation of women in what she was 'proud to call . . . a working-class constituency' by a network of clubs, for she declared herself 'a club enthusiast'.[51] Mrs Chamberlain's clubs held fortnightly afternoon meetings, with tea and a cake at a penny each, and at 'the request of members a sewing party was started at which materials may be purchased and paid for by instalments; also a dispensary club and a library'. While busy with their needles, there would be recitations, songs and speeches. Quarterly programmes were distributed offering dissertations on, for example, the monarchy, the city's work among children, the political outlook as it affected women, electoral work, industrial action and Bolshevism, and as men were recruited to the association their 'womenfolk' were visited by Conservative representatives too.[52]

Apart from the establishment of their own structures, the party began training women agents, and strong women's representation was inscribed in the arrangements for national conferences, to which women were admitted in 1920. Showing an extraordinary commitment to the female presence, associations were required to elect delegations comprising one-third women to the 1921 National Unionist Associations (NUA) conference, and Women's Unionist Organisation (WUO) secretaries were invited to confer with agents 'and arrange mutually that the proper number of women representatives be elected'.[53] The Conservatives were proud not only of the women's representation but also of their appeal to the working class. In its report on the 1924 NUA conference, *Home and Politics* described 'the whole trend and spirit' of the conference as 'to urge the need for the entry of working class supporters into the Association. It was in very fact a striking sign that we are determined not to allow even the suggestion of our party being a "class party".'[54]

Stung by a *Daily Herald* report that no women spoke at the NUA annual conference in 1925 and, therefore, 'very few of these Tory women had been brought there by a genuine interest in public affairs', *Home and Politics* parried:

We should rather like to know how many resolutions at the recent Labour Party Conference were moved by women, and how many spoke. It is also singularly interesting to know that at that Conference out of 1,100 delegates only 60 were women. At the Conservative Conference, out of over 2,000 delegates, nearly 1,000 were women.[55]

Either Labour women were too apathetic to attend, it concluded, 'or else the men of the Labour Party, who are so keen on the principle of equality (but not the practice), see that little chance is given to their women of doing so'. Apparently, Conservative women themselves were disappointed at the lack of opportunity for women to express themselves at the party conference. 'All around one heard regret that there had been no women speakers, who with their high idealism have roused enthusiasm at other Conferences and lifted politics from the mere material plane to something saner and more inspiring,' wrote C. Isabel Green, from Abingdon, in *Home and Politics*. 'We must see to it that women are ready to take their fair share at next year's Conference.'[56]

When the 1927 conference discussed a refinement of the party rules governing conference delegates, Dame Caroline Bridgeman and Lady Elveden, two of the women's organisers with a powerful base in the constituencies, intervened with a controversial amendment to consolidate women's right to be represented. Delegations were to include two officials, the chairman and agent, and two lay representatives, one man and one woman. The women proposed that since women could be constituency chairmen, the rule should specify instead that at least one of the representatives should be a woman, and since women could now be association chairmen, delegations could send more women – indeed they could be three women and one man. Their proposal was carried.

Women and reconstruction

Just as women had been central to the creation of Conservatism's social base as a modern, mass political formation in the late nineteenth century, so women were inscribed at the centre of Conservatism's new political discourse after the First World War. After the collapse of the 1918–22 Conservative–Liberal coalition and a couple of volatile years winning and losing elections, the Tories regained power in 1924 and settled in for the evening of the Edwardian era. Tory fortunes began to revive as their new leader, Stanley Baldwin, overhauled not only the party machine but also the party's political rhetoric. Baldwin mobilised traditionalism explicitly against the new social forces which were taking to the streets and aiming for the

corridors of power during the 1920s. In the aftermath of a cata-
strophic war, the irrepressible clamour of Irish nationalism, the
insistent political ingenuity of suffragettes who had invented a
new vocabulary of direct action, and the insurgency of the labour
movement, Baldwin's ideological impact was 'to blur moments of
rupture and breakdown, privileging continuity rather than
transformation',[57] and as a result his constitutionalist ideology was
to conceal the historical conditions of its emergence. After the
First World War the government could no longer resist women's
suffrage – the 1918 Representation of the People Act allowed
women over thirty to vote. It took the Tories nearly another decade
to concede the vote to women on the same terms as men.

As collective amnesia descended upon the Tories, Baldwin was
to be celebrated as the man who quietly complemented evolution
(rather than the revolution) when he promised in 1927 to complete
universal suffrage. There was an exquisite irony in the presence at
that year's party women's conference of Emmeline Pankhurst, who
was adopted as a Conservative prospective Parliamentary candidate.
It was the Conservatives and Baldwin who finally enjoyed the credit
for the completion of the 'universal democratic subject'.[58]

Conservative leaders had for decades been more or less indifferent
to the pressure for the vote, but in the 1920s the Conservatives
claimed it as their own triumph and, more than that, as an exemplar
of constitutionalism. 'Woman has *not* won her present advantages
by force; they were freely and generously given her by the Coalition
Government, once they had been convinced of the justice of her
claims,' wrote Edythe M. Glanville[59] in *Home and Politics* in 1922.

But after the war, the Conservatives found themselves in an
unfamiliar position. They had to subdue a popular power which
they'd hardly even conversed with before. The terms of this conversation were

> indeterminate and open until the period of the most intense
> industrial and class confrontations in 1925–26. It was in
> those years that the democratic advances embodied in the act
> were finally tied to Baldwinite Conservatism, and that hopes
> for a more assertive, radical and popular conception of
> democracy – both representative and direct – were decisively
> smashed.[60]

Bill Schwarz has mapped Baldwin's ideological construction of a crusade for political salvation with the idea of 'national identity' at its centre: 'Englishness and continuity became condensed through an invocation of the temporal rhythms of the natural world.'[61] So, the Sunday morning murmur of men and women in their homes and gardens became emblematic of the English soul. The radio brought Baldwin's voice into the home, and his rustic ruminations on the essence of English identity symbolised the domestication of Conservative ideology. But, of course, the war had cut the umbilical cord between the woman and the home. About 1.2 million women had joined the paid labour force during the war, and 750,000 joined trade unions, special subsidies encouraged local authorities to set up nurseries, and fierce debates raged within the trade union movement about women's access to skilled jobs and equal pay.[62] There were among Conservative women those who, like their proletarian sisters, saw the war and its effects on the economic position of women as great progress. Lady Castlereagh, for example, celebrated working women's contribution to the war in her assertion that 'by the end of the war 80 per cent of the labour in this country was carried on by women'[63], and in her continuing commitment to the women she recalled that the clamour to expel women from the waged workforce left her 'burning with indignation at the injustice of much of this agitation'.

Nevertheless, the dominant tenor of Conservative women's political discourse represented the war as a catastrophe from which the nation needed to recover and socialism as an unnatural practice nestling in the crannies of that catastrophe. National recovery meant both putting the war behind them and putting socialism, alias the devil, behind them, too.

Alert to the impact of the war on relations between men and women, and to the excitement of women's own economic aspirations, the party paper *The Popular View* noted women's flight from the home:

> What should be a highly specialised profession has grown to be looked upon as something ignoble and menial. Woman created the home in self-interest, and now in self-interest she is leaving it . . . But perhaps even at the eleventh hour self-interest may win woman back.[64]

By the encouragement of a new contract between men and women,

> a woman may help her husband to acquire a fortune; she is
> certainly worth a living wage, and he must meet the
> competition of other industries to give her a share in his
> property. In other words, if he is willing to pay he has the
> means of keeping his wife at home.

Here was proposed a renaissance of respectability: men's responsibility was to earn enough to keep their wives at home; woman's right was to have her domestic labour valued.

The ideology of separate spheres, which had been ruptured massively by the First World War, was rehabilitated with the labour movement's participation after the war. Women (well, some of them) got the vote but lost the right to hang on to the jobs, nurseries, wages and union rights they had enjoyed during the war. The effect of the 1918 Restoration of Pre-War Practices Act was to treat women as if the war had never happened.[65] There were clear trends towards a greater, more gainful women's employment, but the trade union movement was unable to abandon its patriarchal past. And so, going against the economic grain, its past defined its present. Many of the men of the trade union movement still regarded women as competitors rather than comrades, and like the Conservative Party, much of the labour movement still harboured what the pro-feminist William Thompson had described almost a century earlier as 'sexual Toryism'.[66]

Out of the war-time cauldron – characterised as much as anything by sizzling conflict within the labour movement over the relationship between the sexes – emerged the Labour Party, which was to bring organised labour into the political sphere with its own party. *Organised* was the operative word. Female labour had been disorganised, the trade union movement had once again been masculinised, and the Labour Party was the creation of that men's movement. (The wider labour movement also embraced a formidable feminist-socialist tradition and those neglected radicals, the Co-operative Women's Guilds, but neither had any real power within the Labour Party.) The party had a women's section designed 'to create a national representation for women within a party whose affiliated organisations were overwhelmingly masculine'.[67] For decades to come the party spoke with two voices, the voice of patriarchy and the voice of women.

Labour women had their own agenda; their Women's Charter advocated economic equality between the sexes, public ownership of utilities, and the expansion of social provision of meals and other household labours; their debates concerned the vote for women, housing, the conditions of orphans, unemployment among women, family allowances, mothers' pensions, and so on. But in practice, the Labour Party endorsed the 'sexual Toryism' of the dominant ideology. When it came to the territory of the household Labour, having failed, so to say, to put its own house in order, conceded the political initiative to the right; the Tories colonised the politics of home and hearth, and that became their base against the new enemies: Bolshevism, sexual equality, British socialism and strikes.

A crusade against socialism

Women were conceived by the Tories as a category outside the labour movement. They represented 'moral influence' and 'common sense' on the one hand and an innocent and vulnerable citizenry on the other, a de-politicised disposition which wedded them to the project of Baldwin who 'resolutely presented himself as non-political, as the little man thrust unwillingly onto the public stage, talking to others of his type'.[68] He appeared to speak the language of women, placing their sphere of influence, the home, at the centre of his litany of a new kind of Conservatism – a domesticated, everyday ideology of common sense.

The Conservatives launched their crusade against social democracy, which, with the demise of the Liberal Party, became the enemy within. The home was represented as the bastion against statism and socialism; it was seen as the imperative for capital accumulation and self-improvement; it was the source of women's power over their children and therefore over the future. But even before Baldwinism established itself in the mid-1920s, women's separate sphere within the home was seen as the essence of a *natural* national character threatened by an imaginary Bolshevik armada with its fifth column already in place in co-op halls, factories and even classrooms where communist teachers and indoctrinated children insinuated their alien ideology.

The spectre of socialism haunted Conservative women throughout the inter-war years. Their tradition since the greatest years of the Primrose League locked them into a defence of institutions which were now besieged by the demands of the increasingly insurgent 'masses'. Socialism was no longer only a gleam in their eyes – it had taken power in 1917 and established a 'new social order' in the Soviet Union, and its echoes sang across Europe, music to the ears of radicals, tumbrils rattling the nightmares of anyone with anything to lose.

Bolshevism was the context in which Conservative women's ideology took on the ideas about sexual equality that were displacing the old pre-war puritanism expressed in the suffragette slogan 'Votes for women, chastity for men'. Sexual equality was represented not only as an impossible ideal but as the denial of nature, the suppression of sexual difference, and thus the annihilation of women's special sphere of influence. Socialism and sexual equality were seen, therefore, as unnatural, as sinister social engineering.

The liberated woman was a woman denied both sanctity and sanctuary. Sylvia Pankhurst's advocacy of free love and a new domestic contract between men and women in 'Communism and the Family' prompted a critique in *Home and Politics*: 'Under Socialism there will be no more marriages as we know them.'[69] Not only were mothers and daughters 'to be at the mercy of "free love"', but the state would 'map out their lives'. The state and men would see off women's 'separate sphere': 'The home will go. Naturally where there is "free love" there can be no homes.' No doubt, many Labour candidates in forthcoming elections would have hardly recognised themselves as sexual libertarians, particularly given the culture of patriarchal respectability within the labour movement, but the Conservatives nevertheless identified fellow travellers as the enemies of home-loving women:

> As we do not want to be subjected to 'free love' or our daughters to be given to men in this way; as we wish to keep our homes and 'our' children . . . we must give our votes to keep out candidates who incline towards these views . . . we can keep ourselves from socialist servitude, for we should be slaves of the state under socialism.[70]

Radical sexual politics was conflated with the challenge of Bolshevism, and the critique of it in Conservative women's ideology was deployed not so much against sexual reformers campaigning in

Britain for birth control and for women's right to sexual pleasure as against family legislation in the new Soviet socialist state.

The woman voting in general elections for the first time after 1918 had the extra duties of citizenship to be exercised not only in her own interests but in the interests of the nation:

> She now has the power of defending and advancing home-life, which is the very basis of our civilisation . . . To do the socialist justice, he knows that his cause will advance but little unless he destroys the home, and orders our lives from birth to death.[71]

Women as mothers were warned to watch out for creepy communists, usurping the power of parents and staining the minds of the innocent. The Duchess of Atholl, formerly an anti-suffragist, but by now an MP, warned the 1924 mass meeting of women at the end of the National Union of Conservative Associations conference that communists and socialists were trying to 'win the children for the "class struggle" by means of their Sunday schools'.[72] And at the conference itself, Miss Felix Jones of Sutton Coldfield 'drew attention to the number of school teachers who had left our Party to join the Socialists'. Conservatives, she said, should be elected to local councils to 'prevent Communist teachers being appointed to posts in Council schools'. The growth of socialist Sunday schools became an obsession during the 1920s, when the Conservatives promoted anti-blasphemy legislation to wipe them out and alerted mothers, in particular, to 'be very careful not to let their children join any Sunday school, society or organisation without making full inquiries as to its objects and the character of its promoters'.[73]

Conservative politics in the schools was, of course, only natural. The Welsh writer Gwyn Thomas's first novel, *Sorrow for Thy Sons*, set in the Welsh valleys during the Depression, reports the visit of a local VIP to lecture schoolboys on their future:

> The Empire was formed by your fathers to give you succour. Take it and the traditions of our land and the Empire will not fail you. Do not lose heart if an occasional pit happens to close down here. New worlds are being opened up in Canada, Australia, South Africa. There your hopes should lie.

The headmaster stands to address the bolshie boys:

He instinctively repeated some of the Primrose catchwords that had run thematically through the visitor's speech: 'Be brave', 'New worlds, new lives, new opportunities'. 'Be brave', 'Avoid discontent', 'Be loyal', 'Be brave'.

The newly formed Labour Party was a linguistic as well as a political problem for the Conservatives. The arrival of a popular mass party with a clear class alignment challenged the Conservatives' claim to be a party of one nation and all classes, to which they responded by recruiting among working-class voters and reviewing the modernising of the inner-party structures. 'We must go into the back yards and into the little alleys, where people live, often in the greatest hardship and distress, and where nobody goes but the Socialists,' Mrs Neville Chamberlain (as she called herself) told the Conservative women's mass meeting in 1924. The party would not rest with the title of the new working-class party, and seeking to repudiate its class alignment it pre-fixed Labour with 'socialist', a device designed to connect the Labour Party with the allegedly alien internationalism of Bolshevism:

> 'What's in a name?' goes the old saying. But the 'Labour' Party
> know there is a great deal; that is why they refuse to come
> out in their true colours as the Socialist Party and continue to
> delude people with the harmless sounding 'Labour Party'
> label.[74]

John Whittacker, the chairman of the Conservatives' Labour Sub-Committee, insisted that 'there is no scheme of social reform which has for its object the amelioration of the conditions under which the working classes live and labour which cannot be obtained by and through the Unionist Party'.[75] The Conservative Party believed itself to be the friend of the workers and their unions, and under pressure from Tory trade unionists began to set up labour sub-committees, attempted to integrate their representatives in constituency structures and urged its members, both men and women, to join trade unions.

The thick red wedge which had to be blunted was the trade union movement – and this was one of Baldwin's triumphs. The Tories declared themselves not to be opposed to trade unions as such, but 'to their use for the propagation of socialism, as is done by the

"Socialist Labour" Party'. Unlike the first three decades of the Primrose League, the post-war Conservative women's movement was forced to address itself to the world outside itself, the other Britain where they were encircled by mass movements which were also 'British'. The Co-operative Women's Guild or the miners' federation were no less expressive of national identities than the Dames of the Primrose League, but theirs was a culture of challenge which drew inspiration not only from exotic revolt elsewhere, but from their own experience. That's what made them dangerous.

In her review of the 1925 party conference, C. Isabel Green lamented that there were seven resolutions on the problem of trade unionism, 'but I was struck by the fact that Women Trade Unionists were never once mentioned!'[76] The decade began with an all-time high in trade union membership – 8 million. In 1925 women held the first of their own TUC conferences, although their membership declined through the 1920s and 1930s (as it did among men), even while the proportion of women in the waged workforce increased to one-third (not counting all the unregistered washerwomen, cleaners and babyminders).[77] Aware of the rise of women's trade unionism and the quest for women's support during men's strikes, *The Popular View* in July 1921 presented an alternative vision of a wife with distinctly different interests from those of her husband. It was an early incarnation of a dominant Conservative image of women's pleasure in consumption:

> Groceries are snugly packed into her basket, and her work
> ends with a visit to the fruiterer's where she buys potatoes,
> greens, a little dessert for Sunday, and a bunch of flowers. The
> world pours its treasures into her lap, because her husband
> is in work and earning a regular wage. In every great strike the
> woman pays . . . The outside world often marvels at the
> heroic obstinacy with which certain classes of workers deprive
> themselves of pay for weeks, or even months in pursuit of
> some impossible ideal. Nothing is heard of the sufferings of
> women and children.

The Conservatives were not unaware, however, of the engagement of women and children in the 'heroic obstinacy' of their communities. *Home and Politics* noted that Labour leaders realise no doubt that the 'solidarity of the men' in certain industrial disputes has been considerably weakened by the half-hearted support or common sense condemnation of 'such goings-on' by some of the women – who, after all, bear the brunt of strikes.[78]

Smiling but determined women, including both nurses and pilots, stride forth on the cover of *Home and Politics* during the summer of 1926, hauling behind them the be-flagged barge of Britain:

Unionist women have never doubted the magnificent qualities of our leader. Our Prime Minister *is* a man of peace, but there are some who have thought him a man of 'peace at any price'. They know, as we have long known, that Mr Baldwin's actions are governed by wisdom and not by weakness.[79]

Trade union membership was one thing, action was quite another, and struck at the heart of Conservative constitutionalism. The strike was represented as an attack on the community and subsequently 'direct action' was represented as an affront to the new democracy implied by universal suffrage: it was anti-Parliamentary and it was anti-constitutional.

Family chancellors

In Conservative women's propaganda during the 1920s, woman's responsibility towards the Empire was articulated in her special role as the family's 'chancellor' and as the universal mother to an empire of infants. 'The family remained the basic institution of society and women's domestic role remained supreme, but gradually it was her function as a mother that was being most stressed, rather than her function as a wife.'[80] Empire-buying was to the women of the right what the apartheid boycott was to the left in the 1980s. At the 1924 party conference, Mrs Stewart from Newcastle asked Tory leaders to back the proposed Merchandise Marks Bill so that British men 'and especially British women' might have an 'unmistakable indication as to whether they were purchasing goods produced by workmen of our own country and Empire'.[81] The government did indeed bring in the Act. The Empire shopping campaign organised among Conservative women in the 1920s had often been thwarted by the absence of any indications of origin. Amidst the economic crisis of that decade the Conservatives appeared to mobilise women as protectionist shoppers on the side of the British working man. 'The price of Empire was, in a large degree, first paid by countless women of early emigrant days,' wrote Women's Unionist Organisation chairman, the Viscountess Elveden, when she elaborated 'The Empire's Appeal to Women' in *Home and Politics*.[82] For a start, women pioneers had created a new life 'in new lands, where the comforts and protection of civilisation had not yet dawned'.

Racism was inscribed in the eugenicist analogy between motherhood and imperialism. The mother holds dominion over her children as England over her infant dominions:

> The Empire's appeal also lies in the conception of Empire as
> a great family – a family in which the children have grown
> up and gone their ways, developing on lines new to their parents
> and, from their novelty, perhaps distrusted by them, but who,
> like human children, in times of stress and trouble turn again
> to the old home.

And racism yet more explicit is expressed in Viscountess Elveden's challenge to democracy: 'Will it permit the survival of the race and its progression to the highest types of which it is capable, or will it check it and cause a retrogression to lower types?'[83] The cover pictures of *Home and Politics* during this period show 'Little Imperialists at Play' in their snug living room with their own toy, 'British Empire Stores'; 'The Legacy ' with a mother holding her young son towards a globe as she stands in her living room beneath a framed wall photograph of a young officer; and above the caption 'Learn to Think Imperially' a young mother holds her child as she sits, Britannia-like, on the cliffs overlooking the ocean – beyond which there will be brothers, uncles, family . . .

Where the Primrose League celebrated the idea of Empire in its Victorian high noon, the new Conservative women *worked* for imperial preference. Their work as shoppers became work for the cause: Home, Nation and Empire.

The masses

There was by the mid-1920s a considerable mass movement among the working class and women which the Conservatives watched with a jealous eye – the co-operative movement. A recent historian of the Primrose League, Martin Pugh, compares the Primrose League favourably with smaller radical organisations, but he overestimates the extent to which the Conservative tradition politicised women and underestimates the challenge of the radicals in the early twentieth century. This is not least because he tends to assess the Primrose League in terms of scale and form rather than content. The co-operative movement had six million members in 1,000 societies by the end of the twenties; it involved its members in the 'visionary' aspiration 'of those who desire to see the Community in control, instead of the Capitalists', and as one of the largest manufacturing and trading organisations in the land shared its profits among the purchasers.[84]

The co-operative movement was more than an idea; all over the country it had concrete monuments to its capacity for self-help, a virtue not exclusive to the Conservatives. And apart from its wholesale and retail industries, it had what were often caring and combative Co-operative Women's Guilds garrisoned in hundreds of communities. The Co-operative Women's Guild was formed in 1883 and had 67,000 members by 1930. Unlike the Primrose League habitations and the Unionist Women's Associations, it had resolutely 'come out' for women's suffrage, and not only for the propertied few, but for all women – a commitment poignantly expressed by Mrs Wrigley, a plate-layer's wife who said: 'I joined the suffrage, because having had such a hard and difficult life myself, I thought I would do all I could to relieve the sufferings of others.'[85] The Women's Guilds had forfeited the sponsorship of the co-operative societies over their support for reform of the divorce law. They campaigned for a minimum wage, for raising the school leaving age and for maternity benefits and clinics.

This working-class women's movement created its own agenda designed to meet the infinite needs of millions of poor women. It was the guildswomen above all who 'effectively voiced the neglected needs of married working women'.[86] The guilds forced social policy reforms on to the Parliamentary agenda, and in their inner life made some space for women to bear witness to their pain as well as their personal and political aspirations. Here was a space in which working women could create their own consciousness. And the Tories envied it: they couldn't create a rival but neither could they leave it to the left. In the post-war scramble for the support of the working class, the Tories proposed raids on the co-operative movement to save it from socialism.

'We desire also to prevent the "Socialist Labour" Party capturing the great co-operative movement and using it for political purposes,' declared *Home and Politics* in 1921.[87] Appealing mainly to women, both as shoppers and Co-operative Society shareholders, *Home and Politics* urged 'all anti-Socialist Co-operators' and 'Co-operative women in particular, to organise their forces without delay' to block the proposed affiliation of the movement to the Labour Party. They failed.

Comparison with the priorities of the labour movement is useful here in clarifying not only Conservative women's difference from women to their left, but also the boundaries of women's politics within the Conservative Party. Women were undoubtedly recognised as a massive presence within the Tory Party, whose rights to representation were, as we have seen, inscribed within the party's rules. But their political orientation was towards the grand causes of Conservatism rather than the detailed concerns of women themselves, and Conservative women seem to have kept aloof from an engagement with the new prospectus proposed by organised women on the left within the co-operative guilds, the trade unions and the Labour and Communist Parties, who were campaigning for birth control, nurseries, unemployment benefit for women, pensions and, not least, for their own space within working-class politics. It was not that Conservative women did not have a women's agenda; but rather that it was contained within the needs of Conservative renewal. Theirs were the politics of paranoia; women were assigned the special task of monitoring the invasion of the national culture. An idealised vision of the home, ne'er touched by the domestic crises of millions of working-class women, was recycled and mobilised against the threat from without and within.

Within the labour movement, however, there was a different agenda, which implied a different relationship not only to the experience of women but also to the problem of sexual power. During the mid-1920s Labour women became embroiled in a wrangle with the party over government instructions to local authorities preventing maternity centres in receipt of public money from giving birth control facilities to married women. The Labour women had discussed birth control in 1924, and in 1925 came out against the ban, asking for the party's endorsement of a campaign to get the government to withdraw this ban. They failed to carry the Labour Party conference, however, and at the 1926 party conference the issue erupted again and the executive was asked to rethink its position. At the 1927 women's conference the executive was asked for the third time to reconsider and the conference decided to send a deputation to the executive and to urge the 1,728 women's sections to organise meetings on the birth control ban. Mrs Cowell (Chelmsford) stressed the class component in the campaign: 'working class mothers should have the same knowledge as middle class mothers,' she said. And Mrs Harris (Croydon) reminded delegates that 'in industrial troubles women had stood four square with the men, and we should ask them to stand four square with us'. A trade unionist who had been jailed five times during the suffrage struggle, Miss Quinn, from the tailor and garment workers, was appalled, however, and regarded birth control as 'capitulation to capitalism'. After a stormy debate, the women's conference reaffirmed its stance. There were strong protests at the 1929 women's conference against the national executive's resistance, particularly because the women were being repudiated by men in the party.

During this period the Labour women also contested the methods of electing women to the national executive: they wanted the women's conference to elect four women to the executive and to have the right to put three resolutions direct to the party conference. Suffragette and trade unionist Jessie Stephen (Camberwell) explained the balance of power within the party when she said that without these rights the women had to canvass the big trade unions before they could be elected to the national executive. The women lost the argument – and it is one that reappeared on the Labour Party's agenda in the 1980s. But the Labour women's concerns went wider than this: they discussed the need to involve women in housing policy; they condemned the Conservative government's restrictions on widows' pensions and cuts in milk grants for pregnant women; they had contentious debates on family allowances and protective legislation, and detailed reviews of the crisis of maternal mortality and the tragedy of botched illegal abortions.

One reading of this comparison between Labour and Conservative Party women could be that Labour women were losing the argument while Conservative women were more surely integrated within the party. Another would be that Labour women pushed their priorities as women to the limits and challenged the patriarchal culture of much of the labour movement, while Conservative women subsumed their concerns as women to an agenda determined not by them but by the paternalist leadership of the party. Either way, the leadership of both parties was patriarchal: the difference was that Labour women challenged and Conservative women gave their consent. Labour women exposed the poverty of working-class women and sought to intervene in the contradictions within the patriarchal culture; Conservative women sought to protect their separate sphere within it. Labour women tried to renegotiate the terms of their alliance with the men's movement within the party, and thus dared to be defeated, while Conservative women spared themselves the humiliation. Finally, by challenging, the women of the labour movement consulted their own experience and expanded the frontiers of progressive women's politics; Conservative women coded their consciousness according to the dominant discourse of their party.

The rank and file revolt

The Tories lost power to Labour in 1929 but when Labour self-destructed by failing to deliver an anti-unemployment strategy, the Tories were back in business in 1931 with an anti-socialist coalition led by former Labour Prime Minister Ramsey MacDonald, who had deserted his comrades. After the 1935 general election the Tory–Liberal coalition remained in control, this time with Baldwin as Prime Minister. By the 1930s, the decade in which the government despatched commissioners to examine the sufferings of the distressed areas, while the distressed people themselves organised Hunger Marches to London, Tory Party women became increasingly concerned with the domestic crises of British society and defence, the issue which dominated the election. During debates on enduring unemployment, the government faced strong criticism from the women who expressed the anxieties of the grassroots over the Conservative government's failure to relieve the distressed areas during the great Depression of the 1920s and 1930s. Mrs N. Gower, OBE, JP (Pontypool), told the 1936 women's conference that she was fed up with deputations, petitions and commissions on unemployment. In Monmouthshire unemployment was 33 per cent, and she asked for the government to show good faith by putting new factories into South Wales: 'whether you like our districts or whether you do not, business is business. We want work.' Mrs Fyfe (Newcastle) reported 40 per cent unemployment in West Cumbria and asked for help in better utilising the area's resources. And Miss Rachel Parsons (Newcastle), a qualified engineer and company director, insisted that 'something must be done'. The 1939 women's conference again heard criticism of the government's unemployment measures, but equally strong resistance was expressed by several speakers to criticism that could be misconstrued to show that Conservative women believed that their government had not tried their utmost. As ever, Conservative women felt compelled by loyalty to constrain their criticism.

The women's debates on British rearmament and the rise of fascism in Germany and Italy revealed conflicting tendencies among Conservative women: the long tradition of Tory anti-communism found expression in support for attempts to appease fascism in Europe, while critics of German rearmament sought to defend British rearmament. Although defence had featured strongly in the 1935 election, the threat to world peace posed by events in Germany and Italy 'demanded an answer which they never got'.[88] Baldwin's 'policy of drift' was succeeded in 1937 by Neville Chamberlain's policy of appeasement.[89] At the Conservative women's conference in 1936 Mrs Western (Chelmsford) tried to amend an anodyne motion supporting the government by proposing an accommodation with Germany, and argued that First World War reparations against Germany had been punitive. Her attempt failed, but Mrs Whitfield complained that 'we have been playing straight into the hands of communism first of all by imposing sanctions against Italy which a very great number of us were totally against from the start'. The government was implicated, she said, in 'an unholy alliance aimed at nothing else than the encirclement of Germany who has made such a stand against Bolshevism'. But the critics were defeated after a skilful defence of the government by the Duchess of Atholl, the former anti-suffrage campaigner who was now an MP. Reparations against Germany had been scaled down, she said, and yet far from disarming there had been evidence that German rearmament was resumed even before Hitler had taken power, 'namely to re-conquer her old frontiers and a great deal more by the sword'. Loyalty prevailed again when the Conservative women endorsed the government's appeasement of Hitler in Munich in 1938. At the 1939 women's conference after fascist armies invaded Czechoslovakia and Abyssinia, a speaker who complained that 'while London was rejoicing Czechoslovakia was in mourning' was interrupted by a voice protesting, 'We ought not to criticise.'

It was law and order which became the medium for Tory women's dissent in the late 1930s, and thereafter broke the habit of loyalty to the party leadership. Law and order became the cauldron in which Tory women let off steam, a discourse which set them at odds with their own party leaders and set them apart from the preoccupations of women on the liberal or left wings of politics. Campaigns for contraception and for women's right to pleasure were associated with the post-war sexual radicals. But in the absence of a feminist movement to sustain a critique of patriarchal practices and to monitor physical abuse and sexual exploitation, women's sense of themselves as the endangered sex kept surfacing and searching for safety. In such situations women's sexual fear becomes a cuckoo: homeless, it nests in another bird's debate.

This is what happened just as war was about to break out in 1939. The Conservative government supported the Criminal Justice Bill which proposed to abolish flogging, which by then was largely out of use except in schools. This ignited the Tory women's fearful imagination. 'There is a terrible risk for the women and children of our villages and in our more lonely places,' said Miss R. M. Harrison (West Midlands) who, on behalf of 'the women of England', proposed a resolution which not only deplored the abolition of corporal punishment but sought to extend it to 'male offenders in respect of convictions for indecent assault upon women and children'. She was not a parent, she explained, 'but I do feel that the ugliest injury that is done to little girls and little boys, and which is so horrible that it is never spoken about, should be met with some very strong punishment'. She was supported by Mrs Churches (West Midlands), the mother of ten children, eight of them girls: 'It is not of our sons I speak; it is of our daughters, of those people who so forget their manhood as to criminally assault our children . . . inhuman fiends who assault our girls.' It was not so much a manifestation of masculinity against which she protested, as certain categories of men:

> all sorts of imported labour . . . and believe me some of them are not at all desirable. I therefore appeal to you, as a mother, to protect the honour of our children. To my mind, the only way to protect them is to allow something in our laws that will

hurt those who injure them. You know the class of men concerned. I should not like to touch them with a pitchfork.

Viscountess Davidson, MP said she was 'convinced that the government are making a mistake', and urged 'very definite and sharp treatment' of offenders.

But Mrs M. Tate, JP, MP, who had been a member of the committee which recommended revision of the law, proposed a further amendment which removed the reference to indecent assault and replaced it with violence against the person. But she warned that 'you may have satisfied your desire to punish the criminal but you will have done nothing to protect the children, which is the real desire you have in your heart and in your mind'.

The debate turned nasty when the irreverent Viscountess Nancy Astor, the first woman to sit in Parliament, made a typically provocative intervention on the side of progress. 'You are making a great mistake,' she warned the women. 'May I say that the Home Secretary in bringing in his penal reform has won the support and admiration of every social worker in this country.' This provoked cries of dissent and interruptions. 'Will you allow me to speak in silence . . . too often in this hall I have been howled down in connection with matters which four or five years afterwards you have deeply regretted, and the government had to bring in. So that I am not in the least frightened of being howled down by anybody.' At this point the chairman had to intervene, but undaunted Lady Astor carried on and told them that the people who had opposed the penal reforms of the pioneering Elisabeth Fry, 'like you, they knew nothing about the matter'. Amidst the uproar, Lady Lucas-Tooth (North Kensington) rose to oppose the government's critics, too. 'I think this is the bravest thing I have ever done,' she said, before asking them to 'not let your indignation run away with you and confuse punishment with methods of reform'. Unconvinced, Mrs J. B. Kitson (Sutton, Plymouth) argued that 'as long as the world is as it is, provisions of this sort will be necessary'. A convert to the reform was Mrs E. Hall (Chelsea) who argued that crime had shown a tendency to rise despite an increase in floggings.

For the government, Captain Osbert Peake, Parliamentary Under-Secretary for Home Affairs, said he would report the debate to his colleagues, but made it clear that 'modern criminal punishment must be either reformative or deterrent. The old idea of retribution has disappeared from our criminal law many generations ago.' That was clearly a matter of regret to the women, who passed the resolution in support of flogging. This was the beginning of a new relationship between leaders and led which after the Second World War erupted into the revolt of the loyalists.

The New World

In 1945 women and men voted for a new world when they voted for the Labour government. The Second World War had ruptured the economic relationship between men and women; would the peace complete the revolution? Well, we know it didn't – the revolution was reversed. Why?

The new welfare state was a minimum condition of Britain's economic renewal, but the reformism of the 1945 government was contained within statism as well as by its own cultural conservatism: the '45ers could not have conceived of cultural or ideological reform because what was at stake, in part, was the sexual division of labour. Sexual revolution was unthinkable in the patriarchal cloisters of the labour movement, or of Oxbridge, or of the Treasury. Women's brief wartime encounter with economic independence and its meaning both for them and for socialism hardly crossed their minds. Women remained the 'other' in Labourist politics: full employment referred to men's employment.

Within the Labour Party itself, men's power and therefore their politics were built into the structure: the women's section of the National Executive Committee (NEC) was the gift of godfathers who were not just men but reactionary men. It was 'regarded as a bastion of political orthodoxy', according to Lewis Minkin's *The Labour Party Conference*, the most authoritative account of how power works in the party. Nothing showed the might of the right-wing trade union barons – whose hegemony was fondly invoked by the Tories in the 1980s as good old *traditional* Labourism – more than their 'determination to fill this section with those whose political orientation was dependably and vehemently anti-left'.[1]

Labour abandoned social childcare and the reorganisation of

working time which would have integrated women into the culture of workplace politics and men into the culture of childcare and the community. The nineteenth-century concept of the family wage which equated breadwinner with masculinity was rehabilitated not only in the workplace but in the welfare state.

Ironically, the post-war labour shortage did not lead the government or the labour movement to remove the impediments to women in the waged workforce. The wartime Royal Commission on the General Economic and Social Consequences of Equal Pay submitted its report to the government in 1946, but the government failed to implement it. Despite the endorsement of the notion of competition between the sexes inscribed in the Restoration of Pre-War Practices Act, the Ministry of Labour encouraged women to re-engage in the labour market. Thousands of women nevertheless lost their jobs: a classic case involved the 4,000 clippies sacked in the 1940s by London Transport. LT said it was 'grateful for the women who took the men's jobs during and after the war' but they had to go, even though Labour women MPs argued that most of the men who the women had replaced had already been re-employed.[2] And yet in 1947 there were still 300,000 vacancies for women, and government-sponsored research showed that if childcare and part-time work were offered then the employment of another 900,000 women could be envisaged.[3]

The Labour government failed to defend, not to mention expand, public childcare provision and so it drastically declined, despite the opposition of many women's organisations and some direct action by women: in the summer of 1947, for example, thirty-five mothers locked themselves into a Yorkshire nursery to protest against its closure by the council.[4] And the government repeatedly refused to implement equal pay. In effect, it encouraged a higher rate of female exploitation, a sex-segregated labour market and women's continuing personal and private responsibility for the household. Women's relationship to waged work was undergoing a quiet revolution, but it was conditional on minimal disruption either to the habits of men or to the practices of the labour movement. All this was expressed in 'the designation of the woman worker *as* female . . . as *essential* difference. And the most strikingly different workers were the mothers.'[5]

Women within the labour movement during the 1940s and 1950s mobilised a counter-attack. In 1947, Women for Westminster, a campaign to secure Parliamentary representation for women, organised a conference at London's Conway Hall where women deplored the government's failure to implement equal pay. The Labour Party conference in 1947 debated a call for 'immediate implementation of equal pay, in line with the United Nations Charter, which it has signed, and with Labour Party and TUC policy'. Eirene White complained that although an equal pay amendment had been carried in the House of Commons during the war, Winston Churchill 'made Parliament eat its own words, and in true Tory fashion set up an unnecessary Royal Commission'. Equal pay was not 'just one reform among many', she argued; 'it is in a totally different category. It is the putting right of a long-standing injustice. If you take women's work and refuse to pay women the rate for the job it is sheer dishonesty. We have waited with increasing interest for some announcement from the government.' It was rumoured that the government intended to let women down on the grounds that it could not afford it, even while it was making 'concessions to the cartels and combines'.

Then she delivered an apocalyptic ultimatum: 'Forty years ago there was a great progressive party in this country called the Liberal Party. That party destroyed itself and will never recover because of the humbug and hypocrisy with which it treated the question of votes for women.' Woman suffrage and the Irish question 'did for them,' she said. 'Would it not be a tragedy if this progressive party of ours, in the full flood of its achievements were to go down the drain in the same way because of the mishandling of the economic enfranchisement of women?'

Her chilling petition was ignored by the NEC. 'All that we are now concerned about is the practicability of the word "immediately",' said the NEC's spokesperson, because it was 'most injudicious'. Despite an overwhelming vote for the resolution – 2,310,000 to 598,000 – the NEC made it clear that it had to be left to the government to determine priorities. 'Rely on the goodwill of a party that has not let the movement down.'

The Trades Union Congress (TUC) endorsed the government's apostasy. It decided 'that a further approach by the TUC to the Government on equal pay would be inappropriate at the present time'.[6] In any case, it had already invoked the ideology of 'separate spheres' to abandon public provision of childcare: 'While the government was enacting legislation to establish the welfare state, the TUC was advocating private enterprise for childcare. Underlying the general council's attitude to day nurseries was its attitude towards the place of women in society.'[7] The TUC General Council in 1947 reaffirmed its belief that 'the home is one of the most important spheres for a woman worker and that it would be doing a grave injury to the life of the nation if women were persuaded or forced to neglect their domestic duties in order to enter industry'.[8]

Women had to wait another twenty years for legislation on equal pay, and more than forty years later Britain had one of the highest levels of women's waged work but one of the lowest levels of public childcare provision in Europe. Women alone took responsibility for their world. They were left to get on with it by the Labour government to which they gave their support in greater numbers than ever before – or since.

A young Labour MP, Barbara Castle, presciently warned her party of the shape of things to come when she told the 1948 conference that capital was being let off the hook while the government was telling 'the girl at the mill, the miners at the coal face, the engineers and the rest of them "you should work longer hours, and harder"'. Meanwhile, she said, the Tory leader Winston Churchill had thrilled the recent Conservative women's conference when he had 'accused the Labour government of having put an intolerable burden on women'.

While Churchill was apparently speaking *for* the women of the Conservative Party, Labour's Chancellor of the Exchequer Hugh Dalton appeared to be *against* the women – and many of the men – of the Labour Party. In 1947 Dalton refused to implement equal pay in the public sector because private industry would follow, and he argued against equal pay on family wage grounds: 'If the pay of unmarried women was raised to equality with that of married men, a married man with a family would be left in a relatively worse position than any other section of the community', and this would lead to claims for occupational family allowances.[9] In 1948 he conceded the principle of equal pay for government employees – but not now: 'The government must be the judge of priorities.' Even the left-winger Michael Foot defended the exclusion of equal pay from Labour's election programme on the grounds that it would cost too much.[10] And in 1951, faced with a national Whitley Council recommendation that equal pay be gradually implemented among government employees, Chancellor of the Exchequer Hugh

Gaitskell said simply, 'No.' The circumstances weren't appropriate.

Thus the Labour government had no new strategy for women, and could offer no alternative to the challenge of the Conservatives. It did not see women's demands as worth defending; it did not take women's side against capital and the Treasury. Having squandered the magic moment after the war, Labour was not to get another chance for nearly two long decades. Having deferred (a euphemism for defeated) the demands of organised working women, Labourism exposed its own dependence on the familial ideology of the right. It must be said that there were voices among Tory women supporting the movement among working women. There was the Tory MP Mavis Tate, for example, who ended her own remarkable life in 1947. She had been an airwoman, had visited Buchenwald after the war, fought for equal compensation for men and women injured in the war and for many years campaigned for women's rights. In 1946 she argued that 'Britain is still run to the advantage of men.'[11] Labour women said it, Tory women said it, but the Labour leadership would neither say it nor change it. And so the main political parties shared a new consensus in the patriarchal reconstruction of Britain.

Labour was implicated in the constitution of women as a new kind of social subject – the consumer. But since its government was associated with austerity, this hardly worked well for Labour. Rationing was already another source of dissension within the party, and during the 1947 party conference debate on production, Mr J. Benstead, from the railway workers' union, poignantly reminded delegates that

> there is one class of worker whom we forget and that is the
> poor little housewife, standing in the queue and struggling
> to get the food. Let us do something to wipe austerity off our
> banner and remove some of the misery and worry that is the
> daily lot of the housewives of this country.

Out of austerity rose the Conservative sphinx – consumerism. Labour had jettisoned the economic demands of women as workers and the childcare needs of women as mothers, but the Conservatives raised the banner of women as consumers. Their ideology had cherished women's domestic skills as a social value worthy of chivalrous reward and recognition, while in the Labourist culture of post-war reconstruction women's domestic responsibility was mobilised to *defeat* women's demands for a redistribution of time, labour and money at home and at work. Among Conservatives it appeared as positive; in Labourism it appeared as negative, an excuse for women's exclusion.

Olde Worlde or New World

The homely parameters of Conservative women's politics did not prepare them for the new world. The creation of the welfare state and the new Tory leadership's participation in what became known as the post-war consensus disturbed for decades the serenity of Conservative women's loyal liaison with the men who led the party.

Conservative ideology had constituted women and their homes as a private domain with privileged status in the circuit of capital accumulation and consumption. The war, the welfare state and the continuation of wartime rationing of essential goods to ensure equal distribution changed all that. This was the age of social democracy and a new generation of Tory leaders who knew they had to go with it.

How were women placed in the reconstruction of the Conservative Party? After all the traditions of right-wing women had not prepared them for this moment of modernisation. Throughout the twentieth century they had built their alliance with the traditionalist cause of Conservatism itself rather than with the causes of women. In the 1940s Tory rank and file women showed signs of growing restive in the face of the modernising initiatives of the new party leadership – what Andrew Gamble in *The Conservative Nation* has called the new conservatism. Their unease erupted into open revolt in the 1950s and 1960s, forming the moral basis for what was to become the new right and Thatcherism in the 1970s. Commentators have rooted the rise of the new right in the 1960s. Their accounts stress the importance of the family, morality and the role of women in Thatcherism. What they have not done, however, is track the active participation of women in the making of the new right. By this exclusion, women, once again, have been rendered the objects, not subjects, in the political process.

At the end of that process what we saw was Thatcherism triumphant, incorporating the traditionalist women's agenda – but all too late. Thatcherism contained confusion about the role of women, but it was masked by the success of its uneasy coalition of populists, moral authoritarians and libertarians.

Housewives' power

The banner of the Tory women's tradition was initially carried after the Second World War by the British Housewives League, an autonomous maverick organisation which at one time claimed 100,000 members. Independent of the Conservative Party, though enjoying Conservatives' support, it organised raids on the new political consensus to harass both the demons of the left and the new generation of Conservative leaders who were represented as appeasers and collaborators with the new enemy – social democracy.

The Housewives League was born in the cold, cold crisis of the Labour government in 1947, the child of Mrs Irene Lovelock, a London vicar's wife who seems to have begun her political career by organising an Anti-Queue Campaign in June 1945. Its programme was the point of continuity with the tradition articulated by the Primrose League and the inter-war Conservative women's associations. But the world had turned, and the Conservative Party was finding an accommodation with the welfare state. To the ideologues of the British Housewives League, however, this was a betrayal begun in the Tory Party's great overhaul after the First World War. They believed that 'the last vestige of Conservatism vanished with Mr Bonar Law, and that the Baldwin government of the 30s paved the way for socialism and planning'.[12]

Representatives of 200 branches of the British Housewives League met in October 1946 and adopted Mrs Lovelock's programme, which aimed to provide a voice for housewives; to resist 'over-control by the state' in the interests of 'happy home life and the development of personality in accord with Christian principles', and to encourage housewives to become MPs, councillors and representatives on other public bodies. Its immediate aims were directed against a Labour government trying to manage an economy starved by depression, war and capital's failure to modernise. It demanded ample supply of reasonably priced food, housing and clothing, the abolition of rationing and an end to the universal enforcement of the National Health Service on clients and doctors. Its animus against Labour rapidly extended to the Conservative Party too; it declared that its campaign to get Labour out and, in the short term, to force the resignation of Labour ministers, particularly Bevan, Strachey and Shinwell, did not mean that it wanted to get the Tories in. It made a revealing declaration that it was not advocating the 'immediate formation of a women's party'.[13] Not yet anyway.

The League's targets were twofold; state intervention in general and Labour's austerity measures in particular. These objectives were asserted as a defence of what they prized – women's domestic power. The League opposed waged work among women and it opposed the welfare state as a form of state intervention in the home. It found itself pitched against communists, socialists and those whom it regarded as Tory fellow-travellers, and against the working-class women's movements campaigning for progressive legislation in support of women as wives, mothers and waged workers.

Although it insisted on its non-alignment the League found allies among some Tory MPs, and some Conservative women were prominent in its leadership, which led to accusations that it was a scion of the Conservative Party. It wasn't, but prominent Tories, like Sir David Maxwell-Fyffe, spoke from its platforms. It seized upon the introduction of bread rationing as a clue to creeping communism: 'Bread rationing, imposed on the country by this Government, ostensibly to save wheat, is Russia's favourite political weapon against the individual.' It condemned state control of supplies and distribution as a kind of cartel between organised labour and the state: 'In this country, it is obvious, any extension of rationing puts the population increasingly at the mercy of "unofficial strikes", for where stocks are low the slightest disruption of supplies is an almost fatal blow to the community.'[14] A *laissez-faire* economy and the autonomy of the home were represented as barricades defending freedom of the individual against the incursions of socialism and the state. Compulsory National Insurance was vilified as 'a definite move to get women out of their homes and into the factories and shops. The insurance scheme is one of the few bribes to get them there.'[15] Worse still, all parties in Parliament were culpable because they had capitulated. And the League campaigned against the terms of health insurance and the National Health Service as totalitarianism. Here they found allies among doctors organising in the British Medical Association against the democratisation of health provision. An antique political and economic liberalism underpinned the League's campaigns against rationing, fluoridation of the water supplies, compulsory pasteurisation of the milk and National Savings.

The League was *populist* rather than *popular*. It was organised around widespread discontent with rationing, perpetual shortages and queues, but it was not concerned with extending ordinary people's power in the new institutions of the welfare state. And so its critique of red tape and state bureaucracy never took root among the working class. After all, that was the class who lost their teeth as teenagers, to whom illness had been an economic as well as a physical catastrophe, whose mothers were nursing babies while suffering themselves from malnutrition, among whom one of the highest causes of death were botched abortions, who were wearing spectacles scavenged from flea markets, who had neither had health insurance, nor holidays nor homes of their own.

Not that the new institutions of the welfare state 'belonged' to the working class. They didn't. It was just that the electoral power of the working class had made them finally inevitable.

Certainly the Labour government was vulnerable to criticism within its own ranks, but it was the Housewives League, sometimes supported by corporate vested interests, which organised guerrilla war against it. Insofar as it scored palpable hits it was in the sphere of consumption. Labour's prioritisation of production, the export drive, its attempts to cope with the dollar crisis and finally the reallocation of vital resources towards rearmament stripped resources for the domestic consumer.[16] The black market flourished, the rebellious middle classes complained, and the importation of strange foods and even reindeer meat became, like mothers-in-law and the Irish, the butt of little Englanders.

A classic case was the importation of 'snoek', a South African fish. Food Minister Dr Edith Summerskill recalled that

> we were so preoccupied with our success in finding a
> nutritionally adequate food that it never occurred to us that its
> name would prove unpopular and suggest unpalatability to the
> British ear. I was given the task of persuading the women of
> the country to buy snoek for the purpose of supplementing the
> rations. From the storm of abuse which greeted my efforts
> one would have thought that the Ministry was trying to force
> some inedible, unwholesome concoction into the family
> larder. At least I derived some comfort from the knowledge

that most of the protests at our public meetings came from a noisy element calling themselves the Housewives League, and it is not irrelevant that these ladies were opposed to the government on political grounds.[17]

Summerskill admitted that the government's decision to stop the importation of dried eggs to relieve the balance of payments deficit 'caused a domestic revolution'.[18] The Housewives League also mobilised a tough campaign against the cancellation of a Canadian meat order, likewise to relieve pressure on balance of payments and Britain's dollar crisis. Rationing of bread and bacon continued to be among the most unpopular of the government's consumption tactics, and the poor quality of some domestic coal provoked a campaign by the Leeds branch of the League, which sent Hugh Gaitskell some coal containing lumps of slate. Mr Gaitskell thanked them for bringing it to his notice.[19]

As the Labour government became encircled by the post-war economic crisis, compounded by food and fuel shortages during the terrible winter of 1947, the Conservative Party coined the slogan 'Shiver with Shinwell and Starve with Strachey'. The Housewives League claimed that Shinwell's demise in the aftermath of the fuel crisis was their triumph. Their other target was Bevan, whose supposed leftism and class loyalism, the Conservatives hoped, would do for him. Bevan addressed a meeting in Bermondsey in April 1951, in the midst of bitter conflict within the Labour Party over soaring arms expenditure, health charges and the forthcoming trial of seven dockers. It was a meeting 'where all-comers felt entitled to "have a go" about anything'.[20] Local MP Bob Mellish recalled that 'many of the hecklers were members of the Housewives League, asking questions and shouting protests about the meagreness of the meat ration'.[21]

The League's endorsement of the view expressed by a Councillor Feather, during a rally in London in June 1948, that 'in the 1930s there was food and clothing in plenty for all' did not win the hearts and minds of those for whom the state's control over distribution meant at least a minimal equity, and among whom rationing seemed the fairest way to deal with shortages. Insofar as the League enjoyed any popular resonance, it was in its campaign against the *effects* of rationing on housewives' *work*. Tory MP Maxwell-Fyffe complained at the League's biggest rally in London's Royal Albert Hall in June

1947 that the government was 'trying to get a 40-hour week for men at the expense of an 80-hour week for mothers'.[22]

Its opposition to the principle of equal distribution clearly bewildered some of its supporters, however. *Daily Worker* reporter Florence Keyworth talked to some of the 'ordinary housewives tired of queuing and puzzled by shortages' who had turned up. One of them said she had joined the League 'because I wanted a better deal for housewives but I can see from the speeches that these people are just a gang of Tories'.[23] The secretary and most of the Stockport League's executive had already resigned because the organisation was too political and they couldn't support its anti-nationalisation campaign.[24]

The Albert Hall rally was a riot. Communists and Co-op Women's Guild members turned up to heckle and communist leaflets fluttered down into the hall from the galleries saying 'Never mind the label on the packet, the stuff inside is a Tory racket'.[25] There were brawls – the *Daily Herald* carried a picture of two men fighting on the floor – and the League's chairwoman Dorothy Crisp 'stood on the platform blowing a police whistle in a vain attempt to restore order'.[26] And 'In many of the scuffles the demonstrators were charged with being "dirty Jews" – Moseley propaganda was on sale outside the hall.'[27]

The rally was followed by a weekend 'housewives' hunger march' through London led by Miss Crisp in a chauffeur-driven saloon, but 'somehow, somewhere the anti-nationalisation contingent of vehicles of the Road Haulage Association got lost'.[28] The RHA was one of the most formidable privatisation lobbies in the country, and was later to prove an embarrassment to the League.

After this summer bust-up political dissent erupted in the leadership troika of Mrs Lovelock, Miss Crisp and a Conservative Party woman, Mrs F. E. Bloice, who backed a rank and file revolt and complained that Miss Crisp had taken control of the League's headquarters together with Mrs Lovelock's husband. One of the rebels told the *Daily Herald* that 'several times lately Miss Crisp has told us she means to form her own political party and become Britain's first woman Prime Minister. We are strictly non-political and we don't intend to let Miss Crisp's ambitions change the character of the league.'[29] For four hours a meeting of the League was 'unrelieved uproar' and when deposed Treasurer Helen Hart tried to put her case her microphone was unplugged and she 'dived' for Miss Crisp's. Another woman brought her own megaphone. When Miss Crisp defended herself by saying that she had hoped to tell the meeting of 'a very substantial sum placed in our credit by certain individuals', there were cries of 'the Road Haulage Association'. Miss Crisp insisted that this was an 'absolute lie' but later admitted that a Royal Albert Hall meeting had been paid for by the association. She also explained that a party in the Mayfair hotel allegedly for 'Miss Crisp's wealthy friends' was in fact 'a party for influential people'. Crisp and Lovelock only just won the day, but at the end of the pandemonium an exhausted Mrs Lovelock fainted.[30]

The League's authoritarianism was revealed in its attitude to the working-class electorate who would no longer be banished to the basement of politics. Those who voted for Britain's 'expensive programme of bureaucratic control' should be made to pay more than those who wanted to contract out.[31] It appealed to *all* women as housewives *against* the party of 'the people' which had deigned to take power. Appealing to people to 'stand up and fight' against bureaucratic control,[32] Irene Lovelock invoked the memory of the suffragettes, as have so many who have claimed them in retrospect and yet who would have disdained them in their day: 'Think of the suffragettes. They did a great work, a great work. They built the foundation on which we women are allowed to speak on a public platform at all; and what is more, many of them suffered and died for what they thought was right.' But that democratic project was reclaimed for an anti-democratic purpose. In the wake of outbreaks of industrial action among organised rank and file workers, often led by members of the Communist Party, the League came out against the long-standing Conservative campaign for secret ballots by trade unions to sanction action. Secret ballots 'enable people to vote for a Communist candidate without showing their hands – and their treachery. It is an ironical twist that a valuable reform in our electoral system should now be a danger to Socialists and Conservatives alike.'[33]

'The people' had become the problem. By 1950 the League saw politics only in terms of consumption and the electorate as prodigal rather than prudent shoppers:

When we look at the political party system of this country, we are appalled. Under present arrangements, where the votes of those who can scarcely sign their name have equal value with the votes cast by such people as the Archbishop of Canterbury, or Miss Dorothy Sayers, it only needs for a Party to delude several millions of the irresponsible with lies and promises that will never be fulfilled . . . These misguided persons become the 'majority'.[34]

Apart from the British Housewives League, there were other local variations of this kind of organisation up and down the country, often involving or inaugurated by Conservative women. The London Housewives launched an anti-statist 'Manifesto on Protection of the Home' in 1949, proclaiming that the 'worthy husband and father is proud to support a family and the respected wife and mother is happy to care for the home and family . . . The greatest responsibility of all rests with the housewife.'[35]

Erdington Housewives Association had in Mrs L. Wallington an ingenious activist who reported to Conservative Central Office that she had sent fourpence worth of 'horrid frozen fat' supposed to be pork to the Conservative candidate in her constituency. The Scottish Housewives Association formulated its own charter proposing a home for every family, no more nationalisation, an end to the bulk buying favoured by the Labour government and to purchase tax. It wrote to Central Office in February 1949 suggesting a tribunal to investigate the Ministry of Food. Central Office thought 'there would be very little point'.[36] And Marjorie Maxse repudiated one Housewives Leaguer's attempt to get the party to disown a divorced Tory MP in 1950. 'It's still a free country,' wrote Miss Maxse.[37] But by the end of the decade the party was perhaps becoming a little wary of the vigilantes' public image. Mrs Carrington-Wood wrote to Mrs Wallington in February 1950 that although she 'strongly supported the setting up of a Housewives Vigilance Committee' in each local party association, 'we must be careful not to become cranks!!!!'[38] We shall see that although the Housewives League was passing its peak, the Conservative Party took the challenge of the housewife to its heart.

Central Office keeps watch
True to tradition, Conservative women entered the deeply polarised politics of post-war reconstruction with an ideology which simultaneously asserted and suppressed the politics of gender. Conserva-

tive women had always placed the home at the centre of their economic, cultural and political objectives and they could ultimately support women's presence in the political world as an extension of women's private destiny. For the right, the 'private' always had its place in the social firmament. That has always been its great strength. It has attempted to unite the private and the irrational with the public and the rational. But the notion of women's separate sphere was an idealisation; it did not address the impoverishment of women in the home – their economic crisis, the crisis of maternal mortality, the crisis in the care of children, and the crisis of women's sexuality expressed in fear and 'frigidity'. All of this had long preoccupied the working-class women's movements and many of their professional sisters.

For women involved in radical suffrage campaigns the vote challenged the ideology of women's 'separate sphere'; it was a moment in the quest for the holy grail: a new social relationship between the sexes. And of course, Lord Cromer was right: that implied new demands on the economy, civil society and the state.

There were Conservative women who supported equal rights, but the women's organisation as a whole moved into the post-war era estranged from the other women's movements of the 1940s. Sectarian suspicions of everything socialist left it at a distance from some of the organisations which were setting the terms of post-war women's politics and often unable to consult the feelings of Conservative women themselves, many of whom came to feel that the war of liberation from fascism was also, incidentally, a war of *women's* liberation. Just as some Conservative women came out of the First World War believing that they could no longer be denied the vote, some came out of the Second World War believing that they deserved a wage. But there was little in the culture to affirm their regretful reminiscences about their wartime work.

Internal Central Office memoranda reveal that the Conservative Party women's organisation contemplated participation in other more radical women's organisations but was often cauterised by party chauvinism. In some instances, this took the form of what could be described as small-scale political espionage. A clue comes from the correspondence between Marjorie Maxse, who was responsible for women's work at Central Office in 1945, with a party member, a Mrs Allen, about monitoring other organisations. 'The general scheme [is] of attending outside organisations' meetings and reporting to us fully upon them, and she is starting right away,' noted Marjorie Maxse.[39]

Hot-foot, Mrs Allen made a tour of inspection around some of the many women's organisations which mushroomed in the 1940s. She went to the Women for Westminster group, and reported that 'it appears to be entirely non-political'. She decided to join. Then she went to the Duchess of Atholl's anti-Communist League for European Freedom, which seemed to her to be 'older and less go ahead' with a 'slight leaning towards sentimentalism rather than reason'. Nevertheless she found them commodious enough to decide to work with them. During her tour, she told Miss Maxse, 'I have just walked in and asked all the questions I could think of.' Miss Maxse thought well of this research and suggested in May 1945 that 'perhaps you could keep a watchful eye to see that at no point is political influence brought to bear'.

A West London Conservative, Janet St John, a former party organiser who had joined Women for Westminster, wrote to Central Office asking for a speaker, since the group was inviting spokespersons from the main political parties. The speakers' department was surprised, but 'pleased to know that someone with her strong Conservative views was endeavouring to be in a position to exercise a certain amount of sway over the many branches of Women for Westminster'. However, by November the speakers' department was complaining that Women for Westminster had 'rapidly veered over towards the socialist camp' and Miss Maxse warned Richard Law, MP that although she did not want to reject an invitation for him to address the group without consulting him first, Women for Westminster 'has got some very undesirable affiliations'. Undaunted, Law agreed to go into the lionesses' den.

The cautious approach was again evident in the observation of a Conservative representative at the conference organised by the Married Women's Association, another non-aligned group which also involved some prominent Labour women. It held a joint conference with Women for Westminster in May 1946. Some Conservative women went, and were advised that although it was not necessary to stay for the duration it would be 'useful to know what the different women's societies and leading personalities have to say'. In a report to Central Office on the conference, another Tory woman, Robin Clifton-Brown, described the despised Labour MP Edith Summerskill, who was hardly a revolutionary, as a 'cobra mesmerising its prey'. The association's programme included equal guardianship rights for women, joint ownership of the home and the joint income of a marriage, equal pensions for married women, and equal rights in taxation for married and single women. Robin Clifton-Brown did not like 90 per cent of the women present, whom she described as looking like the 'nurses of Belsen', and decided to protest to her diocesan Mothers Union, the conservative and Christian movement of which she was a member. Her reaction to the idea that wageless wives should be entitled to an income of their own – a demand many Conservative women were subsequently to entertain – was contempt. She didn't want to lower herself to the level of a woman of the street, paid for her services.

By 1946 Janet St John had become a little disenchanted with Women for Westminster. She reported to Central Office that its October conference was 'definitely in favour of equal pay' and was just 'a meeting of the converted'. In May 1947, a Women for Westminster conference to which the Conservative women sent only observers, not delegates, heard the indefatigable socialist and feminist Dora Russell and the feminist writer Vera Brittain condemn the Labour government for its failure to implement equal pay. Janet St John reported that her branch was going to demand all-party representation in future.

But this was then a problem for Conservative women, whose caution about sexual equality was determined by ideology and sectarianism. Their coupling of sexual difference and separate spheres subsumed any programme for social equality, and their sectarianism blocked co-operative alliances with women coming from a different political culture. A confidential Central Office memorandum on the programme of the Married Women's Association and Women for Westminster in May 1946 revealed its problem with the meaning of equality: 'It is dangerous to commit oneself in any general way to equality, as different organisations will put entirely different interpretations on the meaning.'

Felicity Lane-Fox, a member of the Conservative Women's Advisory Committee, suggested in October 1948 that Conservative women should consider expanding the involvement of Tory women in 'social welfare activities' because

I understand that Labour women's organisations in towns make a great deal of this kind of work . . . In strict confidence I am told that Conservative members of the WVS [Women's Voluntary Service] are rather concerned that their work at the moment is designed to support the government and they would rather see their efforts being credited to the Conservative Party.

Conservative women were profoundly committed to charitable work, and this expressed not only an ethic of service (one which would be served by many employees in the public services) but an ideological commitment to voluntarism versus statism. They were more than a little irritated by what they regarded as attempts by Labour to assimilate the contribution of the WVS to the ethic of the new National Health Service, and in July 1950 Marjorie Maxse wrote that she would try to 'see whether it is possible to drop a hint' in someone's ear to repudiate such a manipulation.

The Conservative women's organisation was feeling its way around the labyrinthine movements of the new world and was clearly curious about what its more radical sisters were up to. But the party also had a women's agenda of its own, and although they sometimes found common cause, their overall strategy, as we shall see, did not easily synchronise with the objectives of those who wanted to do more than influence women – who also wanted to change the world of women.

Austerity versus affluence

Two key words signified the Tory image of what the main political parties in Britain stood for: 'austerity' and 'affluence'. In 1947 the Conservative Party conference passed a resolution condemning 'the persistent attitudes of the government in ignoring the claims of the housewife to a fair deal' and called upon the government to take steps to increase the available supplies of food and household commodities. By the 1950s, the Conservative Party was able to deploy consumer-wife as its weapon against austerity. Consumer-wife was the 'sign' of Conservatism's success.

In 1951, the election in which Labour secured its highest poll, but in which the Conservatives secured the majority of Parliamentary seats, the main issues for Labour were nationalisation and peace, while the Tories capitalised on the cost of living and the housing crisis. Their propaganda showed a pound note with a quarter torn away. Both Tory and Labour Party political broadcasts tackled the cost of living – and therefore addressed women in their capacity as consumers. For the Conservatives, Patricia Hornsby-Smith argued that Labour wasn't just soaking the rich but was soaking everyone, and that if houses had been built cheaply before the war, then they could be built cheaply again – an attack on Labour's commitment to quality in public housing rather than simply quantity.[40]

Housing was perhaps the sign of Labour's inability to satisfy more than the working-class base which it undoubtedly held during the 1940s and to reach beyond it. Aneurin Bevan, who had responsibility for housing in his brief as Minister of Health, tried to transform public housing from architectural minimalism and philanthropic policing of the working class into a model of both excellence and democracy. His project was to politicise housing by making local authorities the single instrument of provision and by setting high standards to which they had to conform. Gone would be the 'silly little bungalows' built by pre-war private builders capitalising on the economic slump. 'Builders made a fortune in putting them up, and fortunes are now being made in holding them up,' he said.[41] His courageous commitment to quality survived precariously in the chronic housing crisis of the forties – there were 200,000 fewer homes after the war than before it, and often the homeless took their cause into their own hands by organising a radical squatting movement: they occupied aerodromes and army camps, they symbolically squatted premises in London's West End and they converted old boats and garages. Anything habitable became a home. Bevan engineered the 'biggest engagement of local government activity, in degree if not in kind, in the history of local government'[42] when he handed over responsibility to local councillors and direct labour organisations. Although his approach was apparently endorsed by the civil service, keen to regularise housing standards, it was implacably opposed by the Conservatives.

Tory women carried their campaign for privatisation into women's organisations, and with some success. The National Council of Women (NCW), an autonomous federation of women's organisations throughout the country and the political spectrum, organised a nationwide chain of meetings on women and housing which provided opportunities for Conservative women to campaign against local government controls. They focused on opening up the housing programme to private builders. Labour replied that most of the work was, in fact, carried out by private builders but that standards and the distribution of the new homes were controlled by the local authorities.

Bevan had what now seems like a premonition when he prophesied that 'if we scamp our work at present we shall never be forgiven'.[43] But it was Bevan's defeat, first by his own government, which after 1947 cut back his housing resources, and later by the Conservatives, who abandoned quality for quantity, that did for the principle of public housing. The Conservative campaign stressed abolition of controls, minimisation of facilities built into the new homes and liberation of the private sector. A Tory, Lady Elizabeth Pepler, reported to Central Office in November 1949 that the feeling on the NCW's housing committee was 'strongly Conservative', and its annual conference that year supported the full participation of private enterprise.

The Tories went into the 1950s with an unassailable weapon – the revolt of its own rank and file over housebuilding targets. At the party's conference in 1950, Miss Irene Dowling (London County Council) moved a motion deploring Labour's housebuilding record and urging the government to 'encourage closer co-operation between parliament and local authorities in order to achieve more satisfactory results'. Another representative, Lionel Heald, moved an amendment which called for a 'high priority in the party's election manifesto to a strong and courageous housing policy'. Heald spoke for the women. It wasn't just Tory-talk when he referred to the personal tragedy caused by the housing shortage. 'Every woman in this hall knows the value of a good home and she knows how the absence of a good home leads to separation of the family and to broken marriages.' Tory MP Harmar Nicholls pointed out that there were twice as many resolutions on housing than anything else. The party should top Labour's targets, he said, by aiming to build 300,000 new houses a year. 'I've been to many conferences. I know the feeling from this body of the hall can influence the leaders of our party,' he said, and when they held up their hands, 'You must shout in one voice "We support this 300,000." Let us quote a figure with our vote and I am convinced that our leaders will follow that support.' Amidst procedural uproar, the party chairman, the Rt Hon Lord Woolton, MP, intervened: 'This is magnificent. You want a figure of 300,000 put in. The platform would be very glad . . .'

Michael Foot concedes that 'no effective answer may seem possible' to the Tory target of 300,000 and their subsequent success in achieving it: 'Macmillan's success compared with Bevan's failure is now enshrined in the mythology of the Conservative Party, and historians accept it with the suave docility of *Daily Telegraph* leader writers.'[44] Bevan did manage to build 227,616 units in 1948 and by lowering standards the Tories were able to meet the 300,000 target. The point was that to hundreds of thousands of homeless or ill-housed people the Tories promised – and delivered – most.

Sleeping Beauty stays at home

The secret weapon in the Conservatives' recovery, fired across the bows of class loyalty which, with such pride, had animated the left's advocacy of state solutions to the housing crisis, was a sexual stereotype. Alone at home, the housewife became the heroine of Conservative populism: the busy beauty, the artful dodger, who took the laws of nature into her own hands against the ugly sisters, social scientists and socialists who seemed to want to change the world. The party's paper for women, *Home Truths*, was a celebration of the housewife who, it seemed, single-handedly defeated austerity and socialism. Mixing comic strip with knitting patterns, homilies for life and useful political quotations, a homey heroine of the 1950s, 'Winnie Welcome', appeared on the front cover. Marking her second wedding anniversary in their two-room home, she's behind hundreds of other families on the waiting list, and concludes that 'the only hope of more houses, built faster, is a Conservative government . . .'

In July 1950, Winnie's husband tells her she is 'a splendid thrifty housewife, darling! If only the government were as good at national housekeeping as you are at managing our home –' In September Winnie is having a tea party with her friends, sharing an old family album. As they enjoy a photo of 'my grandmother when she was a suffragette!' her friend Joan declares, 'We could do with more of that sort of spirit among women now I say . . . I mean we housewives ought to do more striking against the way shopkeepers are profiteering!' Husband arrives home with a friendly neighbourhood shopkeeper who points out that 'the government itself puts the price up'. In February 1951 Winnie is only able to offer her husband 'fish again and savoury spaghetti for you to fill up on'. Jim understands. 'You do your best old girl. So do the shopkeepers and wholesalers! But if this is the best socialist planners can do after six years of government then it's high time they went out and the Conservatives were given a chance.'

An analysis of the women's page in the Conservative Party monthly, *Onward*, during the early fifties shows how the Tories consolidated their emphasis on the wife as a woman *with rights*. The page was populated by successful wives – mainly of MPs and ministers – writing on favourite themes ranging from gardening to housing. There was Lady Isobel Barnett, the 'perfect television mother' and a Conservative councillor; Clarissa Eden, the wife of the Foreign Secretary, writing about gardening; Dorothy Macmillan writing about housing, not so much because her husband was the housing minister, but because 'I ought to know a lot, as I have lived in a great many of all sorts and sizes'; and Sylvia Maxwell-Fyffe, the wife of the Home Secretary and herself a party vice-chairman. Heroines with their own careers were profiled, like the 'lovely and efficient' Joan Vickers, a social welfare worker, who was adopted for Devonport in 1953, and Mervyn Pike, the managing director of her own ceramics factory.

Wives were not represented as having rights in general, but as women able to pitch their *individual* domestic skills against collective or corporate power. Notions of state-imposed equality and food shortages were posed against choice and individuality as the rigours, not to mention rights, of wartime were finally buried.

'Freedom of choice this Christmas', proclaimed *Onward* in December 1953 with a picture of a young mother in a grocer's shop full of de-rationed goods. Conceding that de-rationing brought with it higher prices and therefore less freedom of choice for many women, the emphasis shifted away from the government's inflationary measures and on to the young wife's difficulty in coping with her new-found freedom to choose. For the first time, women were having to learn to shop.[45]

At the Conservative women's conference in 1954, Mrs G. A. Worth thanked the government 'for filling the shops and restoring the housewife's proper job'.[46] Conservative women stage-managed de-rationing celebrations, and following the example of Dr Edith Summerskill, organised ration-book bonfires. The new freedom of choice cost housewives dear, but *Onward* declared that 'cooking is fun again' after fourteen years of rationing. One of *Onward*'s regular writers revelled in 'Housewives Heyday', a bonanza of special offers and free samples. The housewife's craft as a discerning shopper was invoked as woman-power against tradesmen and bureaucrats:

The bad tradesmen would joyfully have my scalp if they got the chance. For they know that I . . . and the tens of thousands of other women who take a pride in good shopping . . . CAN PUT THEM OUT OF BUSINESS. And we can do it better than any Board of Trade official or any prosecution for selling shoddy goods. All we have to do is stop buying from them . . . oh the relief of not being spoonfed any more . . . in short the satisfaction of knowing that housekeeping is a skilled job once again . . .[47]

So, the shopper as vigilante pitched her will and her wits against the men behind the counter and the men from the board. The language of sexual difference was written into the way the Conservatives represented the housewife not as a downtrodden drudge but as wily and wise, the better of her traders and the better half of her class. Such images of women fully cemented the separation of the sexes, their interests and their sensibilities, upon which Conservatism depended.

Busy Beauty goes to work

Women were thus absented from the renaissance of trade union militancy, which was represented not only as class war but as men waging war on Britain's economic revival. Trade unionists meant men. 'When it comes to this business of going on strike, I'm simply not with them,' wrote Marion Slater in *Onward*, in August 1955:

What woman in her senses (and most women I've met are very much in their senses) would think of taking some definite action without considering what effect it would have on the family . . . But do men work on these commonsense lines. Not on your life as far as I can see . . . All this trouble ahead . . . because the men don't think hard enough. And I still say, no *woman* would let it happen.

Here, women's wisdom was articulated against their potential solidarity with other workers because it was asserted as wives, not workers. What this disguised, of course, was the Conservative lacuna about married women – that during the 1950s, Sleeping Beauty was joining the seven dwarfs and getting a job.

In 1951, 43 per cent of gainfully employed women were married, and by 1961 this had risen to over half. Throughout the fifties, working women mobilised a formidable campaign within their own unions for equal pay. In some unions women were going further than the limited equal pay orthodoxy and also arguing against the deployment of differentials – in effect sex differentials – within collective bargaining.[48] Half-way through the decade, trade union pressure by professional women employed in the public sector became an irresistible force for equal pay. Like the Labour government before it, the Conservative government demurred and deferred until by 1955 a schedule for the introduction of equal pay was conceded, though only for the professional women.[49]

Conservative Party women at their conference in 1957, rather late in the day, supported a motion moved by Dame Lucile Sayers which argued that 'the position of women in employment is prejudiced by out of date legislation' and demanded a review 'in the light of twentieth-century standards'.

Conservative ideology focused on the commonsense values believed to be shared among women. They drew on an implicitly shared consciousness of 'we women' pitched against groups of powerful men, whether traders, state officials or trade unionists. These Conservative women represented themselves as nobody's fools. While they stood against supposedly careless trade unionists, or state officials, they were more circumspect about their own leaders – but did, however, take them on from time to time. They may have accepted economic powerlessness but they saw themselves, then as now, as the 'moderate' but firm defenders of women's sensibilities. At the 1955 Conservative women's conference, where Anthony Eden made the ritual genuflection in paying tribute to 'the part you play – the *dominant* part you play – in the life of the party', the representatives told Harold Macmillan 'firmly' that they wanted reform of married women's tax. 'Married women are classed with lunatics, idiots and insane people as incapacitated for tax purposes,' complained Mrs Prior Palmer.[50] The women 'showed their independence of mind, and, in gloved hands, their political power' by opposing government proposals to increase MPs' incomes 'until other priorities were helped'.[51]

But it was in the political sphere that they had no difficulty in fighting the women's corner. In the 1950s, the women's page of *Onward* consistently carried profiles of women councillors and prospective candidates and offered space for the wives of prominent Conservative men, many of whom were activists within the women's networks of the party. Reminding her readers – and us – of the Conservatives' capacity for retrospectively laying claim to successful political struggles, Sylvia Maxwell-Fyffe noted the death of the last suffragettes and reminded her readers 'how far the battle for political equality for women is already slipping away into history'.[52] She later celebrated the 'silver jubilee of the Flapper Vote' and warned that although it was twenty-one years since women got the vote, 'their sex is underrepresented in Parliament'. Had it become more difficult for women to become MPs? she wondered. Dorothy Macmillan's essay on new houses asked 'whether the women who have to run them will find them comfortable and convenient'. To ensure that they did, she urged that 'every woman, by voting at local elections, has a real say in what should or should not be built. It is up to us to see that we get the right kind of house.'[53] The paper's promotion of women in politics located Conservative women in the long history of women's struggle to belong to political society. While economic equality might have contradicted their rehabilitation of the house-wife, the politicisation of women seemed to represent no such conflict of interest.

The domesticated Conservative woman was not exiled from the community, she was the community. There was, therefore, in Conservative ideology little sense of crisis in domestic isolation, and little sense that becoming 'involved' was a break in continuity from a woman's work in and around the home, the neighbourhood or village. Her transition from the community to politics was less an expression of her transformation from a private to a public woman than of Conservative women's long traditions of 'public service' in the charities and now in the municipalities. Labour's failure left socialist politics in Britain with a hole in its heart. It abandoned the cultural modernisation of the working class because it abandoned women. Its promise of full employment and equality applied to men, and it therefore consigned women to the 'separate sphere' of the Conservatives.

Law and order

In his consummate history of the crisis of modern Conservatism, *The Conservative Nation*, Andrew Gamble argues that the real achievement of the post-war Conservatives was not the destruction of the Labour Party but the rebuilding of the Tory Party by the architects of the new conservatism, the 'right progressives'. But during the 1960s, the new conservatism itself descended into crisis, nowhere more than in the party itself, and this was expressed in the estrangement of the rank and file from the Macmillanite modernisers. The new conservatism's historic compromise with the welfare state went with the grain of the post-war British state, but it did not go with the grain of the party's moral rearmers on the reactionary right.

The Conservative Party was a prisoner of the very traditions of 'respectable' morality which were breaking up in the 1950s and 1960s. Gamble locates the manifestation of crisis in the law and order uprisings within the party during the late fifties and early sixties, when the party's progressive leadership found itself up against the rank and file's reaction to penal reform. But the revolt erupted first in the late 1930s. And there was another, typical feature of it: the law and order revolt was also the revolt of the women. Gender was in the eye of the inner-party storm because the women's movement carried the spears of the counter-revolution, and because law and order was the language in which women interpolated themselves into the politics of Conservatism.

As Gamble reports, demands for law and order expressed inarticulate anxieties as well as individuals' desire to feel they could determine solutions, and it was on that terrain that rank and filers felt that they, too, were experts. But law and order was already a well-established *gendered dialogue* between the leaders and the led. The revision of the Criminal Justice Bill in the 1930s had occasioned the first wave of women's dissent over law and order reform: the revolt then was organised around women and children as the victims of men. It was in the 1930s, as in the 1950s, a populist plea for a statist politics of punishment in the name of protecting the weak: it was populist in that it did not alter the balance of power and safety between men and women: if Tory women felt empowered by their revolt against the party leaders, they did so in the name of weakness, not women's strength.

Anthony Eden, then party leader, was being more than courteous at the 1956 women's conference when he acknowledged 'the part you play – the dominant part you play – in the life of the party'. This the women already believed, and they had a strong sense of their *potential* power: 'It is my bet that these men – who know the power of the women – would rather face a packed and critical House of Commons.'[54]

The women, in an insurgent moment, led the Tory mob against their government when at their 1958 women's conference they deplored 'the leniency of penalties' and demanded that the government think again about corporal punishment. The offensive moved into the mainstream of the party later that year, when the party conference became the theatre of a duel between the leaders and led. A motion criticising the 'existing methods of punishment and reform' also made it clear that the leadership had been given a chance to prove its case for reform and had failed. What the delegates now wanted was 'more effective measures' against crime. The conference confrontation brought a packed house to bear witness against the new spectre haunting the suburbs. 'Why is it that the so-called fashionable lout of today considers himself inadequately dressed unless he has about his person a cosh or a knife?' asked Esher representative P. J. McNamara Ryan.

This and many other speeches took the form of a highly *sexualised* discourse in which the causes of crime were clearly felt to lie in a disturbance of proper sexual difference. Louts were the legacy left to society by working wives, broken marriages and television programmes full of 'sex, savagery, blood and thunder'. Miss D. Turpin (Denbigh) advocated 'flogging for adults and birching for juveniles' for crimes which included 'violent sexual assault upon women and children'. Invoking women's experience of powerlessness, she wondered why corporal punishment was still available to 'husky prison warders' but not to 'the ordinary private citizen, particularly women and children'. Mrs J. Tilney (Liverpool) berated 'groups of these make-believe gangsters strolling about as if they were monarchs of all'. Shouldn't they 'deflate these cocksure young men'? A good beating was the tried and tested solution, 'otherwise we shall find ourselves in a society dominated by young toughs who violate our girls or savagely attack the older people'. Class fear loitered around sexual fear – Mrs Tilney united all women in the category of the victim and specified not all men, but young working-class men as the culprits.

'Those young toughs who beat up harmless women' and the reforming 'smooth, smug and sloppy sentimentalists' were both indicted by Douglas Clift (Lancaster), who was no doubt pre-empting the tone of Home Secretary R. A. Butler, waiting in the wings to wind up the debate. Butler stood his ground, firmly opposing any return to nineteenth-century retribution and trying to mollify the rebels by proposing the 'de-Teddying of Teddy-boys'. If he and the rebels shared anything it was a classic Tory project – to get the working class off the streets. What he did not do was address the speakers' sexualisation of crime and punishment, and in particular the gender-fear of women.

The 1960 party conference returned to the theme. 'Let us introduce the stern discipline our fathers knew,' suggested Mr F. T. D. Prescott (Dorking), and Mrs H. Margary (Chertsey) reminded the conference that the Tory tradition 'has been noted amongst other things for its chivalry in regard to women and children'. She wanted more policing and stiffer penalties to honour that tradition. Home Office Under-Secretary Dennis Vosper tried to hold the mob at bay by appropriating their rhetoric and shifting responsibility away from the state to civil society. He located the origins of alleged degeneracy not in social conditions but in the home; therefore 'the family, and society, or the public as distinct from the government, can do much to remove the seeds of discontent at an early stage'.

The crunch came in 1961 when Butler faced another direct challenge from the constituencies on corporal and capital punishment. Geoffrey Howe represented the government's position when he successfully moved deletion of the specific punishments, but it was a tight fight and exposed critical divisions within the party. Mr H. P. Lucas, who moved the original motion, reckoned that 'if a vote was taken 95 per cent of the women of this country' would vote for corporal punishment. He brought the gender factor into focus when he declared, 'what upsets me so much is that a motion on corporal punishment has been passed so many times at women's conferences . . . It is time the government listened to the wishes of the people.'

But lest the world equate hanging and flogging with the Tory woman, Miss Erica Spinney (Wessex) insisted that there was another voice. Conservative women, it was clear, represented both reaction and reform. 'As a statement of fact,' she declared, 'I am a woman. I am also a Conservative. I am wearing a hat, and I am not so obviously owning a hunting whip', but she opposed the retributionists: the real problem was that the government had failed to put across Mr Butler's message. She was supported by Lady Elliot of Harewood, DBE, a prominent Conservative and a member of the

Home Office Advisory Committee on Offenders. As someone involved in the probation service, she warned the conference that no
one dealing with crime and criminals wanted to return to corporal
punishment. Undaunted, Mrs Olive Roberts protested that 'it is the
women and children I am concerned about. They are in need of
protection . . . women know what can happen to them. Eighty per
cent of the victims are women.' Butler defended himself, supported
by Howe, and they won by a whisker. Again they did not address
the specifically sexual subtext of the debate.

Although that factor of gender has not been explored in the
histories, the party itself seemed well aware of the connection
between gender, sex and violence, and it knew who all the aggravation was for. The chairman of the 1961 law and order debate (who
seemed surprised to find many more applications to speak from men
than women) pointed out for the record that, 'I understand this
controversy was supposed to be entirely for the ladies.'

So the conjugation of sex and violence became the ideological
loot taken by the rank and file from the princes of Tory enlightenment. But questions come to mind here about what the
confrontation really revealed about the power of women in the party.
The form of the 'ladies' controversy' never transcended the problem
of women's powerlessness which infused the debates. Ironically,
and yet typically, it was one of the very occasions when the women
used their power to challenge the leadership. Implicit, but only ever
implicit, was some sense of patriarchal domination, but of course
the case for capital punishment also implied an appeal to another
form of patriarchal dominance, the judiciary. Conservative women
wanted to avenge the victim, not to challenge the drama of dominance in which masculinity and femininity was and is caught.

Gamble argues that law and order was the site of the crisis of the
new conservatism in the early 1960s, for this was the one issue about
which 'most Conservatives felt that they had at least as much
understanding as their leaders'.[55] (Abolition of capital punishment
remained the one issue of 'social' reform that was never endorsed by
the electorate.) The women clearly felt they had more understanding
than most, since they identified with the victims. But as we shall see,
the specifically sexual dimension of the revolt became subordinate; it
was absorbed.

In the same year that the Tory leadership contained the hangers
and floggers, the rank and file turned to another side of the law and

order prism: immigration. Racism which had for years focused on the Irish found a new target in the Afro–Caribbeans, and fully came out of the closet in the 1960s. The moral reactionaries may have been out of synch with the changing sexual mores of the 1960s – a majority of public opinion was for reform – but they touched a seam of rampant racism. In 1961, a resolution calling for a halt on immigration was carried in the face of resistance from Nigel Fisher, who was later hounded by his constituency party for a speech defending the principle of freedom of movement within the Commonwealth, and from R. A. Butler, who defended the contribution made by Commonwealth workers to the labour force and argued that any ban would mean 'departing from a great tradition'.

A measure of how far the British state conceded ground was that although at the beginning of the decade a Tory Home Secretary felt obliged, in all honour, to defend the principle of freedom of movement within the Commonwealth, by the end of the decade a Labour Home Secretary abandoned it altogether in an Immigration Act which split his party and set the terms for the racism subsequently inscribed with impunity in British immigration legislation.

Sex and race deluged the agenda during the 1960s. Suffering defeat on immigration, and barely recovering from the trial-by-hanging debate, in 1963 the party leadership was snared by the 'Profumo affair' – Tory minister, John Profumo, was involved in a web of 'sex and spying' involving upper-class men and diplomats and 'call girls'. The Establishment rounded on the government and its promotion of mass consumption as being in some way responsible for the nation's descent into barbarism.[56]

Who does she think she is?

Around the same time, one of the best-known right-wing populists of her day was getting organised. Mary Whitehouse was a secondary school teacher whose political career began long before she emerged as 'just a housewife' having a go. She had been involved with Moral Re-armament, a religious movement which was associated with appeasement of Hitler before the war, became an anti-communist crusade during the cold war and turned its attention to 'permissiveness' in the 1960s. Mary Whitehouse's cause had a similar genesis to that of Victoria Gillick in the 1980s: as a teacher, she had worried about sex education being handed over to Marriage Guidance counsellors, particularly if it was to be stripped of moral guidance.[57]

In 1963 her fundamentalist Christianity was affronted by the way, in her view, the BBC opened its door to 'the exponents of the New Morality and censored, by exclusion, the exponents of established morality'. Sex and the Profumo affair, she believed, dominated the small screen and playground chatter.[58] She rained complaints upon the BBC and politicians about 'sex and violence'. When the BBC's charter was renewed in 1964, she was so disappointed that she felt there was nothing left but for the parents to 'rise up',[59] so she and a friend launched a women's manifesto, which became the Clean Up TV campaign and later the National Viewers and Listeners Association. And so began her crusade against sex education and the liberalisation of laws regulating sexuality and censorship. In the absence of an appropriately authoritarian agenda from the leaders of the Tory Party, a new salvation army gathered among the ranks inside and outside the political institutions.

After the Tories' general election defeat in 1964, a new 'modern man' was elected leader, Edward Heath. He inherited the moral crisis erupting on the right; indeed his leadership coincided with the ascendancy of the moral authoritarians around Mary Whitehouse. Heath's project was primarily economistic and technocratic: he was opposed to the moral rearmers, although his confrontational stance in relation to trade unionism appeared to place him to the right of his predecessors. For him, good management was the mantra of good government, but Heath's preoccupation with economic renewal evacuated the arena of popular politics – unlike the new right, which, Gamble argues,

> grasped what the modern wing of the party did not, that a competition policy, however necessary, did not recommend itself to the electorate and to the party on technical grounds alone, but had to become part of a much more general and ideological offensive.[60]

Heath's cool corporatism could not have distanced him more from the keepers of the party's moral conscience – women. The ideological crisis was the party's own gender crisis. The conservatism assigned to women had always been less about policy than personal values. In a party founded on the marriage of the family, the empire, the traditional institutions and capital, the crisis of the 1960s produced a divorce – the leaders and the led just weren't talking the same language.

Who does he think he is?

The new right emerged out of the law and order lobby, and was to become the party's 'moral majority'. Gamble suggests that it was the rise of racism during the 1960s which expanded the social base for the populism of the new right, and that it was Enoch Powell who generated a new electoral ideology reaching beyond the boundaries of party and class affiliation deep into the heart of the electorate. Powell's maverick political career peaked in 1968 with apocalyptic diatribes against black immigrants in Britain, whose presence, he alleged at the 1968 party conference, 'in the very heart' of the nation would 'change the character of England itself'. Edward Heath insisted in front of his own hostile party that everyone already in Britain should be treated as equal, but by 1,117 votes to 958 the leadership lost to an anti-immigration amendment. Powell, who was deposed by Heath forthwith, had articulated a post-imperialist chauvinism which resurrected an English nationalism reaching deep into the Tories' past when it was gaudily celebrated by the Dames of the Primrose League.

For sure, racism was the new right's secret weapon, and it was with racism that it reached a wider and deeper coalition than sexual moralism, which had rendered it a moral minority, albeit a vocal and powerful one. Nevertheless, sexual politics must be written into the chronicle of the new right's ascendancy: racism and sexism were critical elements. Racism excluded black people from the new right's forward march, because it celebrated a *white* nation, but sexism conscripted the women of the right because its ideology celebrated family and femininity. The feminine ideology women brought to the new right, however, could be absorbed because it represented *active subordination*.[61] It sought to influence and to civilise patriarchal domination, not to challenge it.

By the end of the 1960s, the inner-party revolt had expanded beyond the highly sexualised discourse of the law and order debates a decade earlier. They now expressed a general sense of siege in the face not only of 'permissiveness' but also of student rebellion, mass demonstrations against the United States' war in Vietnam and industrial insurgency by the trade unions. The party's unrequited rebels on the right felt that they were not so much the silent majority as the silenced majority. Years of resentment was expressed by a redoubtable Keighley Conservative Joan Hall, who at the 1968 party conference moved a motion deploring the lack of a clear distinction between socialism and conservatism: 'A great deal has been said about the middle way in politics, and this means the majority of us in the land.' People were preoccupied with demonstrators, but what did the law-abiding taxpayers and ratepayers feel, she asked;

> who is going to champion them? It seems that the politicians
> are always talking about someone else somewhere else who has
> been neglected and who needs all our thought and help . . .
> traditional voting patterns are breaking down. We have a
> void, and woe betide the Conservative Party if it ignores these
> feelings.

The party leadership was not only at odds with the moral crusade of the new right, but was also its prisoner. The Conservative ethos was grounded in the fastnesses of respectability, family and tradition which were occupied by the ranks in the constituencies. The moral crisis seemed to leave the leadership speechless. It hated the moral regression of the constituencies, but neither did it have a clear moral agenda of its own. All it could do was try to contain the contagion. And ultimately it could not.

It was these crises which later became resolved in the realignment of the party in the 1970s around the radical right. *Race, class and sex*, in fact, were the key terms in what became Thatcherism. The first blow was struck by Sir Keith Joseph who defined the parameters of the reunification of the moral and the economic in a cathartic speech which provoked a storm of protest after the Tories' election defeat in October 1974. Throwing down the gauntlet to the Heath leadership he declared, in a speech published in full in *The Times* on 21 October 1974, that 'During the election, discussion focused almost exclusively on economics; and we lost the election. Were these two facts unconnected? I don't think so.' Voters had been presented with promises by all parties to maintain growth and social security benefits and keep down prices – an 'auction' in which Labour was bound to win. Meanwhile, he said, egalitarianism had led to the decline of educational standards, the invasion of the academies by 'the bully boys of the left' and, echoing the eugenicism of an earlier era, he lamented the degeneration of 'our human stock' by a growing proportion of children born to working-class single mothers of mostly 'low educational attainment'. In the 1960s, sex and race were thrown together in an ideological constellation *outside* the party as well as *inside* it. Although the crisis over crime and immigration was once again articulated as law and order, the discourse of the revolt originated in the very architecture of commonsense: *home* meant many things; it meant England in her Empire and it meant house-wives and houses and high streets. The English were *peculiarly* English. The concept of the Conservative nation, therefore, housed many meanings – from sexuality, the family and the state, to the soul of the cities and the colour of skin. Not surprisingly, the perpetual themes were violence against women and children; the nature of national identity in a multinational society; the nature of homes and neighbourhoods; the crisis of the patriarchal family, destabilised both by the working mother and by parental panic over loss of control; the spectre of 'youth' stalking the streets brandishing their surplus cash and their surplus sexuality. Women became the metaphor for loss of control – they were the victims, the victims of strangers.

Labour's road to Thatcherism

During the Tory turmoil over values, the Labour Party embarked on a programme of economic and cultural modernisation. Labour's mind had been turned to its chronic loss of support among the young by private polls conducted by Mark Abrams. In the 1959 election the gender gap had closed slightly, but 51 per cent of women voters still cast their votes for the Tories. Abrams had shown that the youth were more likely to vote Tory by 2–1, but the enduring alignment of a small but significant number of women to the right had seemed unworthy of analysis or action.

In the 1964 general election Labour, counselled by Abrams, did not so much target specific social groups as direct its advertising at target categories: motorists, the badly housed, pensioners, and so on.[62] Nevertheless, British politicians still seemed 'to view the electorate as a remarkably homogenous entity',[63] and there was no recognition that women existed as a political category in and for themselves, although the gender gap narrowed slightly. Only in the 1966 general election did Labour make real headway among women, when they voted in greater numbers for Labour than for the Con-servatives for the first time since 1945.

It has been argued that this was another case of women's natural conservatism working for Labour, especially since in that election Labour presented itself as not only radical but also reasonable and responsible. But another reading of that election could be that women began to align themselves with the more progressive values associated with Labour. It was hardly socialism, but Labour was breaking out of its old repressive respectability; it was going with the mood of the time rather than hibernating from it, and so were women. In some respects, of course, the social revolution was a sexual revolution, and women themselves embodied the change. If the 1960s was not yet the era of equality, and if women's time hadn't yet come, it was on its way. The sixties and the political fissures among men and women within the left after all gave birth to the modern Women's Liberation Movement at the end of the decade.

While not profiling a political programme for women as women, Labour had targeted a number of social policy reforms, particularly in health, housing and education, for which there has been greater support among women than men, and which may be one of the ways (in the absence of any other) in which women might have been able to articulate their progressive consciousness *as women*. After all, no political party has prefigured a feminist future in its electoral strategy. It could be argued that women's progressive political consciousness as women has been coded through social policy rather than economic policy, just as the reactionary law and order tradition has provided a coded context in which other dimensions of women's consciousness as women have been articulated.

During the late 1960s there was a renaissance of industrial action around equal pay, particularly among engineering workers, and in the aftermath of what was to become the most famous women's strike of its time, by Ford women machinists in 1968, the Labour government introduced the Equal Pay Act. During the 1970s the women's TUC and the Labour Party women's conference both began to be transformed by the new wave of feminism, and in 1975 both adopted bold policies in favour of abortion on demand and freely available contraception. These were then adopted by the TUC and the Labour Party. However decorously, the labour movement was thus committed to defend the abortion legislation which was under siege from the right wings of both the Labour and Conservative Parties throughout the 1970s, and by the end of the decade there was an unshakable alliance between the Labour women MPs

and the women's movement outside Parliament. While not necessarily perceived as such at the time, all this began the transformation
of the labour movement. It was very different from the patriarchal
resistance of the 1920s and the cultural conservatism of the Labour
leadership in the 1940s.

However much the Women's Liberation Movement was vilified,
and however many women appeared to place themselves outside it
by the caveat 'I'm not Women's Lib but . . .', feminism was once
again inside the culture and on the agenda. The culture clash was
arresting. Women's Liberation was predicated on the principle of
'the personal is political', the mantra of the movement from its
formation in the United States in the late 1960s. The movement's
practice was guided by the belief that women formed their feminism
for themselves through the activity of consciousness-raising and a
commitment to direct democracy. All of this ruptured the separation
of private and public. Its challenge to both the left and the right was
a politics which *integrated* the public and the private, the personal
and the political, and in so doing disturbed the assumptions behind
all those categories.

Labour's Equal Pay Act was a limited state intervention in collective bargaining against the anomalous treatment of women, and it
was a measure which secured consensual party political support.
But it did not address the problem of the *typical* poverty of women
in relation to men. It was not until the 1970s, when the trade union
presence in the Labour leadership broke with the traditions of their
conservative antecedents twenty years earlier, that women's interests
as workers found a place in a new and more egalitarian approach to
incomes. The 1975 social contract was a deal sold to the trade
unions as a trade-off for pay restraint and was much criticised by
the left of the labour movement, who repudiated its architects, Jack
Jones and Hugh Scanlon. Yet this was the first national wages
strategy to give any priority to the demands of women, the low paid
and the elderly.

Both Tory and Labour governments from the end of the 1960s
to the mid-1970s attempted piratical incursions upon the power and
autonomy of trade unions, particularly the rank and file, and both
suffered humiliating defeats. The Tory manifesto in 1974 still
stressed the beleaguered notion of incomes policies and promised
national reunification. The Labour leadership came out of the
debacle of the three-day week and Heath's humiliation with a

manifesto proposing a new reconciliation with the trade unions. Instead of gladiatorial trials of strength, Labour embarked upon a programme carefully crafted with the trade unions themselves: the social contract, industrial democracy, pensions reform, land and housing reform. Both the Tory and the Labour manifestos briefly endorsed the economic equality of women. Labour won the February 1974 general election and returned to the polls in October, when it won with a bigger majority among women. As in 1966, more women voted Labour than Conservative in that second election.

Taken together, the first two phases of the social contract containing flat-rate pay rises (designed to erode differentials), the Equal Pay Act and the Sex Discrimination Act, both implemented in 1975, represented a limited yet significant state intervention in the distribution of incomes between men and women. It began to detonate the patriarchal ideology which had dominated collective bargaining practices for a century. But it was short-lived – the demise of the social contract into undisguised pay restraint in its third phase, and the labour movement's reaction to that, opened the door once again to the assertion of anti-egalitarianism. As the social contract foundered in the midst of the Labour government's financial crises, the dominant tendency within the labour movement was to regress into anti-modernism. The TUC and the left of the labour movement, too, abandoned the 'collective' in collective bargaining for a tactical realignment against the government's 5 per cent pay limit – from which neither the poor nor women were exempted. One trade union leader told a TUC Congress in 1976: 'We all know that differentials have been squeezed . . . what we are saying is that in a freer situation ability must be rewarded, skill must be rewarded, effort must be rewarded.'[64] He didn't mean the re-evaluation of millions of low-paid women's ability, skill and effort, of course; what he meant was the good old traditions by which men had defended themselves. It was almost identical to the language of Thatcherism.

So-called free collective bargaining was resumed at the end of the 1970s in the name of differentials. But there was still an egalitarian flame flickering within the labour movement: the public employees' union NUPE launched a pay campaign based on a national minimum wage and a shorter working week. A coalition of unions with low-paid members went into the winter of 1978 with industrial action for low pay and against cuts in social services. The 'winter of discontent' ended in a deal struck in a smoke-filled room between the lions of the labour movement: out went shorter working time and a minimum wage, and in came a Standing Commission on Pay Comparability. It rejected NUPE's proposal to compare women's pay with men's and consequently came up with deeply discriminatory pay settlements, reinforcing the sex differential which had already started to increase in 1977–78. The defeat of the egalitarian initiative found an echo in Thatcherism's incomes ideology – which no doubt helps explain why in the 1979 general election the biggest swings towards Thatcher were among skilled men.

Labour was moving in contradictory directions in the 1970s. Part of the movement was travelling towards a new egalitarianism and part was behaving according to the patrician habits of a lifetime. Labour's Prime Minister until the party's defeat in 1979, 'Uncle Jim' Callaghan, was still telling Labour women's conferences in the 1970s to beware the lure of waged work. Callaghan, who took control personally of Labour's 1979 election campaign 'can be seen as the most conservative Prime Minister since Baldwin, cautiously presenting consensual politics and presenting himself as a kindly uncle, responsible and firm'.[65] His debacle with the trade unions during the 1978–79 winter of discontent and his intuitive conservatism destroyed the Labour government in 1979 and with it the legislative space for radical women's politics. From women's perspective in this, the decade of women, sexual Toryism rose from the ashes and beckoned the labour movement. It was the kiss of death.

That was Labourism's road to Thatcherism. But what was happening among Conservative women during the prelude to Thatcher's ascent?

Hats off at Central Office
During the late 1960s and early 1970s, the preoccupations of Tory women ran along two distinct tracks. Their traditional demonology appeared to co-exist with egalitarian ambitions shared with women's politics in the world at large. Their party women's conferences were concerned with the impact of 'the present social revolution on the family', the 'nation's need for woman-power', the expansion of nursery school provision, equal rights for women, and an end to tax discrimination 'against marriage', as well as the familiar Tory women's themes: capital punishment, immigration, stiffer sentences,

permissiveness, supplemented by the new demons – revolting students and unofficial strikers.

During Edward Heath's era, Central Office tried to keep the Tory mob under control and took on board the modernisation of the women's organisation. Modernisation was embodied by Sara Morrison, who had been a county councillor and whose political world was voluntary organisations. Hers was a typical trajectory for a Tory lady, perhaps, but the political context and, therefore, the concerns of many voluntary organisations – the traditional terrain of Tory women – were changing fast in the 1960s with the emergence of key words like 'poverty' and 'participation' and of the more radical community action and voluntary agencies like the Low Pay Unit and the Child Poverty Action Group. Heath persuaded the reluctant Morrison to take on the party's women's organisation and when she did finally agree to her appointment as a party vice-chairman with responsibility for women, she set about making the environment of Central Office more consonant with the changing culture of women outside.

As one party functionary recalled, the constituencies were still populated by members of the old colonial middle class who had once inhabited the empire 'where they made life tough for the natives, and who returned to make life tough for the natives here'. But there were within the regional and national hierarchies and the voluntary agencies, women who wanted change and who were themselves part of it. When Morrison arrived on the scene and appeared to have 'whipped the hats off them and told them to belt up about flogging' she was not alone. According to Morrison, 'There was already a strong feeling that the non-conformist liberal thing was under way', and in her view that was the authentic voice of Disraelian Conservatism.

Heath set up the Cripps Committee within the party to look into the new legislation affecting women which was being introduced by the Labour government in the 1960s. Its brief was to look at the position of women in society in general and the legislation in particular. 'We were all in favour of it at Central Office and on the women's advisory committee,' said Morrison, 'and by the time the committee reported the cast of woman had changed and they were very aware of the changes and were 100 per cent for it'. The Tories wanted more limited equality legislation than that being proposed by Labour, but Morrison remembers no opposition to the legislation among Tory women: 'I can recall opposition from some MPs, but not the women.'

There was also some security in the knowledge gained through the regional structures of the party and among women prominent in the voluntary agencies that they endorsed the Morrisonian approach. Through this kind of 'alternative intelligence service' the women's organisation believed, moreover, that it had the feel of the communities in which the activists moved. There was also a feeling that many of the 'progressive' Tory activists among women were dug into voluntary agencies in the 1960s where they felt they had more clout than in the party 'where women tended to be making the sandwiches and fighting with Mrs Tiggywinkle over who was to make the vote of thanks after a boring speech by the local MP'. One of the women involved in the changing role of the women, recalled that

> until we got our hands on it, the Tory Party was the best vote-harvesting machine there was. But by our time we saw that we had to sow the seeds of politics, too. That was alienating to vast sectors, but we were trying to make the party a political force. And therein lay the rub – we were a catastrophic failure, we kept losing elections, us swinging liberals – we'd laid the seeds for the right wing.

Another image held by one of the senior politicians of the day was that the problem with the women

> wasn't so much hanging and flogging, but the village flower show and the fête, and what hat they were wearing and what people thought of them behind the stalls. The thing is, those things are necessary – it is one of the advantages we have always had over the Labour Party, we have a lot of organisation in the constituencies. The ladies were working very hard for the cause without knowing what the cause was and being prepared to adjust the cause year by year or election by election as circumstances seemed to demand. That was becoming rather different; we were changing that.

One of the party's problems was that it did not have a sufficiently powerful coterie of professional and businesswomen in the infrastructure of the women's organisation to encourage equivalent women to join them. Consequently the party was not felt to be an appropriate place for the ambitious professional/political women. A politician sympathetic to the modernisation of the women's organisation reckoned that outsiders would look at the party 'and think this isn't really a party that believes in this sort of thing. In fact it must have a deeply dug-in form of reactionary conservatism which is automatically against us.' Nevertheless, the women were a potential, if not an actual force, and the lid was being kept on what one official described as 'the dinosaurs in twinsets' – women who may not have meant 'mischief', but who were 'just old-fashioned. They were odious because they were dangerously out of touch; they were tragically, socially irrelevant.'

One theory about the role of women in the triumph of the right after Edward Heath's defeat in 1974 and the subsequent election of Margaret Thatcher as party leader was that

in trying to reform the party we'd created a right-wing backlash. They were waiting in the wings. When we were mugged by the right, it wasn't the women, and the party organisation stood behind Ted and what he represented: it was the Parliamentary Party that did it. Women weren't part of it, but blimey they were the victims of it. You see, the Conservative Party was full of the facsimile of twinset and pearls who were there before. The floggers had been vanquished, but in 1974 there were still enough around and they came out of hiding.

Undoubtedly, the party harboured apparently contradictory tendencies among women. One was the old faithful familial ideology which had a critique of the decline of moral values from which, implicitly, women and the world could be saved only by the moral authority of women themselves. The other was a cautious endorsement of equality: they affirmed women's movement into men's worlds, particularly the professional and political world. But tactically the latter never abandoned concessions to the ideology of women's special and separate sphere. The fragility of Tory egalitarianism was expressed in their silences; patriarchal power was not on their agenda. Morrison herself recalls that however committed she was to women's equality she was not an angry woman, 'perhaps because I'd never been personally shackled', and she never felt able to go all the way with 'Women's Lib' because half-way through a speech 'I'd get the giggles about it'. Later those typical Tory equivocations enabled the women to hold to their belief in the power of women while simultaneously endorsing the anti-egalitarian regressions of Thatcherism in the late 1970s and the 1980s, because Thatcher herself was the embodiment of women's strength and stamina.

Margaret Thatcher's campaign for the party leadership was not founded on what was to become Thatcherism, but she was soon inventing it. Her purge of the modernists secured a coalition between apparently disparate tendencies: the marriage of moral authoritarianism and economic liberalism reunited a party divided since 1945. In March 1975 she said:

> Self-reliance has been sneered at as if it were an absurd suburban pretension. Thrift has been denigrated as if it were greed. The desire of parents to choose and to struggle for their children has been scorned. In the name of equality, that decent, honourable ambition of many thousands of people is to be deliberately frustrated by the state.[66]

It was in International Women's Year, 1975, that she invited the women of the party at their conference to honour their own specific traditions and political practices. What she could not contemplate was the Tory women's connections, however cautious, with the women's movements of their own time, as Morrison tried to do. People wanted, said Margaret Thatcher, 'to own a piece of personal property', to exercise their obligations to family and community and – in a special word to the women – to go about their voluntary work, which was 'the spirit of a real social contract'.[67] The following year she staked out her assault on 'the progressive consensus' – which by then, of course, included the changing circumstances of women. In a germinal speech in New York, she questioned the support for equality in Britain, and if a gesture towards equality of opportunity represented a concession to the consensus, then it was simultaneously withdrawn in Thatcher's refusal to address, still less endorse, the meaning of equality *for women*.

The politics of pessimism

The party's preparations for the 1979 election campaign strategy, which was handed over to Saatchi and Saatchi with a budget of £2.4 million, show that it targeted specific sexes as well as classes –

particularly skilled men and women. The Tories had for most of this century depended on working-class support, and 'since the 1920s it has had to maintain its working class support against the competition of a party claiming to be the exclusive representative of the interests of that class'.[68] The campaign run by James Callaghan, on the other hand, languidly looked for the 'traditional Labour voter'.[69] But the evidence accumulated in the 1950s and 1960s showed that there were no longer 'traditional' Labour voters, or rather, if there were, they could no longer be regarded as a fallow majority. In any case, during the 1970s there were gender realignments which cut across class as much among men as among women, if not more so.

Historically, insofar as the gender gap was acknowledged, women were assumed to be the anomalous sex by not voting according to their class. But in the late 1970s, it was men who became the volatile sex, who abandoned their class alignment for reasons which could be inferred to be as much about their gender as anything else. Labour, under Callaghan, had jettisoned the 'new women', yet Labour's 'traditional' chauvinist core, the proud and patriarchal craftsman, no doubt felt abandoned by a party that was no longer entirely in his own image, and which in any case had let him down. By backing his 'traditional' Labour voter, Callaghan seemed to be backing the horse that had already bolted. With the modernisation of the women's organisation barely underway in the Tory Party, Thatcherism gave it no positive encouragement, and Toryism thus became the authentic voice of patriarchal values once safe but now challenged within Labourism. It was now the voice of skill and sex sectionalism, the individual against the collective interest.

Contrary to the Tories' reading of their mandate in 1979, an overwhelming majority of the electorate, 70 per cent, preferred the maintenance of services to tax cuts.[70] Yet MORI's research into voter attitudes conducted for the Labour Party disclosed powerlessness and deep pessimism about politics itself.[71] Research for the Tories confirmed this profound depoliticisation, together with a clear separation between 'life' and 'politics'.[72] Into the void rose the Tories with subliminal jingles which addressed voters, particularly women, as consumers in the language of everyday life rather than politics: 'inflation' became 'prices'; the Budget became what any housewife knew. Where Labour had failed to democratise public housing, the Tories promised property-owning democracy. Where skilled men were affronted at the politicisation of collective bargaining, the Tories promised to restore it to its traditional concerns; where people felt alienated from the butch persona of the trade unionist, the Tories threatened to put the 'bully boys' and the 'barons' in their place; where women feared the streets, the night and strange men, the Tories – until the 1980s the only party to politicise women's private fears – promised the protection of the law.

Thatcherism had a populist appeal to both men and women, but for different reasons. And also to different effect. Although the result of the election brought the sexes closer together – which could be seen as an erosion of the gender gap – men and women on the margins were moving in different directions: women tended to move away from the right while men moved towards the right. In the moment of a woman's triumph, men were becoming a more conservative sex.

The post-war election tally encouraged MORI's cavalier psephologist Robert Worcester to conclude after the 1983 election that 'If women in Britain voted proportionately to their incidence in the population and the political "gender gap" favouring the Conservatives were maintained, the Conservatives would never be voted out of office. Women traditionally are more likely (by some 5–10 per cent) to support the Tories than Labour.'[1]

Psephologists and political scientists have tended to assume that women vote Conservative because they are naturally conservative. But if we rely on 'natural causes' as the explanation, how are we to explain, for example, that in the United States the gender gap is working the other way, in favour of the Democrats? In any case, it doesn't explain the tendency for a higher proportion of women voters in Britain to support the Tories, nor the variations among women of different ages, classes (their own rather than husbands') and domestic circumstances. We shall see that until recently these questions have not been addressed by straight psephologists (students of voting) who have tended to see women's sex as sufficient explanation. But complex and apparently contradictory features appear when we look at women's *political* as well as their *party* orientations. We will see that something seems to be afoot among women – they may not be the conservative sex in the future and already on many social-political issues women tend to be the more radical sex.

Sex and nature
How have women's voting proclivities been explained by political scientists, political commentators and politicians? The answer is that

in the main they haven't been. Within political science orthodoxy, we see that women are marooned outside the dominant cultures which are believed to determine political allegiance. Political science has left 'the woman voter' swilling around in a sea of homilies and hunches which we are all supposed to recognise because they come from common sense. Thus women have been deemed to have no class consciousness of their own, and so there has been no sense that their own class consciousness might take a different form, with different priorities, from that of comparable men. Men's political allegiance has been understood to be determined by class, while women's has been, in effect, determined by their sex, not least because their class position was classified according to their husbands' occupations. This not only misrepresents the effects of both gender and class on men's and women's politics, but also how they acquire their politics.

It is implicit in the orthodoxy that men *make* their consciousness actively through their *experience* in the world of work, or in the crucible of class solidarity, the trade union movement. It is rational and pragmatic, specific and self-interested. It implicitly follows that women are *born* with their consciousness, it is in their instincts. So men have social consciousness and women have only their unconscious. It is assumed that women's politics are formed in the home, which frames a quest for stability and security. So their consciousness is acquired passively, it is moral, instinctive and inaccessible. Motherhood is represented as a state of nature: unlike fathers, mothers are not represented simultaneously as workers; mothers are not exploited.

Typically, David Butler's exhaustive studies of each British general election since the war did not include statistics on women until the 1960s.[2] Mark Abrams' *Must Labour Lose?*, which influenced Labour Party electoral planning in the 1960s, refers to women in only one among scores of statistics.[3]

Post-war political scientists have been primarily concerned with the relationship between class and party support, the assumption being that one determines the other. Changes in class culture have prompted studies of the phenomenon of working-class Toryism, an essential factor in the Tories' success at the polls. The subjects of these studies of political delinquency have been men. Butler and Stokes, in *Political Change in Britain: Forces Shaping Electoral Choice*, dodge the problem of women as political subjects in their own right by categorising women according to their male breadwinner's class position, and that disposal of the largest sector of the electorate is achieved in a footnote.[4] This influential book is a paradigm of what two critics call 'fudging the footnotes',[5] whereby women's supposed characteristics are stated as asides, but never substantiated. Butler and Stokes simply say that a 'primary source' of working-class support for the Tories is Anglicanism. In the footnote they elaborate: 'we have here a partial explanation of the greater conservatism of women, who tend also to be more faithful in religious observance.' They admit, however, that this explanation 'is no more than a partial one'.[6] And apparently, it wasn't worth verifying.

Religion may have been important historically in aligning women's politics to the right, but to leave it at that is to consign women's politics to peculiarly feminine forces: religion represents those characteristics imputed to women – a love of tradition, morality and mysticism.

The class of women

The Labour, Liberal and Conservative parties more or less held on to their poll percentages among women in both the 1945 and 1950 elections. It was only after the Liberal vote collapsed in the 1950s and went to the Tories (among both men and women) that the Tories began to collect significantly more votes from women than Labour. But Labour's base among women was remarkably resilient. Having already consigned women to the Conservatives, Abrams *et al* then ascribed women's loyalty to Labour to their conservatism: 'There is even some evidence to suggest that the conservatism of women has made them more likely than men to retain their traditional attachment to Labour.'[7]

When married women's post-war employment began to change the profile of the labour force, the actual or potential political implications were infused with ideas about women not as workers, but as consumers. 'Some social changes appear to have had little impact, at least in the short run,' noted Mark Abrams and Richard Rose in their reflections on Labour's demise during the 1950s. 'The increase in the number of working women and their new buying power does not seem to have influenced their voting behaviour.'[8] Hidden here is a gendered perception: women's re-entry into wage labour was assumed to 'bourgeoisify' rather than proletarianise women. As it turned out, the post-war gender gap often tended to work against Labour and yet the party seemed to have sighed in pious resignation.

Feminism has criticised the ways that both politicians and political scientists have subsumed women's class to that of the men in their lives: 'Most women, whether married, unmarried, deserted, deserting or widowed, whether gainfully employed or housewives, are fed into the computer under the occupation of their father or husband, or male head of household, be the man retired or still in the workforce, dead or alive.'[9] Criticising the methods of political science, Murray Goot and Elizabeth Reid argue that 'while the political behaviour of women has been the principal concern of very few voting studies, it remains an incidental concern of many. Women are of interest only insofar as they resemble or fail to resemble men.'[10]

Important new work has been produced in the 1980s which breaks with the tendency to conflate the assumed decline of Labour with the decline of class support, and instead proposes a revision of the ways class is classified and the allocation of women to class positions according to their own class location rather than according to male heads of households'.

Adopting the feminist critique, Patrick Dunleavy and Christopher T. Husbands, in *British Democracy at the Crossroads*, noted that to classify women according to their husbands' jobs was 'obviously and offensively sexist' and decided to *reclassify* women's class according to women's own jobs. And because 'gender positions are logically and empirically prior to occupational class', they abandon occupational class in favour of social class categories because 'gender effects'[11] can't be collapsed into class when sex has such a determining impact on the occupations men and women do. So they suggest that it is 'very dangerous' to compare the votes of men and women in the same class. Social class is 'much less vulnerable to distortion by gender effects' because it is about power within the production process rather than rank in a hierarchy of prestige. It is also about political power. Dunleavy and Husbands also argue that 'union membership has always figured as the most important workplace effect on voting behaviour', and yet 'there is *no* reliable evidence to show that occupational class is a major determinant of whether people join trade unions'.[12] More important is whether they are employed in the public or private sector, and whether they are men or women. They conclude that 'only when we have correctly analysed union membership as overwhelmingly determined by production sector and by gender, rather than by class, can we move on to understand its full political implications'.[13]

Putting together gender and social class, they find that among women it is the manual/non-manual distinction which is critical, while among men this is less significant than the gap between controllers of labour and (non-manual) workers. When households are added the most Conservative grouping is non-manual worker housewives, while manual worker housewives are most strongly Labour. Among women manual workers in households dependent on a single wage, 65 per cent voted Labour – more than any other group in 1983.[14]

Anthony Heath, Roger Jowell and John Curtice, in *How Britain Votes*, argue that there is no substantial evidence of the decline in the class basis of politics. They, too, relocate women into categories according to their own position in the labour process, and conclude that 'there are no major differences in the voting behaviour of men and women within a class'.[15]

Reviewing the 'class distinctiveness' of the political parties, they state that the Tories 'may be *the* party of the bourgeoisie, but they are not a "bourgeois" party. Their vote is in fact drawn almost as evenly from across the classes as is the Alliance vote. On this criteria the Conservatives and the Alliance have almost equal claims to be called classless parties.'[16] But Labour remains more obviously a working-class party. 'It is still a party of the subordinate.'[17]

Class, however, is not the only determinant of subordination – for women, as for ethnic minorities, no major political party clearly organises around their insubordination, or makes their aspirations a priority within classes as well as across classes.

Will the really conservative sex please stand up?

Do the electoral alignments of men and women conceal the possibility that women are, in fact, the more progressive sex? Does men's greater commitment to Labourism and its economic prospectus make men the socialist sex? Or does it only reflect perhaps their corporate interests as a sex and disguise greater conservatism in social, cultural and personal politics? As Peter Kellner asked in the *New Statesman*: 'Is the Labour Party missing out on an international trend for women to set the pace in progressive political attitudes?'[18]

Kellner points out that the notion of the gender gap depends on only a minority of voters at the margin but they may nevertheless determine the results of an election in the British system. Scanning polling evidence, Kellner concludes that 'the apparently greater progressive instincts of British men concern a narrow but traditionally dominant set of "socialist" issues, mainly to do with work, unions and the State'. But 'on many issues that have little or nothing to do with class struggle against monopoly capital – from social policy to cruise missiles – women tend to be more progressive than men'. Working women were more sympathetic than working men to paying higher taxes to allow more government spending on job creation. But more men than women thought trade unions should have more say in running industry. Might not men's traditional emphasis on their own individual wage rather than the social wage be expressed here, and might women's indifference to industrial democracy reflect not so much opposition as their own powerlessness within trade unions?

By 1986 the strength of feeling against tax cuts and in favour of greater public spending showed a marked and growing opposition among voters to Thatcherism's tax cuts programme. A Marplan poll showed that three out of five voters who backed the Tories in 1983 were prepared to face higher taxes in return for more spending on public services in 1986. Here again there was a slight gender gap: 60 per cent of women compared with 54 per cent of men supported increased public spending, and 64 per cent of women, compared with 52 per cent of men, said that cuts would cause them to switch their votes away from the Tories.

The defence gender gap produced a strong divergence in men and women supporting the Tories after the 1986 party conference season seemed to re-align some voters to the right: among men the Tories were 15 points ahead of Labour, but among women only 2 points.[19]

Surveys of sexual attitudes reveal seemingly paradoxical results. Gallup found in January 1985 that both men and women overwhelmingly believed that young unmarried people should have access to contraception (87 per cent men and 84 per cent women) but that more women than men were opposed to girls under sixteen being prescribed the Pill without parental consent (53 per cent men opposed, compared with 61 per cent women).

Slightly more women than men, according to the Gallup poll, felt that pornography should be available to people who wanted it (54 per cent men, 60 per cent women) but more women than men found the following personally unacceptable:

topless waitresses:	32 per cent men, 56 per cent women
abortion on demand:	41 per cent men, 55 per cent women
male nudity in films:	37 per cent men, 55 per cent women
female nudity in films:	24 per cent men, 40 per cent women

A MORI poll among young people in 1985 found a massive divergence among girls and boys on sex shops and pornography (33 per cent and 14 per cent). But lest these results be read as girls' puritanism, the ratio reversed on homosexuality: fewer than a quarter of girls disapproved, while a whopping 45 per cent of boys disapproved. In sex, as in everything else, men and women do not hold power equally, and sexual desire is never neutral: the question, who has the power of the gaze, and who is the object of that gaze, must affect views about sexuality. 'Whatever their social class, girls are defined primarily by their sexual reputation ... The mere fact that she is a girl affects everything she does. Girls are defined in terms of their sexuality and exist in a culture that is patriarchal, where women are subordinate to men.'[20]

All this suggests that women tend to be the more progressive sex when politics reaches beyond the economic. But what about the apparent discrepancies? These cannot be explained by 'puritan' or permissive criteria which – like the economic – have had different meanings for men and women.

The gender gap

The strongest electoral evidence against the notion of women as the eternally conservative sex appears in the USA, where 'women's rights' has moved into party politics and where not one but disparate gender gaps become apparent from the correlation of sex, class and domestic circumstances: women are the more Democratic sex, and if only women voted the Democrats would repeatedly be the election winners. Research on the 1984 Presidential election revealed differences between employed and non-employed, married and unmarried women, with the greatest level of support for Reagan among married women without a job, and the lowest among unmarried women with a job.[21] When questioned about discrimination and feminist issues, by 'big margins' women said they regarded the Democrats as more sensitive to their experience than the Republicans – bad news for the Republicans and 'it will probably get worse'.[22]

This evidence challenges the notion of women's eternal conservatism. The impact of the modern women's movement has been felt on party politics in the United States. In Britain, that influence, even by the mid-1980s, has not been felt on party politics in any significant way; when we look at women's policy preferences, there is evidence of a gender gap – but that may or may not be reflected in party alignments.

Some feminist and socialist critics of orthodox political science have tended to argue against the very concept of the gender gap. Supporting his thesis that the Tories are declining, John Ross boldly argues that women are the most important of those groups among whom Thatcherism has had 'no success whatever'. Furthermore, 'about four-fifths of the decline of the Tory party vote since 1955 can be explained by the loss of Conservative votes among women. From 8 per cent more women than men voting Conservative in 1955 the difference fell to 5 per cent in 1964, 2 per cent in February 1974, 0 per cent in 1979 and actually 3 per cent *fewer* women than men voting Conservative in 1983, according to Gallup polls.'[23]

It is 'a nonsense' to talk of a women's vote and a men's vote, Jill Hills argues persuasively, because results are 'affected by the disproportionate number of elderly women in the electorate'.[24] MORI's Robert Worcester reckons, too, that 'half the reason' for the tendency for more women than men to vote Conservative is the greater proportion of elderly women, and the propensity of the elderly to vote Tory. And Hills shows that men and women in the largest age group, 30–59, supported the three main parties in roughly equal proportions in 1979. Among voters over sixty there was less support for Labour among women and more support for the Conservatives than among men. 'If British women ever were more Conservative than men, they apparently no longer are,' concludes Hills.[25]

But this does not explain different movements in men's and

women's votes and policy preferences. For sure, there has been a
levelling of men's and women's support for the Conservatives in
recent elections. But the direction of these movements has been
different. When we look at the sexes' policy and party alignments
in more detail we can begin to speculate that something is happening
among men and women – and it's not the same thing.

Men and women on the move

We now know that, despite the conventional wisdom, in no simple
sense was it women who elected Margaret Thatcher's governments
in 1979 and 1983. Despite some divergences in the statistics produced by different polling organisations, they showed that the most
dramatic swing towards the Conservatives was among men.

MORI swing to the Conservatives:	men 7 per cent, women 5.5 per cent
BBC/Gallup	men 9.5 per cent, women 3 per cent

A similar divergence appeared in their 1983 general election
percentages:

	BBC/Gallup		MORI	
	men	women	men	women
Con	45	42	42	46
Lab	29	29	30	26
SDP/Lib	24	28	25	27

Hills and Ross argue that on the basis of these proportions, men
and women were voting Conservative in roughly equal proportions
in the Thatcher era. But that does not dispose of the phenomenon
of the gender gap. We have already seen, from the Dunleavy and
Husbands data, divergences between men and women and between
different groups of women. We have also seen that although men's
and women's support for the Conservatives evened up, this was
because many men's and women's votes were moving in different
directions. *Men have been moving to the right and women have been
moving away from the right.* Among women manual workers, according to Dunleavy and Husbands, the Labour vote was 11 percentage
points higher among women than men, mainly because 20 per cent

of women voted for the Alliance compared with 30 per cent of manual men. In none of Dunleavy and Husbands' social class categories did a higher proportion of women vote for the Alliance than men, although in the Registrar-General's occupational class classifications more 'intermediate and junior' non-manual women voted Alliance than men.

Of course, in 1983, the success of the Alliance was primarily at the expense of Labour, and it is sometimes argued that women, being moderate in all things, have been moving away from the 'extremes' towards the centre. This has not been borne out, however, by opinion polls conducted after the 1983 general election. By summer 1985, according to MORI, for the first time in many years, more women supported Labour than Tory:

1985 (July–September)	men	women	gender gap
Con	31	32	+1
Lab	37	34	−3
Alliance	30	32	+2

It was still among older women that the Tory preference remained powerful, but among women between 18 and 24 only 26 per cent declared their intention of voting Conservative, while among women over 55 that rose to 36 per cent.

Thinking about women's voting patterns over the decade of Thatcherism, the picture that emerges is not that of a straightforward gender gap, but several gender gaps and, more interestingly, a remarkably volatile movement among women voters. Women are on the move, but although it looks like a crucial minority are beginning to jettison the right, it is not certain where they are going and which party they are going with.

We have seen from the drift of opinion polls and surveys of voting habits that women's marginally greater support for the right may be declining. The language of class or of sexual subordination is no longer enough to secure women's vote and yet without it, no party – and the Conservative Party most of all – can secure power.

5

WAR AND PEACE

The 1983 general election seemed to have settled one of the most contested issues in British politics in the 1980s: the defeat of the disarmament party (Labour) seemed to sanction the impending deployment of US Cruise missiles in the heart of the English countryside. Or that's how the Conservative Party read the result. But anti-missile feeling in Britain before and after the election was a mainstream response. A paradox.

Unable to dishearten the peace movement, despite the best efforts of the then-Defence Secretary Michael Heseltine, all the Conservatives had to do was defeat the Labour Party in an election. The Conservatives won the election – but they didn't win over the many dissident hearts and minds among their own supporters, and they did not cure thousands of women of their aberrant illusions. The Conservative Party underestimated the degree to which many women integrated their Conservatism with their considered opposition to the new nuclear missiles. It was the irony of that integration of apparently disparate, not to say contradictory ideologies, which kept the Conservatives in power. And it was Labour's failure to work upon those contradictions that produced its defeat. The Labour Party had squandered the potential hegemony of peace politics in 1983; while there was no mandate for unilateral nuclear disarmament by Britain, Labour had been unable to maximise a more limited disarmament initiative by capitalising on the strong opposition to the impending arrival of Cruise missiles. But after that general election, a combination of the resilience of the peace movement, widespread discontent with the United States' use of its British bases from which to launch its raids on Libya in the spring of 1986 and the impact of the Chernobyl nuclear power catastrophe in the Soviet Union in the early autumn put an end to complacency on the nuclear issue. By the autumn of 1986 the Labour Party, emboldened by the anti-nuclear winds of public opinion, boldly came out as the anti-nuclear party, committed both to the removal of US nuclear missiles and to phasing out nuclear power. Nuclear politics were possibly the only aspect of the national agenda not defined by Thatcherism. In 1983, the year of Cruise deployment and the climax of the Greenham Common women's peace camp, 67 per cent of women were opposed to the United States' missiles. By the autumn of 1986, Libya and Chernobyl extended the women's majority to the population as a whole – 54 per cent were opposed to the US missiles[1] and 65 per cent were opposed to the use of bases in Britain for the Libyan raid.[2] So it's worth looking at the ways in which the minds of Conservative women were caught by the women's peace movement.

Women's ways
The forms of direct action adopted by the Campaign for Nuclear Disarmament (CND) and Greenham Common women's peace camp in the 1980s reached into the political heart of surprisingly many women in Britain. Greenham had an extraordinary impact because it was a women's camp: it engaged women's sympathies as well as their antipathies *as women*. Conservative women were drawn into a new 'feminine' discourse about war and peace and political action.

The Greenham Common activities transformed the culture of direct action: they enabled the intrepid and the fearful to take part, to keep watch, to act upon that space, to reclaim it. On their television screens women saw the ingenious invention of new forms of non-violent direct action that enabled women to climb over the fence, rock its concrete pillars until the fence came down, cut through the wire with bolt cutters, and in one magic moment to lock the gates with a bicycle lock that couldn't be broken by the camp's guards even with giant bolt cutters. And where the fence was left standing, it was transformed by women adorning it with memorabilia signifying their organic commitments to life by babygrows, outgrown teddies, and photographs of loved ones, be they grandchildren or retired teachers' past classes. A whole new culture drawing on 'feminine skills' wove its way on to the fence; rags became rainbows and doves and hometowns; the spectacular needlework of peace banners revived lost or scorned skills, and some of the art created by peace needlewomen now travels with the American artist Judy Chicago's 'Dinner Party', a triangular table laid with ceramics and needlework for heroines from history. Skills and sensibilities associated with the subordination of the feminine were rehabilitated for strength and for radicalism. Women's gentle but implacable inhabiting of that space signified another form, a subversive form for femininity. And women's relationship to the military, too, signified a new kind of confrontation: women looked the men on the other side of the fence in the eye and searched for their humanity.

Diane Charles, who lives on a respectable estate in Birmingham rarely talks about politics: 'It's a private matter, like religion, I've never admitted what my politics are.' She never admits her age either. Privacy, if nothing else, is her prerogative. But she thinks about the world constantly as she goes about her housework and listens to the radio. She has one or two women friends. 'I talk to one woman, a sort of friend and if things are boiling up in my mind I don't take rash decisions, I'll think about it and then throw it at her to see what she thinks.' Many years ago she was listening to 'Woman's Hour' on Radio 4 and discovered a charity which she threw herself into: 'I want to do my bit.' Her parents, she thought, were Conservatives like her, 'but they never argued about it, it was always private. I've got two lads and my husband – the men in this house! It's a battle for me to keep my head above water.' Her politics are animated by wishing people well and by fear. It is fear above all which undermines the kind of personal fulfilment promised in Conservative values. 'The biggest fear is cancer. Every woman is afraid of death, every woman is afraid of having a breast chopped off.' When asked if she were able to define the priorities of the Conservative Party in ways that would be good for women, and that women would endorse, she said: 'If only they'd stop all the missiles money and put it into cancer and screening for everyone on the national health! I'm surprised she [Margaret Thatcher] hasn't done that, I'd have thought she would have.' This woman supported Margaret Thatcher not only because she was the leader of the party, but because she was a woman, 'because she's showed 'em'. But as a woman who thought about politics as a woman, and always consulted her own feelings before making up her mind, she thought that Margaret Thatcher's militarism, rather than her own anti-militarism, seemed anomalous.

What did she think of the Greenham Common women's peace camp during their most visibly active years, 1982 to 1985? 'I think they're marvellous, I really do, because they believe in something and they've gone out and stood up for it. We've all got the right to do that.' It's not a right she personally has ever exercised. But part of her pleasure – and it was *pleasure* – in the women's peace camp was that the women there exercised that right for her, and in so doing they changed her mind. 'Before Greenham Common I didn't realise that the Americans had got their missiles here. Then I realised. What a cheek! It was the fuss the Greenham Common women made that made me realise.' The peace camp became the source of endless attrition over the kitchen table: 'The men in this house think they're butch, queers.' Did she? She thought for a moment. 'No.' Would it have bothered her if they were butch or if they were lesbians? She thought again. 'No.' Women irritated her men anyway, she said, not without affection. 'They never stop talking about Land Rovers and bikes, and they've not finished their dinner before they're asking for their tea.'

She is a big woman, stout and serene, who used to have longish hair to her shoulders. Greenham Common was much on her mind, 'and that's why I got my hair cut off. I came home one day and said to them, "Look, I've got a Greenham Common haircut." You see, I'm fighting them off every minute.'

Betty Zikel, a retired businesswoman living in a London suburb, admired Margaret Thatcher 'because she's strong' and enjoyed her premiership: 'I'm pleased she's a woman, women are stronger than men and they have a different approach, all through the years women have to be very strong.' But despite, or perhaps because of these convictions, she was resolute in her support for CND and the Greenham Common peace camp. Peace was one of the issues that disturbed her life-long alignment to the Conservative Party, even though she would not find it in herself to vote for any other. Nuclear weapons 'are beyond . . .' she sighed, stared at her hands, searching for words . . . 'devastating'. Many Conservatives shared her distaste, but did not support disarmament, so did she think Britain ought to have the missiles? 'Certainly not! I feel very strongly about it. I've felt it from the beginning, that such a device could have been thought of by man!' The Greenham Common women had secured her support 'because I believe in anything that can stop it'. She thought they had been 'terrific'.

We have had arguments about it, my husband and I. He believes strength is the only way against the Russians. I believe quite the reverse. He says it's bought peace. What kind of peace? I'm sure the Russian people have suffered too much themselves. I'm not afraid of the Russians. The Conservatives have got it wrong and they're wrong about the Russians.

While the politics of war may often have excluded women, the politics of peace have often been represented as womanly. But the conventional wisdom that women are in any sense *naturally* pacific is dubious. Conservative women's historic longing for law and order, and their rugged campaigns within the party for corporal and capital punishment, suggest that their positions are not in any sense 'soppy' or 'sentimental', nor can women's feelings about war and peace be ascribed in any simple way to the notion that they may blame men for war but don't expect men to take responsibility for peace. The high profile of apparently admirable women in the 'second wave' peace movement of the 1980s, and the Greenham Common peace camp in particular, engaged women as women – whatever their positions on nuclear weapons.

'The missiles? I'm neither for them nor against them,' said Eleanor Hartshorn, a Northerner in her thirties, studying on a Second Chance for Women course. 'They are a deterrent. I didn't have a lot of time for the Greenham Common women, though they were probably necessary because they showed that we're not a warlike nation, and they did a job in that area.'

Elsie Ward, a retired countrywoman in the North-East, a long-time member of the Women's Institute who has always voted Conservative, except when she voted Liberal 'tactically to keep Labour out', was disappointed by Margaret Thatcher, not least because of Cruise and Trident. 'I'm against her on the missiles. It's folly. And I don't like the Americans having control of the nuclear button. I've always disliked the nuclear weapons – I hate war! But it seems to be getting worse – I'm a Christian but there are all these holy wars going on.' However, she had strong reservations about the women's peace camp. It wasn't Greenham Common which had encouraged her anti-nuclear beliefs, and she held on to them despite her dislike of the camp:

I wouldn't care so much if they didn't leave so much filth and rubbish. Protest by all means, but it's not fair to camp there. I don't think anybody would like to be surrounded by all those rag, tag and bobtails. Mind you, they expressed what most people feel. I said to my husband, I'd love to go to Downing Street and tell her where she's going wrong – she doesn't seem to know the feeling of the country.

Despite the successful deployment of Cruise missiles, other dimensions of nuclear politics erupted, and nuclear anything became a volcano that continued to disturb Conservative women. 'The Greenham women – I used to sit there and think what a load of creeps,' said Barbara Stone, a middle-class woman living in the Borders, who began attending New Opportunities for Women courses in the mid-1980s when her children were almost grown up.

But then I had a feeling of envy that they'd got out of their boring lives. I still have that, and a tremendous admiration – they'd been despised, the butt of everyone's jokes, but I admired their courage for standing up for what they believe in. I have very mixed feelings, though, about whether we'd be better off without the nuclear deterrent. But Sellafield has affected me because it's quite nearby. It obviously can't be good, people being contaminated – and all those lies!

She was referring to radioactive leaks, cancer clusters associated with nuclear locations and the plutonium traffic between civil and military operations. She developed 'a large feeling of mistrust for Mrs Thatcher. I feel they play with the truth and mince it up.'

Nuclear dissent has appeared in the unlikeliest quarters. 'The whole thing worries me,' said Sara Keays, the former Parliamentary secretary and lover of Cecil Parkinson:

The debate on nuclear matters should be opened up. What's most important now is access to information, and interestingly Margaret Thatcher who used to talk about open government seems to have carried on the secrecy thing as much as her predecessors. The best protection for all of us is some check on the government of the day.

She admired the Greenham Common women in much the same

way as she did Mary Whitehouse, 'because they've made people think. I admire any woman who risks being attacked, sticking to her guns in the face of a hostile reaction. A man wouldn't be attacked in the same way.'

And while some unsympathetic men and women felt that the peace people were sincere, their own political fatalism – a characteristic of conservatism – was expressed in their pessimism about the capacity of pressure groups to change anything. Lorna Walters, a young single civil servant in a Border town who had belonged to an unusually heterogenous range of groups, from a feminist action group to the local branch of Business and Professional Women, explained her commitment to Conservatism thus: 'It's about doing the best you can with what you've got, standing on your own two feet, bettering yourself. It's a Conservative thing. Labour represents the disorganised mediocrity, levelling out and bringing people down. There's nothing in Labour and left-wing politics that appeals.' She resented being 'set up for a limited nuclear war and I'd rather the missiles weren't here. I'd be happier with good conventional defence and everybody knowing how to use a gun, and everybody knowing about civil defence like in Switzerland.' She felt that the Greenham women's camp had been

so badly represented on the media. But again, it was so disorganised, it was so sad because there was so much good heartedness and commitment – there must have been to live in that appalling squalor. They don't repel me, they have my admiration, but they're wasting their time, they could have been doing other things. I don't know what really, but maybe they could lobby MPs, get into the government, organise, get some strength.

Women hostile to disarmament expressed not only a fatalism about protest but a positive belief in the efficacy of the deterrent. Dorothy Love, a retired woman living in a small northern town, was adamant:'Oh, you've got to have them, the missiles.' Hitler came to her mind and, like many supporters of the deterrent, she equated the Soviet Union with Hitler's Germany. 'You've got to be strong. If you're not strong people will trample all over you. And if you're not a strong woman your husband will trample over you. It's the same in the world. It's most important, you've got to be strong! We've got gypsies up here,' she said, pointing out of the window of her flat. 'I'd rather have the missiles than them, they can bring the missiles up here any day.'

The culture of the peace women also polarised women around contested meanings of 'woman' and revealed how 'woman' is not an essence universally recognised and claimed. The Greenham women's evacuation of their own homes and encampment outside the fence was for some an heroic act of womanly sacrifice which simultaneously usurped the female condition, and yet for others it was a source of disturbance and disgust because Greenham Common offended against the standards for their sex: the peace women were unwomanly women.

'It's the sordidness that upset me,' said Judy Worth, who lives with her builder husband and children in Birmingham's middle-class villadom. 'Revolting! They left their homes. Why go there? Why not stay at home and make their protest? They've just got no responsibility about their children.'

If only women voted

If it was once a truism to suggest that if only women voted, we'd have only Conservative governments, then it would also be true to suggest that if only women voted on nuclear weapons, Cruise and Trident would not be deployed. The missiles and the campaign against them have provoked an enduring gender gap which is the inverse of the party gender gap. This is what the opinion polls found:

	Men	Women	Con	Lab	Lib	All/SDP
			(both sexes)			
Marplan April 1981						
against Cruise	43	56	35	59	54	
Trident	48	38	36	69	57	
Gallup October 1982						
against Cruise	51	64				
Trident	53	60				
reason:						
because of Trident's cost	30	14				
because it's nuclear	43	68				

	Men	Women	Con	Lab	Lib	All/SDP
			(both sexes)			

MORI November 1983

| Cruise | 43 | 57 | | | | |

MORI April 1984

| Cruise | 49 | 58 | | | | |

Gallup May 1984

No to US missiles in UK	50	62	32	75	62	77
Don't trust US to consult UK before launching missiles from UK bases	64	68	53	75	66	76
Reagan not seriously tried to halt arms race	65	66	55	73	59	77
Reagan should take up Soviet freeze proposals	78	78	75	79	77	88
Oppose UK defence system that depends on nuclear arms	44	56	29	69	51	59

Shortly before Cruise missiles arrived in the winter of 1983, there was, according to the political columnist, Peter Kellner, a 34-point gender gap. That gender gap was 'the largest, as far as I am aware, that any poll has ever found on any major political issue'.[3] By 1986 the nuclear agenda had broadened, and still there was a significant gender gap:

Gallup August 1986	Men	Women
UK should get rid of nuclear arms, whatever anyone else does	39	49
should not	54	39
nuclear arms do not keep you safe	53	47

Gallup August 1986	Men	Women
do keep you safe	35	45
for Euro-bomb	26	18
against	66	70
for phasing out nuclear power	48	56
against phase-out	45	24

Trouble in the party

Nothing mobilised by the right managed to match the effect of the peace movement. When he was Defence Secretary, Michael Heseltine failed to see it off despite his own strenuous efforts. Even in his own party there was evidence among women that he had not entirely won the argument for the missiles. In 1985 Heseltine was mocked in the British media for having conceded everything to the United States in the Star Wars negotiations. The hero appeared as a wimp. At the party's Younger Women's conference in Solihull in November 1985 he was challenged by Jane Ellison, an Oxford student and active member of the Young Conservatives. 'I would like to raise people's worries,' she said. People were worried about lack of consultation between the US and its allies over America's offensive military actions. People were worried about Star Wars: 'the British people have reservations. Mrs Thatcher has reservations.' People were worried, too, about whether 'we are listened to in NATO'. Heseltine, she said, 'should be answering people's worries'. Although all the other speeches supported the presence of US bases and Heseltine's representation of the Soviet Union as the enemy, Jane Ellison received a surprisingly strong echo of support in a solid round of applause.

In a meeting of Greater London Conservative women in the autumn of 1985, Heseltine complained that the peace movement had taken to the streets in an attempt to frustrate negotiations, whereas the Soviet leaders had been brought to the negotiating table and were talking to the leaders of the Western alliance. The only way to reach agreement, he claimed, was through a process of dialogue. This was 'in direct contradiction to what the protest groups and the Labour Party said would happen,' he said, for their argument had been that modernisation of intermediate nuclear weapons would threaten the world and create instability. The British people had 'taken our view and gave us one of the largest majorities in history because they thought our judgement was much to be preferred to that of the left'. While it was surely true that the Tories had secured a spectacular majority, it was as surely not true that the majority of voters shared Mr Heseltine's views on the missiles. Nevertheless, he insisted that the government had secured the right to train Cruise convoys on British roads. 'We were right and the protest groups and the Labour Party were wrong.' Part of the problem, he said, was that people didn't understand the process of negotiation, an understandable lacuna among the young who believed the natural condition of Europe was peace when, in fact, 'the natural condition of Europe has been war. The reason today there is such a sense of peace is because the nature of the weapons is such that the concept of war is unthinkable, because there is no prospect of victory. It's that that has secured a period of peace.' It was, therefore, a logical step to suggest that disarmament would 'undermine the credibility of defence'.

Here Heseltine seemed to share the view expressed by Margaret Thatcher in her interview in *The Times* on 26 March 1986 when she said: 'Both the President [Reagan] and Mr Gorbachev have said that they want to see a world without nuclear weapons. I cannot see a world without nuclear weapons. Let me be practical about it. The knowledge is there to make them. So do not go too hard for that pie in the sky, because while everyone would like to see it, I do not believe that it is going to come about.' So, it might have surprised many loyal Conservatives to learn that *neither* unilateral nor multinational nuclear disarmament was on the government's agenda. That possibility was confirmed by Margaret Thatcher's chastening conversations with President Reagan after his Reykjavik talks with the Soviet leader Gorbachev when she made it clear that there was no question of Britain's nuclear arsenal being part of any disarmament deal.

The predictable effusion which rewards ministers facing their troops was not offered when Heseltine appeared before that autumn 1985 area women's conference. 'He didn't show his star quality,' muttered one representative, who didn't clap. Another woman stood up and said, 'I'm worried that the US has still got responsibility for pressing the button on whether to use Cruise.' Heseltine replied that, 'There's nothing new in the argument.' There was an agreement that they wouldn't be used without telling Britain, he reassured her. But it was a 'phoney argument', he said. People wanted 'control over our own situation' but why did that matter to them so much? One scenario he suggested was that the Americans wanted to deploy the

Cruise missiles while Britain wanted to stop them; but say the US ignored Britain and used the Cruise missiles; supposing Britain did invoke the letter of the agreement to say the Americans couldn't? What would happen? 'So they'd use them somewhere else.' In any case, he ventured, 'The whole argument is phoney because they're not going to use them.' The response suggested that he was less than convincing. Another representative proposed a solution: 'Wouldn't it be better if we kicked the US in the teeth and we'd get some respect and get some of their orders, like France?'

Only Lady Olga Maitland, the *Sunday Express* columnist who took to Greenham Common, Molesworth and Trafalgar Square with her defence campaign, really attempted to match the peace movement's practice by challenging it on its own terms, though without success and without endearing herself to many in her party. 'There's a very strong feeling in our area,' said a party activist in the North:

> Everybody's reaction was against Lady Olga Maitland, especially in the North, you don't want that kind of voice. She's not the right image, she makes me cringe because she's too la-de-da and upper crust. I'd want another type of woman and wouldn't want to be associated with Families for Defence for that reason.

But Lady Olga encountered another kind of opposition, too, founded upon distaste for the politics of demonstration and direct action. She explained that she came up against

> that terrible term 'one doesn't' and 'that's not the way we do it'. But my first instinct was to look at CND and to ask why? What? How did it come about? and why aren't we doing anything about it? Perhaps I have a natural feel for grassroots politics anyway, it's where the essentials are, and you serve and feed the grassroots. Politics is about people's needs and therefore you have to get down and go and meet them.

She believed that

> CND and Greenham Common touched women, without a doubt, and perhaps CND hadn't realised their good fortune when the feminist lot arose at Greenham. Having seen that, of

course, quite sensibly, they didn't try to interfere, because it was a brilliant idea to have women only, who are hearth and home by nature, doing a great demonstration which involved great hardship, which I don't think anyone should underestimate. The kind of people who went to Greenham were not what one would call down-and-outs; they came from educated middle class backgrounds. I met them many times and I took them very seriously. I quickly realised that they were not what you'd call riff-raff dropouts, and they had a cause, and because they were articulate they could communicate their feelings to others. What I realised was that it was this aspect of Greenham Common that was fantastically successful. By concentrating on women, mobilising women in this period, women were beginning to think of themselves, take action themselves, so I felt right, let's challenge CND and reassure the women who are being terrified out of their wits.

Lady Olga opted for 'defence' as a key word in her campaign against the disarmers, because 'defence is a uniting word. The country rallies to defence'. Nevertheless, during her campaign opinion pollsters and the peace movement came up with rather different evidence. A MORI poll on people's political priorities at the beginning of 1984 found that defence was way down, while disarmament came high on the list, second only to unemployment.

Lady Olga's own campaign, counter-vigils at the peace camps and demonstrations, too, was the kind of activity Conservatives weren't used to:

Some people say it's not the right thing to do. I think it is. When I started I heard reports of outraged Conservatives in the shires saying, 'Oh my goodness, does she expect us to wear woolly hats and jeans in Trafalgar Square?' and round I'd go saying, 'I haven't got a woolly hat or a pair of jeans, although if I'm down at Molesworth I will put on my wellington boots, but you don't have to change your style.'

Although her campaign began as Women for Defence, she changed the name to Families for Defence when 'the men said, "What about us?" Now, unlike Greenham we're not a feminist campaign and the men are coming on board and playing a role.'

It seems, however, that Central Office didn't know what to do with it. In any case 'Central Office is not capable of helping. They've no idea about presenting material, they don't listen enough and what they do produce is unreadable. I'd say the same about the Ministry of Defence: neither was listening to people on the ground about why they were worried.' After focusing first on the peace camps, her campaign began to change its emphasis to education, and by the mid-eighties 'indoctrination' and 'politicisation' in the schools became the basis of much Conservative activity – indeed *the* theme of the party's campaign in the May 1986 Inner London Education Authority election:

> Families for Defence became very concerned about political indoctrination in schools. That arose out of our youth group. I went to see Sir Keith Joseph [then the Secretary of State for Education] in 1984 – we had rather a curious meeting. He paced around the room like an angry leopard and then he said, 'Why are you coming here?' I said, 'But there's a problem, can't you see it, it's at the ground, can't you see it?' He couldn't measure it, he was only used to hearing intellectuals. I thought, my godfathers, we've got to do something about it – an entire generation of silent, cowed children and parents, we've got to do something about it.

What shall we do with them?

Nuclear politics during the 1980s were unique in British politics because they contained the dossier of mass divergence from Conservative orthodoxy. Well into the government's second term it began to emerge as the only issue upon which Thatcherism had not defined the agenda, and over which it had lost ideological control. The Conservatives celebrated their supposed defeat of the country's biggest protest movement by victory over Labour in 1983, and ignored the threatening minority of nuclear dissidents in their own party who were part of the majority at large. (It was a poignant commentary on the lassitude of British political commentary that no party on the left would have escaped challenge from the media if there were evidence of such a rupture between the party's social base, its leadership and public opinion.) The issue divided the Alliance parties and the Labour Party seemed initially incapable of trusting the evidence before its very eyes. By the autumn of 1986 Labour was beginning to take hold of the anti-nuclear consensus and to challenge Thatcherism with it.

But alliances have to be *made*, not in heaven but on earth. While the anti-missiles majority was made in the informal and intuitive world of civil society, political realignment was to be the specific task of the political party. Labour's task became how to transform a moral majority for limited nuclear disarmament into *political hegemony*. If hegemony, in the Gramscian sense, was the expression of *collective will* radiating outward from the political party, with the party *organising* that will, then Labour was faced with a difficult task: the anti-nuclear stance at its 1986 party conference may have expressed a mainstream mood, but it did not make Labour the mainstream party. The resulting realignment undermined the Alliance and strengthened the Conservative Party. Nothing was simple any more in British politics. Peter Kellner showed in the *Observer* on 5 October 1986 that the Tories gathered support on defence among adherents of other parties. But on defence the Tories' traditional lead among women sank and a significant gender gap emerged: among men, the Tories had a 15-point lead over Labour, but the lead was only 2 points among women. Defence thus reversed the notion of men being more pro-Labour and women more pro-Tory.

Labour has been blinded to its potential as a wedge to split the hitherto hegemonic centre-right coalition wrapped around Thatcherism. Women had never constituted Labourism's social base, after all; and Labour had never galvanised a strategy around the aspirations of women. Nationally it had not, therefore, been a hegemonic party. Women's anti-nuclear kinship crossed party boundaries in a movement of thought and feeling articulated almost entirely at the level of civil society – outside the institutions and processes of state power, outside the traditional discourses of politics. It had been expressed in entirely extra-Parliamentary modes, inspired by the flow of feeling and thought.

It challenged the distinction between 'public' and 'private' which had marginalised women's politics, keeping them in a separate sphere. Conservative women opposed to nuclear missiles consulted their personal passions to order their political perspective on peace. They relied upon feelings usually designated private and, therefore, outside political discourse. In that sense, they adhered, whether consciously or not, to the principle of 'the personal is political'. In any case that principle already formed some of Conservative women's political glossary – it was a language they understood. The culture of the women's peace movement appropriated a term hijacked by the right, *personal responsibility*, and transformed it from self-interest to the global interest – to personal responsibility for the protection of the planet. That spoke to a sizeable minority of Conservative women. But no party, not least their own, it seemed, knew what to do with them.

6

THE FUGITIVES

The stereotyped Tory woman has a hat and a whip. In reality she
is a formidable fugitive.

When Mrs Thatcher first got in she said her first priority would
be law and order. But you have all these horrific crimes. We
feel terribly betrayed.

The gimlet eyes of an antique Tory kidnapped my own as she
showed me the door of her London flat. How could those MPs not
vote for capital punishment? She demanded an answer.

Her flat is high in a block of West End apartments and to reach
it you pass two attendants at the foyer, go down long, carpeted
corridors and up in a whispering lift before you reach her home.
The evidence of better days is all around: a photograph of Winston
Churchill and the ubiquitous bric-à-brac of the upper classes,
hauled across the high seas when they used to rule the world. It's a
high-class dungeon.

'I'm a prisoner,' spits this startling woman. She's very old, still
has her own teeth, and she often rearranges her dress. She still
cares. She's so militantly poised that she almost seems to be bending
over backwards. It's her Edwardian education. But all the elocution
and etiquette can't hide the coarseness of mind as she hallucinates
about the nation:

Capital punishment! When people say there might be mistakes,
you might hang the wrong person, I'm sorry but there's never a
mistake with a thoroughly decent person. It's wicked that a
woman can't walk about alone. Very seldom I go out in the

evenings. My husband always says take a taxi, and I do. I'm not going to walk out alone. Women feel more vulnerable. And the other appalling thing is the poor old-age pensioners. The beasts, they break in and batter women to death. And if they catch these thugs, what do they get? They're barely punished. A lot of people agree with Powell. We should never have let all these foreigners in. You've got daily thefts on the buses, any conductor will tell you. But what can Mrs Thatcher do? It's too late, it's got out of hand. There should have been frightfully stiff laws and tremendous sentences.

An upper-class woman, she appears as a wolf in sheep's clothing, corseted, coiffed and ready to kill. 'Foreigners' signifies not only the racism that has accompanied the hangers' and floggers' agenda, but the presence of any indigenous aliens who inhabit her *own* territory, her country, her neighbourhood; they do not, after all, belong to her at all. Whether her fears are justified is immaterial. For such a woman, loss of a sense of safety is an expression of a more comprehensive powerlessness, for without a doubt the cities, the country, do not belong to her. But her sense of personal and political powerlessness is an upper-class panic at the democratisation of society – 'the people' or the 'lower classes' are the dangerous classes, as they always were, and now they're joined by darker strangers. To such a woman, comprehensive schools are as dangerous as working men's clubs or dark alleys or launderettes or Brixton. They are all populated by strangers. But this woman's fear now has a generic force, shared among all women across classes, and it's found among working-class women living in Peckham or Poplar, Wallsend or Wolverhampton.

In a different world, Carol McKurniss, a Birmingham shop worker, hugs her dog. Beside the sofa there's the *Birmingham Mail* and a book on the Borgias from the library: 'I like history, I love going to Warwick castle.' She reckons that 'Some of these people want a good thumping. They're not hard enough on hooligans – they should be put in the middle of a field and birched.' And in the absence of any other authority, she is the one to do it, you feel; a strong woman, a commandant in her own home, her fortress, but feeling deserted by the politicians who just don't seem to understand, she complains. They are, of course, always somewhere else, in another place and from another class:

They're not down here among us. And the police ought to be
out patrolling. It's the coloureds who cause most crime. The
Birmingham Mail says the majority of muggings are by
coloureds. Muggers should get life as well. What gets up my
nose is the jails: they've gone in there to be punished and they
might think it's hard, but I don't think it is; they're waited
on hand, foot and finger. Hanging should be brought back.
And rape – they should be put away for life. Rape must be
a terrible thing, even if a woman's a prostitute she's got the
right to say yes or no. There'd be more sex crimes if there
weren't prostitutes. They only blame the women, not the men.
But a woman's life is ruined for life.

This woman lives in a respectable working-class area and she
specifies the enemy all around: it is male and it is black.

Another working-class woman in her forties who lives in a quiet
suburb of Birmingham believes that Conservatism is about individual
self-fulfilment. Does she feel fulfilled?

No, I can't do what I want. My life is controlled. Let's be
honest, it's because I'm frightened of being banged over the
head. Especially women, we're completely controlled by
violence. I can't go into the town now, because I'm frightened.
It's this terrible *fear* that women can't go out.

But where does the fear come from? Is it from direct experience?
'Well, nothing has happened to me. I can drive, I'll drive anywhere,
but no way would I drive into town.' Town seemed unsafe, with
danger lurking even in the multi-storey car parks. Public space is
dangerous. But so is private space:

Incest, you don't realise how common it is. There's this line
between making a fuss of a daughter and abusing her. Women
don't do it, you know. We don't do it because we're mothers.
Men haven't got the same emotions as us.

In the common sense of women on the right, women appear as
the endangered species. Men are the dangerous sex. That common
sense they share with women across the political spectrum, but the
Conservative Party has incorporated women's gender-fear into its

doctrine. Too easily, however, have angry, frightened women been lampooned as the barbarians of the suburbs. And they have been even within the Tory Party itself, ever since the stereotype of the Tory woman as an avenging hell's granny was established in the 1950s. Real or imagined, these women's fears focused on real dangers and a real crisis of parental authority. The parental crisis wasn't new; it was built into the structures of the authoritarian family. But it was a crisis that the Conservative Party uniquely made its own.

The feeling of powerlessness expressed in the law and order discourse breathes the sigh of 'shame!' which meets each new outrage. Shortly after riots by Millwall football supporters in 1985, a retired couple in the North-East were reflecting on the scenes they'd seen on television. Both were respectable, Christian and Conservative. The husband commented that, of course, the rioters came from Millwall, which seemed to explain things. 'But where is Millwall?' asked the wife. They discussed the geography of deprivation until, frustrated, the wife protested: 'They blame the environment – but you make your own environment! They could keep themselves tidy.'

To this woman the world is basically dangerous. Like the weather, it is out of our control: parents don't care; there are too many guns; nobody does their bit any more. 'The world is ridiculous,' she concluded. In her view, you may not be able to control anything but your own patch, and there you must make your own law and order.

By the 1970s and 1980s the law and order lobby's culprits extended to those involved in the crimes of political dissent and direct action – 'rioters', 'terrorists', 'trade union bully boys', 'bosses and barons', all terms invoking heavy-duty masculinity and a mafiosi atmosphere from which women were historically excluded.

An arresting image of woman as a solitary vigilante appeared amongst the Tory ranks at their 1985 party conference in the wake of the siege of Broadwater Farm in Tottenham: Ambrozine Neil, a black Brent councillor, who had earlier quit Labour and joined the Tories. A strong and sober woman, she pointed up to Sir Keith Joseph during the education debate and appealed to him, from her heart, to do something for black and working-class children, otherwise they would be prey to the 'bloody socialist revolutionaries'. If anyone embodied the Conservative Party's image of itself as the party of 'the people' at that moment, in the midst of chronic social crisis when they badly needed it, she did. And she did it as a mother, crying for her children to be saved from the incubus of revolt. She appeared as a gift from heaven, the voice of benign but authoritative, not to say authoritarian, motherhood. It took a black woman to show the human face of the Conservative Party's quest for legitimacy among *all* the people.

A recurring theme in the women's law and order campaigns within the party was the sense of parents under siege articulated by Neil. The emergence in the late 1950s of 'teenagers', with their secret life and for the first time enjoying surplus income and surplus sexuality, confronted parents with a relatively autonomous culture which rendered it out of control, challenging the prerogatives of parenthood. The women's conference returned almost annually to what they and their children consumed on TV, to vandalism and juvenile delinquency, student militancy, school discipline and the supposed decline in educational standards. In the 1980s, law and order focused once again on the 'personal' crisis between parents and children, expressed as the breakdown of parental control and discipline in the home for which the solution was represented as the reassertion of parental authority and stiffer sentences.

Two characteristics stand out in the debates: women's fear as women, and their panic as parents.

Women's fears are articulated by the right-wing tabloids' crusades against the enemy – everywhere. 'Violent Britain ... terrifying evidence of the evil infecting our society': an eighty-five-year-old widow tormented and tortured by children under ten on her Hackney estate, where she always left her door open – a typical *Daily Mail* report in December 1985, supplemented by the obligatory comment from an obliging Tory MP: 'I'm writing to the Home Secretary to ask for a change in the law. Prison for the serious offences, fines for the lesser ones – that's what the parents should get.' So, the culprits are not only the children but their parents, too. It's all their fault.

The body

The female body is the object of infinite scrutiny, dead or alive. Nowhere is this better exemplified than in Britain's tabloid press, in which women appear as the objects of men's desire and also as men's victims. In *Ways of Seeing*, John Berger says:

Men look at women. Women watch themselves being looked at. This determines not only most relations between men and women but also the relation of women to themselves. The surveyor of woman in herself is male: the surveyed female. Thus she turns herself into an object – and most particularly an object of vision: a sight.[1]

In European art a woman's nudity is not simply being without clothes; 'it is a sign of her submission to the owner's feelings or demands.' It is for the male spectator that the subject wears her nudity: he has the power. And power is inscribed in the way the tabloids constantly display both women and the worst consequences of that relationship of domination – sexual assault and even death. The *Daily Mail* is a more decorous Tory tabloid which, unlike the *Sun*, does not feature pin-ups; but as a newspaper which has targeted a female readership, it nevertheless encourages women to display themselves, and so reproduces the feeling that Berger describes within women: woman 'comes to consider the *surveyor* and the *surveyed* within her as the two constituent and yet always distinct elements of her identity as a woman'.[2] The paper is interesting because it also treats male aggression as a serious problem for women, and as serious news.

A random selection of editions of the *Daily Mail* during two months in the early eighties showed how sex and violence are typically represented:

October 1982: The police claim made early in 1982 that there was a correlation between race and crime is allegedly vindicated, as the police suggest that people are being more wary of potential attackers and robbers and that adults in the black community are putting pressure on their youngsters. This story is based only on police contacts; there are no comments from potential 'victims', nor the black community itself. Tory MP Teddy Taylor talks about the Tories having 'a huge and special responsibility' for law and order, but the 'crime crisis' is not being overcome. Enoch Powell tells the Tory Party conference that there is a 'continued drift towards civil violence in the inner cities where a minority, alien rather than alienated, is in the course of turning into a majority'. 'Femail', the women's page, reports that women are learning to avoid muggings; the Tory rank and file at their conference demand hanging and tougher punishments. A report on the Peckham by-election, which was won by the Labour Party feminist Harriet Harman, represents her as 'an archetypical left-winger', albeit 'able and attractive', who 'manages to sound more concerned about the rights of suspects than she does about the victims of muggings'. Crime reached a peak in 1981 and Home Secretary Willie Whitelaw is heckled by the police. A fresh 'immigration row' breaks out in the Tory Party. All this is punctuated by stories of rapes, rape trials and the jailing of rapists. Meanwhile the women's pages are mainly preoccupied with fashion, with occasional features criticising Greater London Council grants to gays, and women for sulking, and advising women on avoiding muggers and on job prospects in the media.

December 1983: The month is dominated by printers and 'the stage armies of the left' picketing outside Eddie Shah's new-technology printing plant in Warrington; the 'rioting mob' invading Brent Council Chamber after Labour councillor Ambrozine Neil resigns and joins the Tory side, giving the Tories an overall majority (Margaret Thatcher describes it as the 'fascist left'); the television screening of 'The Day After' and the Embrace the Base encirclement by women of the US Air Force base at Greenham Common, including opinion pieces by *Daily Mail* writers and a lament by a father whose daughter has gone to live at Greenham; and women's protests on British Rail Southern Region against the 'railway rapist', demanding more police protection and 'the right to walk the streets without fear' – a rare occasion on which the *Daily Mail* treated protestors favourably. News that Brook Advisory Clinics are campaigning among boys to use contraception is accompanied by a denial that this will lead to 'promiscuity'. There are stories on baby-battering, teenage mothers being bad for their babies, Judge Brian Gibbens' sympathetic reaction to a man who sexually assaulted a seven-year-old girl ('Hang him,' says the girl's father); a picture story about a mugged woman in hospital. The women's pages carried features on underwear, fashion, how insurers valued a wife and 'shaming sex beasts into confessions'.

Political resistance is represented – with the exception of two women's protests – as the domain of militaristic mobsters, mad or bad, calling up echoes of ritualised male violence – fascism and gang warfare – which finds an answering echo in the emphasis given not to organised crime but to random viciousness, the victims of which are always women. It all creates an atmosphere of organised violence invading public space and disorganised violence invading the privacy of individual women. The portrayal of women as victims carries with it an appeal to the state to maintain public safety in the face of forms of male violence against which women cannot defend themselves. Rape, in particular, is represented as a random violation of women which invades their private and public space.

Absent is any sense of the collective experience of women as a sex in relation to men as a sex; women appear only as isolated, vulnerable victims, whose sole protection is their own spirited vigilance. The emphasis on rape and muggings brings together race and sex to create a sense that the inner city is a warren of shadows harbouring refugees in flight from respectable society. In the *Daily Mail*'s scenario, the 'rapist' and the 'mugger' are set apart from men in general. This separation frees the paper from any need to account for masculinity and femininity as a relationship of domination and subordination. Only some deviant men are dangerous, while all women are potentially endangered.

Ghetto children are now added to the line-up of suspects. Commenting in 1985 on the case of an old woman tormented by children living on her Hackney estate while police and social services apparently ignored neighbours' warnings, the *Daily Mail* leader said that children 'have to be watched. They have to be controlled. Disciplined. Taught right from wrong. In a word, civilised.' The inner city, a 'no-man's land' between neighbourly anxiety and unresponsive officialdom, must be better patrolled. For it is the modern wasteground, where the young are criminalised and the old are terrorised.[3]

What is notable is that the *Daily Mail* deploys the image of an army of 'aliens' to reinforce women's fear. The paper's political antennae are sensitive to what is real and makes crimes against women *news*. Furthermore, the *Daily Mail* has mobilised a whole politics on the basis of women's fear *as women* and generalised it: women are the soft centre of the community, and their dreads have become the medium of general social panic. On news pages women are reported to have been mauled and mutilated. On the women's pages they are not political subjects but objects once again, finding self-realisation not in liberation but in fashion. Style, not politics, is their emancipation. But it is a freedom which they do not make for themselves – Yves St Laurent is featured as 'the man who liberated women'.

Back to real life; women really *are* afraid. A Gallup poll published in the *Daily Telegraph* on 5 March 1986 found that half of Britain's women were afraid to go out alone at night in areas within a mile of their homes, but 43 per cent were not. A crime survey among residents of the inner-London Labour borough of Islington, commissioned by the council, found that crime was seen there to be a problem second only to employment. Among women, 31 per cent (compared to a borough average of 23 per cent) said they *always* avoided going out after dark because of their fear of crime. Nearly two-thirds of all people thought there were risks for women going out at night after dark. The survey found that black people were 68 per cent more likely to be assaulted than white people and women were 40 per cent more likely to be assaulted than men. Those at greatest risk of assault were young white women and young black women. The report concluded that

> women are more likely to be victims of crime than men. This belies the notion that women have an irrational fear of crime. By far the highest rates of crime at any sub-group are those against young women (White, Black and Asian).[4]

Opposing strategies

Until the 1970s, the Conservatives had taken the terrain of policing as their own, but it began to be confronted by a formidable challenge from many groups of people, ranging from liberal reformers to trade unionists, ethnic minorities, and women, who have revealed widespread discontent with the slogan 'support the police' as an appropriate response to the problem of crime. But unlike the Tory response – *more* policing – the Islington study criticised police practices for alienating a most important source of detection, public witnessing. But most of those who witnessed crime in the borough were least willing to co-operate with the police.

Traditional Tory law and order responses have usually involved an endorsement of police practices, and yet those same practices discouraged women, for example, from reporting sexual crimes against them. This only began to change when the police were subject to radical scrutiny by the media, from feminists and some local authorities.

Conservatism seemed to assimilate women's fear not because its ideology contained any critique of the conditions which produced it, nor because it contained any programme for its solution, but because moral panic *is* its politics. The politics of fear is central to the Conservative Party's 'authoritarian populism'.

Conservative women express, albeit hesitantly, a common sense shared among women that has often been expressed by women's movements, not least the modern Women's Liberation Movement, which in the late 1970s added to its programme of fundamental demands an eighth demand for women's freedom from violence. It is on the terrain of fear that feminism and Conservatism meet. And it is on that terrain that socialism has until recently been absent, and in its silence has appeared to distance itself from the preoccupations of women, not least when they demanded the reform of men. But the Conservative Party simply seeks to mobilise the good against the bad. Moral banalities like good and bad, right and wrong are condensed in Tory doctrine in the ideas of personal discipline and responsibility, of eternal vigilance – a kind of permanent war economy.

But among some Conservative women, personal responsibility implies a different response from the politics of punishment, one that attempts to confront women's fear as well as the problem of crime against women. There is a strand of resistance to the racism and revenge of the law and order lobby, and a regret that women are so implicated in it. During a Conservative Party area women's conference in the North-East in 1985 the two ideologies confronted each other. The representatives were introduced to Jackie Lait, their candidate in the winter by-election at Tynebridge. What was going to be done about all the violence, they asked, citing crimes against women as the source of their anxiety. When she tried to stress the difference between crime and fear of crime a murmur of discontent spread across the room. Pressed hard to support a punitive response, she held firm and confided – with some courage in that context – that she could not support capital punishment. It did not make her popular.

In autumn 1985, when Sonia Copland, a member of the minority Tory group on the former Greater London Council and a member of its women's committee, told the party conference that living in the inner city was 'horrible', she was warmly greeted for the rest of the day by representatives who complained that blacks were taking over the cities. But that had not been her message. As a woman who prides herself on her anti-racism, she was appalled.

Wendy Mitchell, a London borough councillor active in the party's women's organisations, reckons that as a result of 'a combination of things, including some of the feminist issues that were being raised', she decided with her daughter to go to a women's self-defence class. 'I know that if I'm in a situation alone late at night in which I could be scared I would have a greater readiness to defend myself. I'm not saying I could do it, but I have more of a readiness.'

These indicate an alternative response to the problem of violence among some Tory women, whose consciousness has been touched by the feminism of their own time.

Since feminism has produced its own politics around violence against women, it is useful to see how it differs from the status of women in the traditional Tory politics of law and order. The most important difference between the mainstream Conservative women's response and the feminist response is that feminism has taken action to transform the conditions in which women experience their fear: it has built battered women's refuges to enable women to run for it and make a new life; it has built a network of rape crisis centres to wrap around the survivors. It *does something*; it is practical rather than rhetorical, and it is about empowering the survivor rather than simply avenging her. The Conservative response is a politics of limited liability. It appeals to women as victims, but at the same time denies that women are oppressed, because to represent women as oppressed is to suggest a *system* of intimidation.

As Janice Winship has shown, 'femininity is not merely a passive acceptance by women of patriarchal domination but represents an *active subordination*'.[5] Feminism, she argues, embraces aspects of femininity, the world of women and the work of women, as sites of struggle, for it also wants to change the world of women. And therefore feminism is characterised by the creation of forms of politics in which it draws on aspects of women's oppression 'but transforms them into aspects of *feminist strength*. As part of under-standing that movement from femininity to feminism and the relation between them, we need to explore the processes by which femininity "manoeuvres" within and against masculine hegemony.'[6] We have seen how within the law and order discourse of Conservatism, women have done exactly that: they have manoeuvred within and against masculine hegemony. Their appeal to authoritarianism affirms and yet constrains women's discontent; it can always be allowed because it can never be satisfied: nature is nature, men are men, and men are beasts.

Implicitly Tory law and order debates were about policing men and protecting women, and they therefore revealed a crisis of *masculinity* which generated a crisis for *femininity*. But while the law and order rebellions represented women only as victims, the reform of masculinity was never on the agenda. The challenge did not require change.

7

THE MORAL CRUSADE

One of the Conservative Party's sources of strength has been its representation of itself as the party of the family and, therefore, of women. It has been uniquely successful in drawing women into political discourse, though rarely in their own right. Women connoted the family, the family connoted the world of women, and together they signified the personal and the private, the natural, the intuitive and the inevitable – all key terms in Conservative common sense. But the complaints which are as much a feature of familial common sense as commitment have always been purged from the official record.

How do Conservative women themselves feel about the family and their role within it? Their women's conferences have always attracted a plethora of resolutions from the constituencies on the importance of the family, and in 1981, when the conference focused on 'family matters', half of the twenty resolutions on economic policy and taxation, which attracted more resolutions than any other, urged the government to reform taxation to encourage mothers to stay at home with their children.

The tone of many resolutions over the years has suggested great concern about the needs of children for their mothers, often expressed as anxiety about juvenile delinquency, and about the need to defend women's full-time habitation of their separate sphere as a free choice. But there is also a coercive injunction at the back of the cult of motherhood in Conservative culture – the idea that not only the child but society needs mothers to stay at home to police their children, and that women in turn are policed by the demands of children.

Contemporary Conservative ideology is increasingly concerned with the *idea* of the family rather than the *work* of motherhood. We know that the tendency to assume that modern motherhood has been liberated by capital investment in the home is a myth: contemporary feminist research has shown that far from the workload being eased it has remained remarkably static, consuming about seventy-seven hours a week of a woman's time.[1] There is an important sense in which many Conservative women share with other women across the political spectrum the desire to affirm the work they do within the family, sometimes in a vocabulary that seeks to unite women across classes: 'I'm working class – I've scrubbed my kitchen floor,' insisted Baroness Platt, the Conservative chairman of the Equal Opportunities Commission.[2] But domestic life as *labour* rarely features in the rhetoric.

When Patrick Jenkin was Social Services Secretary he articulated the traditional, though no longer the only Tory view: 'The great majority of families recognise that the traditional way, with very young children brought up at their mother's knee, does have advantages. That's the way one gets the transmission of culture, the best education for our children. That's the safest way.'[3] He told the party women's conference in 1981 that although 'we applaud' the greater number of women who go out to work, he was not sure that this meant 'we should give an unreserved welcome to the mothers of young children going out to work. I find that people are sometimes confused and uncertain ... Of course it must be right for many young children, particularly for the under-fives, to have the love, care and attention of a mother for most of their waking and sleeping day.' He admitted, however, that 'for many mothers with young children, the isolation, the stress and sheer boredom can become intolerable. For some a part-time job must be the only thing that keeps them sane.' But he qualified this cautionary note that motherhood might mean madness with a loaded warning:

> What I ask in these circumstances is that families – and it must
> be a family's choice, it can be no one else's – should pay as much
> regard to the real interests of their children as they do to their
> own wishes ... the role of the mother who stays at home
> and looks after her child is an honourable one.

Down among the Tory women though, it doesn't always feel like an honoured profession. But political etiquette seems to forbid them from consulting their feelings. There is no equivalent within the manners of Conservative political discourse to the practice that Women's Liberation – that other movement which attaches priority to the politics of the family – has built around the principle of 'the personal is political'. But that is not to say that Conservative women don't have their own feelings, nor that they are uniquely Conservative. The question we have to ask is whether they are heard in the Conservative context, and whether the feelings themselves inform the political discourse within which they are structured. Does the recognition of the importance of the work of motherhood imply support for the conditions in which women are mothers, or does it imply suppression of women's consciousness of the contradictions thrown up by their solitary responsibility for children?

Emma Nicholson, who took over responsibility for Tory women in 1984, believes that Conservative women are 'largely happy with their lives' and the world, unlike socialist women who want to change the lives of women and the world. My own conversations with Conservative women show that this is both true and not true.

'I enjoyed stopping at home, I wasn't bored, I still think women should have the right to choose to stay at home if they want,' said Diane Charles, a housewife in Birmingham, expressing a widely held commitment that this, too, should be a matter of choice. 'A lot of women don't like housework – I don't particularly. But if a woman does want to go out to work there should be the facilities for her, like crèches and nurseries and not just childminders. You should be encouraged to do either, stay at home or pursue a career,' she said.

Gillian Clarke, who looks after her teenage children and her husband, Employment Minister Kenneth Clarke, trusts her own experience. As a voluntary worker for Oxfam, for example, she has come to criticise the government on aid: 'I want aid to be for development not for increasing export markets for this country.' And having been a full-time mother herself since her children were born, she is a strong believer in Tory family ideology. But she also believes that equality legislation

is a good thing because it opens things up. I've made my choice, but it is mine and I wouldn't want to impose it on anyone else. I just wish my priority got a bit more recognition. There's a lot of lip service from politicians about the vital role of women with their children – for instance when they talk about juvenile delinquency.

An MP reckoned that 'After six years of nappies I'd have gone into the loony bin if I hadn't got out of the house and taken up something else.' A middle-class professional woman who abandoned her career when she married, she said regretfully, 'That was what my generation did in the 1950s.'

But there is another dimension to women's commitment to staying at home: this may be the one area in which women feel they have some control over life. It produces an experience of power and substantial responsibility. 'I never had any training,' said a woman in her forties who had several jobs in shops and behind a bar before she married:

> I'm very unhappy about women having children and then going back to work because a mother can't give her all to it if she's got a job too. I feel that children need a parent around. The trouble with the Conservatives today is that it's all new times and they're going with the sway. We're made to feel guilty for staying at home, because of all the opportunities available for mothers to work now. I want respect – this is what we have lost.

A councillor in the North, Isa Smith, was one of the few women of her generation to go to university immediately after the Second World War:

> I taught for two years in a girls' high school, which I enjoyed, because in those days there was no difficulty getting a job. That was in 1949. Then I got married and oh yes I wanted to give up work, because it seemed an infinitely better prospect. I still feel that to be a good wife and mother is a wholetime job, and until my youngest child was at school I felt that the family should come first. Nevertheless, I do realise that a woman doesn't always feel satisfied by that and needs to widen her horizons. That's very real to many women, and anyway more women have had the benefit of education and there's the financial side: in my day somehow a man's earnings were related to having a wife.

Many older women seem to feel that they did what was expected of them, and there is no loss of pride in feeling that although it was expected, they did it well. But they, too, now feel that their experience was specific to their generation. A part-time voluntary worker, Diane Charles adheres to Conservatism, 'because I like to see people get their achievements. We're not here very long so we should get what we want to do.' Has she achieved what she wanted in her own life?

Me? No! I tried to do everything properly, to stay at home and bring up the children because society said you should. Society was wrong. But if I'd had two jobs I couldn't have concentrated. Well, I'm not certain. Anyway, I've done it my way. Actually there's a girl across the way and I'm watching her, she doesn't know I am, but I am, because she's got two little children and she goes out to work, and I just want to see if she can make it work. I could start again I suppose, but if you have babies you should stay at home, then maybe the vandals and the crime rate would be better.

What works for women in the Conservatives' family ideology is the sense that women are important to society because they are important to the family: they take care of it, after all, and the family is important to society. But women live their relationship to the family always in the tension between power and powerlessness, passion and pain, self-realisation and self-denial. The rhetoric of familial ideology is rarely about the *content* of the relationship with children and the work of motherhood, and still less about many if not most women's experience of solitude and abandonment. A housewife who had been active in her village Women's Institute, Susan Maynard, felt that for all the *talk* about the importance of the family, women were just left with the labour: 'You don't have any support bringing up children. I recall my eldest child having an accident. My husband was away for six weeks for his work, and I *coped alone* for six weeks – she couldn't even stand up on her own.' It wasn't his problem.

Among relatively privileged Conservative women, the rhetoric of familial ideology does not describe, and probably never has de-scribed, their lived relationship to motherhood and childcare, and this miscellany of views implies a different programme from that of the theoreticians and the populists. Conservative women's commitment to the family resides, as it does among women in general, in their pride in giving life and in the pleasure of relationships, not least because they feel it is they who know about children and the fibre of family feeling. But they are also concerned about the *conditions* in which women have to organise their commitments, their remorse and their affection. If the familial ideology of the right were to express women's real feelings, then perhaps it would be less about authority and discipline and more about the real meaning of their slogan 'freedom of choice'. There is no debate about that in Tory circles, for that would imply a collective and social strategy for childcare. Nonetheless, many Conservative women are exercising choice – because they can afford to – in ways that challenge the injunctions of their ideology.

An MP with children still living at home believes that although

> children have a right to care, I don't think it matters who provides it, but it must be long-term. I know we're only talking about professional people – I see that it would be difficult for shop workers. You have to consider the fulfilment of people for whom you are responsible. It doesn't matter who provides the care; it could be early-retired grandmothers.

Sceptical about the family cause in the Conservative Party, she believes in

> a balance of sacrifice in the family. I don't think a woman has responsibility for her husband; she has no more responsibility for him than him for her. Victorian values, all that subjugating of women to the husband! I'm saying parents have obligations to their children, but neither has the obligation to subjugate themselves to the other.

A Parliamentary hopeful aligned to the new right of the party and who came from a working-class background, said:

> I was always taken with the idea of a nanny because it left the mother to do her proper job – the nanny can clean up the sick. I despised my own mother because I saw her as a slave and I won't have that attitude to me. I didn't want to be one of them. I felt ashamed of my mother because she didn't work.

Those women in Parliament who are sentimental about this,
I hate them, they're not real Thatcherites.

Edwina Currie, a real Thatcherite, believes that in her own
marriage and career

one of the things that helped me win the snakes and ladders
game was that I started out with no rules at all. You start
constructing your own cave. When I met my husband – he's a
super bloke and I'm very lucky, and I know that – we talked
about it long before getting married. We decided that we didn't
want the standard sort of home in which there's the tea on
the table at five o'clock. So we've never been very traditional.
And I see no virtue in polishing the table. I can't tell you
why, I just don't. In more recent years I've trained myself to
care about some things and not others. What we decided to
do, and we got quite practical about it, was that anything we
didn't like doing about the house – and some things I do
enjoy, I actually like cooking as long as I don't have to do it all
the time – we take the drudgery out of it. We eat out a lot,
and so do the children. We have a freezer and a microwave,
we do without or we get a machine to do it, or we pay
someone else to do it – I've always had someone in to do the
housework. Similarly with childcare, I've never worked on
the principle that I know better how to look after my children
than anyone else. So we tried it and it worked. My husband's
attitude has always been that as long as we don't bankrupt him,
in other words I have an obligation to earn the money to do
some of these things, and as long as I don't do anything
dangerous, he's perfectly happy.

Emma Nicholson had

a lovely old-fashioned upbringing. We had quantities of people
looking after us. Three gardeners – tiny little garden but it meant
we were self-sufficient, we didn't buy things – a cook, a
parlourmaid, all of whom had been with my father since he
was a boy, absolute darlings, nanny, nurserymaid. They turned
over rapidly because this was post-war and really it was a
pre-war upbringing my mother was trying to do, without

realising that perhaps times had changed. I would have preferred nobody except my mother – you know, all these people coming and going – but it was what mama, who was very reserved, a sweet person, an artist, very intelligent for whom everything went into the garden and art, it was what she thought she ought to try to do for her children. The servants were one's best friends.

And friends was what they remained, not employees:

Oh no, you didn't look at them like that, that would have been wrong. To have thought of them as employees would have infringed their dignity, and the point was that they were just as good as you, only they were doing a different job, that's the key. In the 1950s a marvellous Jamaican lady came and that was marvellous because it meant that one had someone who was coloured living in one's household all one's life.

Now in her forties, she is single and a professional woman:

We get job satisfaction from our work, a feeling of achievement, and I've always thought, perhaps wrongly never having been a wife, that it must be fantastically difficult to get satisfaction in just being a wife at home. So I think working in charities offers housebound women those satisfactions. Most Conservative women feel reasonably satisfied with their lifestyle, with the order and patterns of life; they're not by nature out to change society. That's not saying they don't have a target, they've got their family and their husband to promote and care for, but their personal development takes a back seat. The woman develops the family rather than herself. But they haven't got job satisfaction. So, you get personal pleasure from things working well in the family, but you don't get a sense of tasks achieved, and people saying, 'Well done.' You don't get much of that at home I imagine. I'd go mad at home all day.

Emma Nicholson's life, although specific to her class, is also consistent with late twentieth-century Britain, a Britain in which most women work outside the home. While that may have informed

Tory employment policy, it has not shaped the familial ideology of Thatcherism.

The politics of the family

How has this miscellany of voices been heard in Tory ideology? Has its diversity been assimilated? During the post-war decades the traditional family has been destabilised, and instead of being axiomatic has become an unstable concept in Conservative ideology. As we scan Conservative Party manifestos, the ideological interventions of Conservative leaders and theorists, the concerns of the party women's organisation and the private feelings of women, we discern shifting emphases, conflicting priorities and contradictory moods. The party was imprisoned by its own history and yet also by the status quo, and so has found itself forced to respond to diverse pressures on its family policy from within and without.

We shall see that the Conservative Party, which has always had to house different ideological and material interests, has been unable to articulate a homogenous familial ideology true to its old traditions. Rather than waging an ideological offensive to consign women to their separate sphere within the home, thus reuniting women and the family, Thatcherism was concerned with something bigger than both of them: the family as the anchor of the new right's anti-statism and economic liberalism. Citizens were to realise themselves not in their social being, not through politics, but through consumerism. In itself this was not new, but what was new was Thatcherism's deployment of the family while often adopting an almost agnostic stance in relation to women's role within it. Thatcherism's family strategy has not been about any explicit designation of the role of women as only homemakers; it has not prescribed women's expulsion from the labour market, but it has clearly been about the family as its moral bulwark against degeneracy and dependence, and as its economic barricade against the state.

Sir Keith Joseph had on 20 October 1974 given an extraordinary endorsement to the moral rearmers when he'd urged 'let us take inspiration from that admirable woman Mary Whitehouse', described as 'an unknown middle-aged woman' who had stood out 'against the permissiveness of our time'. He singled out working-class single mothers for attack: they were the classic scroungers, degenerates who were producing the future scourge of the cities: 'They are producing problem children, the future unmarried

mothers, delinquents, denizens of our borstals, subnormal educational establishments, prisons, hostels for drifters.' When public
wrath descended upon him from the right as well as the left, he
wrote to *The Times* on 22 October claiming that he had not suggested
that class caused the degeneracy, but rather that single parenthood
produced a 'cycle of deprivation'. But this was an evasion: his speech
had indeed stressed that a growing proportion of children were
being born to unfit mothers 'who were pregnant in adolescence in
social classes four and five'. Their social class, in other words, came
first.

Joseph's speech lost him any chance of succeeding Edward Heath
as party leader, but it mapped out the contours of Thatcherism's
political landscape.

During the mid-1970s equality legislation, reflecting irresistible
pressure from the women's movement and the labour movement,
transformed the parameters within which Conservative sexual and
familial politics could move. The Conservatives led by Edward
Heath were part of that new consensus. He had distanced himself
from the moral rearmament agenda and the politics of punishment,
and by the end of his administration women commanded their very
own, albeit modest, space in the manifesto.

The February 1974 election had nothing on women or the family.
However, the October 1974 manifesto, written as the government
was running into the deadline for implementation of the Equal Pay
Act, declared: 'we stand for the principle of equal pay', and promised
to set up an Equal Opportunities Commission, 'the biggest step
towards a society of real equality for men and women taken by any
government since women won the vote'. Heath's defeat in the 1974
general election and then his demise within the party inaugurated a
new era in which women disappeared and the family resumed its
place on the right hand of god, the manifesto. Nevertheless, the
1979 general election manifesto did not express the old common
sense of the family as the bastion (as well as the burden) of woman-
power.

After the Second World War, family life was transformed by the
forward march of married women into the labour force. Married
men *and* women were now breadwinners. The political problem for
women across the political spectrum in the 1970s was how to make
the institutions, from the DHSS to the CBI and TUC, from
the police to Parliament, ratify the revolution in women's lives.

Thatcherism attempted not so much to reverse this process as to return the problem to the private rather than the political domain.

Not surprisingly, the 1979 manifesto was silent about women. Instead it concerned itself with 'helping the family'. Home was about property: 'To most people ownership means first and foremost a home of their own.' Parenthood was about 'extending parents' rights and responsibilities' by making the authorities 'take into account parents' wishes when allocating children to schools'. Welfare was about encouraging private insurance. Social security was about maintaining child benefit, reducing income tax and running 'scroungers' to earth. The manifesto did not prescribe any particular family form, or rather it did not specify the role of women within the family. However, the offensive by some Thatcherites in the 1980s against the permissive society and the poor pointed the finger at the family, and particularly the different responsibilities of both *mothers and fathers*. This marked a shift not only from the Heath era but from the twentieth-century tradition – the right had always been fixated by the regulation of mothers.[4] The independent single mother, for example, was measured as a threat to men, to social order and as a *cost* on the state: the state supported her in-*dependence* and in so doing supported the dissolution of civilisation.

Patrick Jenkin was to be the family fall guy of the new Tory leadership. As social services spokesperson he made in 1977 one of the few public remarks – now notorious – risked by a party leader which explicitly opposed equality between men and women and which implied a return to the old domestic order:

Quite frankly I don't think mothers have the same right to work as fathers do. If the good Lord had intended us to have equal rights to go out to work he wouldn't have created men and women. These are biological facts.

And later as Secretary of State for Social Services he wove a strict sense of sexual difference into social security amendments. If women's dependency on the state was degenerate, then men's dependency was deviant. It offended against the laws of masculinity. He justified cuts in benefit paid to homeless men on the grounds that people would be annoyed if they got 'more actual cash in hand by being homeless (sometimes by choice) than by contributing toward the cost of a household and accepting the attendant responsibilities'.[5]

Sir Geoffrey Howe repeated the preference for sexual interdependence rather than independence when in 1980 as Chancellor of the Exchequer he questioned the efficacy of the popular child benefit after his failure to maintain its value in his 1980 Budget. He said he was beginning to wonder whether the state had been wise to give this allowance to women, thus departing 'from the idea of the state dealing with the family as a unit headed by the father'. This prompted another, rather more eccentric question in his mind: 'Does the mother feel greater independence because she is not dependent on the father for the children's support?'[6] Jenkin, however, was the most explicit in following logic of the new right's old-fashioned family crusade: 'Perhaps the most important social work today is motherhood.'

Margaret Thatcher's appeal to women in speeches and interviews always emphasised her motherhood as typical and her career as exceptional. Some women needed extra responsibility beyond motherhood, but 'it isn't right to impose it on others'.[7] She articulated her womanhood in motherhood. But her self-image exemplified the Conservatives' problem: women were both mothers and workers. And although the Conservatives' family politics assumed the traditional roles of mothers and fathers, it was not – and could not be – followed through with an explicit campaign to get women out of the workforce.

Thatcherism's moral anti-modernism should not be interpreted as a premeditated and self-conscious campaign to get women back to the kitchen sink – not least because many of the women who formed the Tories' social base were already somewhere else, and many of the younger male Tory ministers were married to women with jobs outside the home. Actually, the Tories' family policy had to accommodate diverse pressures. The party was under pressure to abolish the married man's tax allowance, and if it did, then it had to placate men. Conservative women opposed erosion of child benefit and transfer of state income support for low-paid families from women to men. The party was under pressure from women who'd lobbied for years to make the party do something about tax, in particular to ensure privacy in taxation for married women. Many Conservatives wanted the government to encourage women to stay at home through tax incentives;

others wanted the government to support equality for women in the workplace.

In the year after Jenkin's 'good Lord' revelation, the Tory women's conference, working with a new format of area working papers, discussed 'family matters' and their recommendations included support for nursery education, encouragement of home-ownership and flexible financing of the health service (the North-Western area women also lamented the demise of the matron in hospitals). The working parties did not discuss family life and the role of women within it, perhaps because their brief was, according to Baroness Janet Young (deputy chairman of the party with responsibility for women), to discuss 'matters of particular concern to the family'. With the family more in mind, resolutions from the constituencies weighed towards tax reform to encourage mothers to stay at home. The next Conservative government was urged in one resolution 'to revise the present taxation system which encourages a married woman to work and discriminates against the mother who stays at home to look after her children'.

However, the inference that Tory women were only for hearth and home was to be belied by their 1981 conference. The theme was women and employment, and the area working parties, after conducting local surveys, made the following recommendations: that women be encouraged to 'seek advancement in industry', to acquire mechanical and technical skills and become active in trade unions, 'so that they can have greater influence over their conditions of work'; that part-time workers should get equal pay, pro-rata with full-timers; that homeworkers' pay should be improved in fields 'where exploitation still existed'; and that it should be made easier for women to work at home 'whilst fulfilling [their] role as homemaker'. Worry that employers might be disinclined to take on women because of employment protection law was not confirmed by their research, although one working party questioned the efficacy of maternity leave, no doubt in the interests of small businesses and to pre-empt an employers' backlash. The South-East working party found evidence 'that some employers are avoiding employing women for positions that now enjoy equal pay' and that women still faced 'widespread prejudice'.

In the 1980s, the women's organisation skilfully turned the leadership's family rhetoric against it. During the early 1980s it used its annual commentary on the Budget to persuade the Chancellor of the Exchequer to maintain child benefit, a popular benefit which unites women in both the 'feminist' and 'feminine' camps. After the stiff cuts Budget of 1980, which was greeted with widespread discontent in the party, Patrick Jenkin made a promise to keep the benefit in line with inflation 'subject to economic and other circumstances'. In the House of Commons there was a pro-child benefit lobby among a group of Tory MPs, and the women's organisation, dedicated to establishing women as a political force, had begun to intervene on behalf of women in the annual debates around the Budget. The women were annoyed about the devaluing of child benefit, and the following year their organisation took courage and lobbied hard for child benefit in the discussion on Sir Geoffrey Howe's 1981 Budget. Furthermore they went public by sending their pre-Budget comments to the press. 'The delay in sending the comments was perhaps not quite as long as the party would have expected, to put it euphemistically,' said one Central Office staffer involved at the time. In other words, the women had pre-empted the government somewhat by getting their comments publicised.

The cut imposed in 1980 was restored in time for the 1983 election. But child benefit returned to the agenda only a few years later when Norman Fowler as Social Services Secretary launched his social security review: child benefit was not kept in line with inflation and Family Income Supplement, a benefit paid to low-wage households and usually collected from the Post Office by women, was to be paid as family credit through the wage and, therefore, primarily to men. This meant re-distribution from women to men. Initially, the women's committee seemed to buy the transfer to men. According to one member:

It gives them equal power. At the moment the state gives them no power. The present system is degrading; the state assumes that if the father gets the money it won't go to the family, which is a fairly patriarchal position, which I loathe, it's a disgrace. The other way round actually lifts their wages and that's what people want. They don't want to be taking home a tiny wage packet and going round the corner to get it from the state. If the whole thing goes through the wages system then I do agree with Fowler that it enhances the dignity of the family.

> The state should take a step backwards and let them make
> the decision.

Wasn't she suggesting that, in a situation of unequal power between men and women, women were just going to have to 'stand on their own two feet' and fight? 'No, because after all they'll have their social worker to help them.' Do *all* poor people have social workers, and do they have them just because they're poor?

At first, it looked like the Tory women might trade defeat on family credit for victory on child benefit. However, at their September 1985 meeting the Conservative National Women's Committee came out flatly against paying family credit through the wage packet – and even took a unanimous vote against it! But what else could they do? The women's organisation came under tough pressure from ministers not to go public – as they had done in 1980 when the women quickly told the press of their disagreement with the Chancellor. Positioned outside the decision-making process, the women's organisation could only discreetly counsel a change of heart, and in the hope that delicate diplomacy from their side would be reciprocated by a rethink on the other side, the women kept quiet and tried to avoid a row. But apparently to the surprise of ministers the women's organisation finally gave up waiting for a sign from the government and joined the coalition which had been built outside the party among seventy organisations, ranging from the Child Poverty Action Group to the Women's Institutes and the Confederation of British Industry. They campaigned in 1985–86 to make the government change its mind. It did – Fowler's junior minister, Lady Trumpington, announced in the House of Lords on 23 June 1986, a day of defeats for Fowler and his treatment of women, that the government would pay family credit direct to 500,000 mothers.

This defeat was important because it revealed the ways in which the family represented different priorities to different constituencies within the party. It showed how Conservative women's feelings about the family reached beyond the idea and the institution to a concern with women's conditions of existence within the family.

Theory and polemic

If Tory family policy has not, in reality, matched the ideology, then Tory theory has not been so encumbered. The family occupies a privileged place in Conservative theory, particularly since the creation of the modern state. 'In their defence of the individual against socialism and excessive state power, Conservatives rely chiefly upon the family and private property . . . Man is a member of the family before he is a member of anything else. The family is the centre of affections and the transmitter of traditions.'[8] More than that, the family is regarded as the engine of Tory commitment to private property and accumulation: 'People have a natural instinct for ownership and possession, and private enterprise provides an incentive, other than force, for work. But Conservatives value private property and private enterprise primarily as the protectors of the family and of freedom.'[9] So the family is both the necessary condition for authority and private enterprise, and private enterprise is the necessary condition for the authorities and affections inscribed in the family.

In contemporary Tory ideology, the family had to be maximised in order to minimise the state.[10] In the 1970s and 1980s the family was deployed as a key formation on several fronts in the assault on the 'scrounger' state: the family v crime, the family v class, the family v permissiveness and, more recently, the continuity of the family v fragmentation of the family, and the family v feminism.

One of the most important theorists of the English new right has been Roger Scruton, an alienated maverick of the generation of 1968, whose animus against his contemporaries informs much of his theoretical work. Unusually for a Tory, he not only opposed the theoretical challenge of the left, but occupied much of the same terrain. He argued that conservatism originated in an attitude to civil society in which the motivating forces were authority, allegiance and tradition.[11] Against the trend within socialist or left-wing libertarian theory to uncover the contradictions within the family and in the family's relation to state and civil society, he affirmed the object of allegiance, which is to 'ratify the authority of the state and its traditions'. The state should not be concerned with 'myths of equality and social justice'. Tradition must, for Scruton, mould people's idea of who they are, and there is no better institution than the family, for it is the 'one particular tradition, which both embodies a transcendent bond, and also reinforces social allegiance, [and] has survived all the upheavals of recent history'.[12]

Unlike Marxism, with which he engages in the book, and more recently feminism, Scruton absents the family from history through his argument that the family, in some form, has survived all social upheavals. The point for Marxism and for feminism, however, is that the particular *form* of the family has changed through history, and that the history of the family is also the history of class and gender, of power and politics. Like all institutions, it is never *above* history. And like all social relations, its history is one of power and contradictions. For feminists drawing on and amplifying the Marxist tradition, the family has been a site of unequal power between men and women, and as a sphere of work, the work of reproducing human relations. Scruton acknowledges that he shares with Marxism the recognition that 'the essence of politics is established power'. But for him the family is a natural not a social institution, which is, despite his denial, never immune from the 'upheavals of recent history'. Just as Scruton insists upon the family as a natural formation, so he must insist, somewhat limply, upon sexual difference as a natural phenomenon, rather than a dynamic relationship subject to social change. That insistence marks him as a misogynist marching against the tide of history which is carrying even the women of his own side.

For it is the palpable evidence of the changing relationship between men and women, both public and private, that disturbs Scruton's representation of the family as transcending history. So, history has to be suppressed. That, too, is the project of Ferdinand Mount, a former adviser to Margaret Thatcher at Downing Street. His thesis in *The Subversive Family* is that history is bunk. Deploying the claim that the family is a web of 'private affections' outside history, the state and market forces, he asserts that the family is 'the enduring, permanent enemy of all hierarchies, churches and ideologies'. Like many modern Conservatives, piqued by the extent to which many Marxist and feminist concepts have entered popular vocabulary, he appropriates their alien axioms against them: the family is in 'permanent revolution against the state'.[13] Furthermore, the working-class family is 'the only revolutionary class' because its members work for 'one another'.[14] The family, in other words, is a higher form of solidarity which transcends the allegiance of class.

Far from women's participation in the labour market destabilising the traditional family, it has strengthened it, he argues, because surplus income has been devoted to . . . family holidays. In his ingenious but absurd quest for evidence, he proposes that 'the great Northern resorts such as Blackpool are to this day a living refutation of Marx'.[15] Like Scruton, Mount's project is to demonstrate the autonomy of the family in order to reaffirm its authority. While citing the family as an institution which has subverted class allegiances, his case makes no sense without an account of the history of patriarchy or 'gender hierarchy' within working-class politics. It is not that the traditional family has rescued the working class from socialism, but rather, as Barbara Taylor has argued in her germinal history of socialism and feminism in the nineteenth century, *Eve and the New Jerusalem*, that the 'decline of the feminist impulse within socialism' marginalised 'sexual liberation and the democratisation of personal relations'.[16] Not only were women's aspirations off the agenda, but the socialist project itself became narrowed down to class-based industrial struggles, within which the machinery of organisation was generally denied to women. The means of organisation – if not the means of production – were expropriated by men, so to speak; the labour movement became a men's movement. 'The development of capitalist production on the basis of gender division has meant that no workers' struggle has ever been free of these sexual politics.'[17] And it follows that the history of the working class, and its family, has never been free of the 'sexual Toryism' which secured the power of men and the subordination of women.

Women's subordination is necessarily suppressed by Tory theorists in their presentation of families as homogenous institutions in which genders and generations are united and men and women nestle beyond the reach of the other solidarities of sex and class. Within the family men and women's positions are assumed to be unproblematic and unchanging; they are represented as simple and self-evident because they are biological. Margaret Thatcher in a speech in Cardiff on 16 April 1979 asked: 'What is the real driving force in our society? It is the desire for the individual to do the best for *himself and his family* [my italics]. There is no substitute for this elemental human instinct.'

Similarly, for Mount, it is only within the family that the working class realises itself. There it remains in its natural state, inaccessible to the paternalism of the establishment and the Big Brother of social democracy's super-state. Even the district nurse, a symbol of state interference, has at her disposal a 'Stalinist array of powers'. There is of course truth in this: there is mass discontent with the scrutineers and sleuths of the welfare state, and Thatcherism's rhetoric against the boss class of state bureaucrats no doubt speaks to widely held grievances about DHSS authoritarianism. But of course Thatcherism also drew in the net of scrutiny and increased the surveillance. In an attempt to colonise the language of Marxism, Mount postulates an 'undeclared war'[18] between 'an overclass, bossy, acquisitive of power and security, intermittently guilty about both' and its protagonist, a bossed underclass. Assuming a natural antipathy to the welfare state in the working class (an eccentric view given that the working class fought *for* it), he argues that the proletariat wants none of these bureaucrats poking their noses into its affairs: 'What few have yet grasped is that the working class is the true defender of liberty and *privacy*.' It is only a short stagger then to abandon the idea that the working class has an *economic* interest – the redistribution of wealth – in favour of a familial one – the assertion of the family's autonomy and authority through a 'redistribution of privacy'.[19]

The polemical objectives in this approach are to suppress women's position as subordinate; to pitch the family against the 'servant state'; to discredit class interests and class solidarity as anachronisms; to set biological kinship against political solidarity, and in so doing depoliticise civil society. If the family is the agency of working-class aspirations, then social arrangements can be devolved to the improvised but 'inevitable' notions of nature and private life.

The Conservatives had a problem, however, in their representation of the working class as being autonomous from class consciousness when in the 1980s, as in the 1920s, wives, mothers and sisters – whole families, not to mention whole communities – mobilised to sustain strikers during the government's confrontations with the miners. Family solidarity was synonymous with class solidarity. Where the family has been part of the train of working-class solidarity, it has been mocked as primal, unconscious, out of the reach of cosmopolitan culture and consciousness. Sir Alfred Sherman, *Daily Telegraph* leader writer and former Downing Street adviser to Margaret Thatcher, and Sir John Hoskyns of the Institute of Directors, another former Downing Street adviser, have scorned the solidarities of the working class, within and without the family, as atavistic throwbacks. Class-based trade union solidarity is 'obsolete', they argued. And Sherman inveighs against trade unions in some of the most besieged industries as a cost to their own class because they generate not 'surplus value but deficit value, hence they exploit their fellow workers', and worse than that they struggle to preserve a way of life akin to 'what Marx called "rural idiocy" in an isolated, quasi tribal one-class society'.[20]

The refusal to engage with the history of the working class as a *class*, and then in government the refusal to negotiate with it through its institutions, which marked Thatcherism's radical break with all other post-war Conservative governments, was the corollary to its family theme. Thatcherism mobilised the 'citizen' against class. The trade unions were said to have been returned to their individual members, and individual members shared not class identification but the same 'instincts' – accumulation for the family. By coupling the family and nation in its appeal to Victorian values, as Margaret Thatcher did when she told the 1979 party conference, 'Let us remember, we are a nation and a nation is an extended family', Thatcherism appeared to invoke England's finest hour, in which fathers were proper patriarchs, rulers were proper rulers and England properly ruled the world. Both sides of the tracks had presumably played their part, unmolested by middle-class mediocrity entrenched in the state, which was decried by Thatcherism as the parasite on the people, sucking dry the independence of the working class and the enterprise of the upper class.

Most of this theoretical work deployed familial ideology against the labour movement and the welfare state. But the new-right theorists got around to taking on feminism too: 'The normal family is alive and well and living in the hearts of a majority of the population. But there are forces in contemporary society which are deeply inimical to it', including the 'ideological extravagances' of the feminists, argued the Social Affairs Unit of the Centre for Policy Studies set up by Sir Keith Joseph in the 1970s.[21] The argument against feminism rests on the case that the family hasn't changed, that it is still the typical household, that women are powerful in families and that children living in fatherless families are feckless and violent. *Sunday Telegraph* columnist Mary Kenny wonders why feminists want to attack the family as a 'patriarchal body' and 'transfer power away from women as mothers to the state' when 'the working class woman is queen of her home, the empress of her kinfolk and sometimes the Boadicea of her neighbourhood'.[22]

But Boadicea is no match for the wanton offspring of fatherless families. Patricia Morgan's petulant essay 'Feminist Attempts to Sack the Father: A Case of Unfair Dismissal?'[23] typifies the right's shift of emphasis away from the role of the mother to the necessity of the father. For her, the children of fatherless families are under-achievers and prone to violence *because* of the absence of patriarchal authority. Boys, apparently, will be boys unless they are policed by real men. That was what veteran 'moral majority' man Rhodes Boyson told a Church Society fringe meeting at the 1986 party conference, too. The phenomenon of single mothers was an 'evil' because it exposed society to the 'wild and uncontrolled male young' who needed to be 'civilised by firm and caring fathers'.

The mass presence of many mothers in the labour market, easier divorce and the rising number of single-parent families has displaced the Edwardian preoccupation with motherhood as the source of and the solution to family crisis.[24] Thatcherism's preoccupations have focused on the crisis in the *patriarchal* family. 'If there is a "war over the family", then one of its principal battlefronts is whether homes need fathers,' argues Morgan, who misrepresents the feminist critique of fathers' abstention from fatherhood and its support for women's economic parity with men when she suggests that there is a strong lobby, informed by Marxist feminism, to produce a situation in which 'fathers have faced not only the *dismissal*, but a positive *denigration* of their role'.

On the other hand, feminist and socialist attempts to re-think social policy in the light of changes in household composition are dismissed by Robert Chester, who challenges the evidence of the '*pluralism* of contemporary family forms and the alleged minority status of the conventional family'.[25] Only about 5 per cent of workers are men with dependent wives and children, and only 32 per cent of households are made up of married couples with dependent children. These figures challenge the stereotypes of typical bread-winners and typical households around which incomes and social policy are organised. But Chester argues that if people and not households are calculated, then a majority of people still live in families. There have been changes in family behaviour, he concedes, but these have operated within a strong framework of continuity. So, everything has changed and yet nothing has changed. For these theorists, who argue that the 'normal family' desperately needs political and economic support against anti-family propaganda, there is an unresolved tension between the assertion of family stability and panic in the face of its instability.

Thatcherism's rehabilitation of the family may not be explicitly directed towards a reversal of the changes in women's relationship to the family – it wouldn't dare – but the crusade nevertheless involves a suppression of women's experience. This places Conservative women in a contradictory relationship to the family crusade. Thatcherism brought to politics a womanly vocabulary:

> Thatcherism is concerned to construct an alliance with women-wives – an alliance which, if successful, would create for it a powerful consensus on which to carry out its overall strategy. This alliance is concerned to construct its ideological strategy as if it were common sense.[26]

But it did not establish itself as the common sense. What the Conservatives have not done is promote the exclusion of women from the labour force – unprecedented in peacetime economic crisis – because they are themselves the captives of common sense: the world has moved on and even the law now ratifies the rights of women in the labour market. But what the Conservatives have continued to do is to treasure the non-working mother: after all she has been the backbone of the Tory Party, and her husband is prized by all the political parties.

Margaret Thatcher presents herself to women as a mother, but an exceptional mother, a mother with other needs represented as being as instinctive as the maternal instinct itself. So what's exceptional about being a working mother? Nothing – it describes most British women. But Margaret Thatcher does not represent herself as identifying with the world of women who go out to work and have children because even in the 1980s that is not the Conservative world. In Conservative ideology woman as working mother is still individualised, and the most famous working mother of all is still trying to explain herself in the rhetoric of the 1950s rather than the realities of the 1980s. As a political calculation it would seem inept. Certainly, there is a strong sense of regret among many Conservative women that she has not identified herself with the majority of women. But Thatcher's idiosyncrasy makes some sense not only in the context of Conservative culture but also as an index of how far working women's politics have been silenced in British state institutions. Working mothers are typical and yet, to all but themselves, still regarded as exceptional. So much so that women's – not to mention children's – needs for childcare have had no impact at all on the political agenda. Working women in Britain have had to go it alone and make their own arrangements. No field has been so successfully consigned to a private market as childcare.

In 1945 there were 62,200 public-sector nursery places. This number dropped to 43,600 in 1946 and declined every year thereafter until it reached its lowest level in 1969, at 21,100. Not that social childcare decreased – all other kinds of voluntary and private provision increased steadily, more than covering the demise of public-sector provision. Voluntary and private premises provided only 6,900 places in 1949, but reached 203,100 in 1969, and places offered by childminders increased from 1,700 in 1949 to 70,500 in 1969. At the beginning of the 1970s, when the women's movements were influencing the political climate, all forms of childcare increased. By 1983 childminders provided 107,500 places for children, private and voluntary premises and playgroups 420,900. The slowest increase was in the public sector, where the 28,800 places offered in 1983 remained fewer than half those provided nearly forty years earlier.[27] All British governments consigned supply to the voluntary or private sector, despite the evidence of massive demand.

While the Conservative Party may not have tried to turn the clock back by purging mothers from the labour market, what it has done is refuse to look the clock in the face and tell the time. It does not represent the typical working woman, who is – or may be or has been – a mother and a wage-earner. And insofar as it invokes the principles of the welfare state, it assumes a welfare state founded upon a model family that is no longer – if it ever was – typical. In several speeches Margaret Thatcher restates, with irony and with pride, the values embodied in the Beveridge plan upon which welfarism was based. It assumed the economic dependence of women. And so does Margaret Thatcher.

Carry on crusading

Among its many failures, one of Thatcherism's most marked and yet least remarked upon was its failure to create a 'moral majority'. Its moral agenda was characterised as much by silences as by speeches, by its abstentions as by its interventions. For sure, Thatcherism created an aura in which the moral rearmers enjoyed some ministerial endorsement, but that begs the question: were the moral rearmers a moral majority?

Norman Tebbit's moral crusade of the mid-1980s can be seen as an attempt to recreate Thatcherism's historic achievement of the 1970s: the unification of monetarism and moralism which reunited the party. Tebbit tried to repeat history in the 1980s by revamping Sir Keith Joseph's 1970s assault on the 1960s.

Delivering the first Disraeli lecture in 1985, he offered 'a vision of society profoundly more in keeping with the character of the British people'. He prefaced his programme for Britain's economic renewal through tax cuts, expansion of share-ownership and eradicating state subsidy, with the promise that

> at the front of that campaign for a return to traditional values of decency and order will be the Conservative Party, for we understand, as does no other party, that the defence of freedom involves a defence of the values which make freedom possible without its degeneration into license.

In 1986 before a congregation at St James's Church, Piccadilly, he expanded his theme:

> a large part of the difficulties Britain has had to contend with over the last six years really has its roots in the 1960s. Those were the years when relative economic decline and the trend towards spending and borrowing which we could not afford dug deep in our nation's life. The debasement of currency has run parallel to the debasement of standards.

He located that debasement in

> what Roy Jenkins and others thought marked a triumph of civilised behaviour – the permissive society. Legislation on capital punishment, homosexuality, abortion, censorship and divorce – some of it good, some of it bad, but all of it applauded as 'progressive' ushered in quick succession an overwhelming impression that there were not only going to be no legal constraints, but that there was no need for restraint at all.[28]

From this, society slipped towards sympathetic tolerance of the wrong itself. 'Love for the sinner slipped into love for the sin.'

And yet, there were no significant legislative reprisals against the progressive guerrillas of the 1960s. Despite some successful skirmishes, the contras could not mount a coherent legislative counter-revolution because they had no clear mandate even within Thatcherism. Thatcherism's re-unification of the right around a moral-economic matrix disguised what was perhaps only a tactical realignment within the party. The theory may have mollified the party's authoritarian right, but action would have risked revolt, not least among Tory women. However evasive about the role of women, Thatcherism's moral authoritarianism, expressed by Sir Keith Joseph and Norman Tebbit, certainly implied the incarceration of women in a separate – and dependent – sphere from which they were already on the run.

The limits of Tebbit's appeal to women lay not only in the way that he appeared dry to the point of dehydration, but in his patriarchal stream of consciousness, revealed in the raw when the musings of the Family Policy Group, a Cabinet committee, were leaked in 1983. Tebbit was one of its members and reckoned that one way to solve the problem of unemployment was to get women out of the labour market. That view was by then unsayable in public.

One prospective Parliamentary candidate, for example, agreed to accept Norman Tebbit as a speaker in the constituency only on condition that he did not go on about permissiveness and traditional values.

'I think all this moral crusading stuff by Norman Tebbit and the Victorian values stuff is just a cop-out for social problems,' complained a prominent Young Conservative, Jane Ellison, expressing a widely held disdain among Tory wets.

> It's just old-fashioned chauvinism. Tebbit sees himself as the great inheritor of the Thatcherite tradition. It's trying to seek easy explanations for the problems that British society has, like inner-city degeneration, the riots, rising crime, that sort of thing. They've never gone as far as defining what they mean by the permissive society. It is just assumed that people know what they mean. The tenor that Tebbit tends to hit, anti-sloppy morals, anti-sloppy attitudes, get on your bike, tighten your belt, it's just looking for easy answers. I don't happen to view the permissive society as the source of all our ills. Instead they should be admitting that they've been in power and that although the government isn't totally responsible, it is partly responsible. They need to look at where policy went wrong, they should be transferring the centre of debate to what the

real causes are. Instead it's just an exchange of clichés,
Thatcher and Tebbit saying sloppy morals, Kinnock saying
unemployment, bad housing, as if people had no responsibility
for their own actions.

As Tebbit closed in on the 1960s he closed down a potential
alliance with women, because although he might have appeared to
sing the traditional right-wing woman's refrain, he was only doing
his thing; he was speaking the prejudices of the public bar, the
patriarchy of the pub. Whatever else it might have been, that was
never the culture of Conservative women. And even when women
tried their best to support his standards, their own pain bled into
the argument and coloured it red with another kind of rage.

'Return to traditional values? Oh yes!' declared a well-off Birmingham housewife, Sue Lake, a teenager during the 1960s who enjoyed
her memories of sharing flats, the Beatles and swinging London:

> The family unit again and helping your friends. These days
> the family is so split up. Tradition is what keeps a home happy
> and ticking over. Abortion? I had one when I was young, it
> should be allowed if a child isn't going to have a good life,
> but otherwise it's wrong. Sex is too easy; but on the other hand
> there was so much hypocrisy about Victorian values, I don't
> want the Victorian way of life – those poor scullery maids,
> upstairs downstairs. But people were happier then, they
> didn't want anything, I suppose because there was nothing to
> have.

This was a very angry woman, angry with black people, angry
about homosexuality ('AIDS is the best thing that's happened to
them, at least it'll keep them with one partner'); angry about crime,
strikes, social security ('They'll pay all your standing orders, it's
terrible'); angry about schools ('This country is so shabby. What
would impress me now is more discipline in the schools, it's education that is the crux of everything. School uniform! There's no
discipline'). She was angry about everything, and about her own life
perhaps most of all:

> Our husbands work very hard, we see very little of them. I get
> very dissatisfied. It was hell with the kids when they were small,

I felt so deprived, I hated it and cried at night, I loathed it. But when I think about my poor husband slaving away, whereas we women have a lot more freedom . . .

She plays squash every day . . .

But of course he's meeting people all the time. I do moan though. I've resented it that I couldn't get my job back after I had the kids. My kids are at public school because that's the finest way of educating children and because in the long run we'll be kept together as a family.

Traditional values appeared to Marjorie Williams, a middle-aged lingerie saleswoman living in the Borders, as 'jolly good, but not as far as women are concerned, because women were downtrodden'. She saw herself as a tough Tory, but unlike Tebbit felt that the legal changes had been 'good for women, because now they can decide whether to stay with a man. The abortion law is wonderful. A woman should have an abortion if she wants to.' In any case she believed that the legal changes affecting personal relationships 'happened because women were asserting themselves. Women themselves brought those changes about.'

Though most of the women I interviewed shared Tebbit's angst about education, safety in the streets and personal responsibility – they wouldn't be Tories if they didn't – there was little sense that they endorsed his tone, his animus against the progressive legislation or his preoccupation with permissiveness. Yet within the party structures they appeared not to have taken him on. That absence of challenge was a function not of political support, however, but of the party's structure. The rest of the world might have been forgiven for assuming that Tebbit had picked up the gauntlet thrown down by the Conservative women decades earlier, that his agenda was the women's agenda, that he was thinking their thoughts. He wasn't.

Emma Nicholson wasn't surprised that women didn't go for Tebbit's crusade:

Conservative women are very realistic, they're nearer the ground, they're in the Citizens' Advice Bureaux, they're on the bench dealing with delinquents, they're not ladies in kid gloves eating cucumber sandwiches, they're not distanced from life, they're at the sharp end of life. Many political pronouncements are taken with a pinch of salt.

No sex please, we're British?

Part of the problem about deciphering the attitudes of Conservative women to permissiveness and sexuality is that they are *assumed* to be represented by the anti-permissive crusades of the moral right. But are they? Can we simply read off Conservative women's feelings from the pronouncements of the populists on the right? It's as if we think we know what they think without asking them – and that goes for the right as much as the left. But conversations with Conservative women show that they are more diverse and pluralistic than we might assume. It is one thing to assemble the tracts of the new moralists and call them an ideology; it is quite another to suggest that this ideology is hegemonic. What is more likely is that the vocabulary of puritanism may codify discontents that find no political expression elsewhere. But the question remains: did the puritan populism of the 1980s describe the sexual politics of the modern Conservative woman? Did it express her desires as well as her disappointments?

The answer is that it did not. But it still remains important to find out why the moral rearmers enjoyed resonance among many women and yet did not represent many more.

What is our image of the Conservative woman as a sexual person? Has the stereotype been so unqualified that Tory women are seen rather like the Queen – we assume there are some things they don't do?

One woman who comes to mind is in her seventies, Dorothy Love. At one time she was a Conservative committee woman in a Border town but she's given that up, although she still enjoys going to the Soroptimists. She is a tough Tory who hates scroungers and vandals and communists. Her hair is a bold bob, barely changed since the 1940s, which became very stylish again in the 1980s. She hasn't liked her life much, despite all the appearances of middle-class respectability:

> I regret my education, because if you were a girl you were just pushed over, I was just ignored. And in my family my sister

was the beauty. I was the ugly duckling – that spoilt my life.
And I had three brothers who kept me down, I had to fight
that. I'd never been out to work, because we were brought up
as ladies of leisure – my father was in business, you see. I
thought about having a job, but my husband said, 'You could
never get a job!' So I got dressed up and I went out and got
myself a job for six weeks over Christmas to prove that I could.

The bravest thing she felt she ever did was to divorce her husband:
'I'd been brought up not to feel good about myself, and I didn't
until I stood on my own two feet and left my husband. Something
kept saying to me "Dorothy don't", because I couldn't face old age
with him.' Since then she takes tea alone or with women friends in
department stores. She wears good coats, good shoes and good
corsets, although these days no one sees or feels her big body. This
is a matter of some regret to her and so I like to think that sometimes
she sees and feels and pleases herself.

She has strong views about standards:

These young girls having babies to get a home; they get it all
on the DHSS, and then they have another. Children today are
just wanting to get out and live in flats. We didn't have flats in
our day and the council shouldn't be paying out all this
money. My attitude is you can't expect everything from the
taxpayer, you've got to go out and earn it. That film *ET* just
proved how indifferent the modern mother is: she just packed
the fridge with food, there was no discipline and ET was
there but she didn't know! Standards are going down. I'd never
dreamt it would be like this. I don't know who's to blame –
it's the mothers going out to work too early!

About the Abortion Act she had equally strong views:

If you don't want a baby you shouldn't have to have one. I've
had personal experience of this. I was pregnant and I couldn't
face it because it was during the war. The doctor was going to
do it and he let me go four months, which he shouldn't have.
But I didn't know anything about these things. The pain! And
the baby was formed! I was climbing the wall with the pain.
They had to wrap up the baby and burn it and the doctor had

to put his hand right up to get the afterbirth. It was a terrible experience. Sex was never mentioned in those days, everything was hushed up. If you don't want a baby I don't see why a man should dictate to you that you should.

And about sex itself: 'Sex has got more vulgar today, whereas it was sweet in our day. I enjoyed my sex even though I didn't love my husband.' One of the most pleasurable memories in this woman's life was a brief romance enjoyed while on a holiday cruise with her mother. There she met a widower, also middle aged and also with his mother. 'Oh, it was marvellous,' she said. 'We didn't do anything, but we did enjoy ourselves.' She brought out photographs of a fancy-dress ball aboard ship, in which she was being carried over his shoulder.

'I can't wait until I'm an old lady with a string of very unsuitable and very young lovers,' said a civil servant, Lorna Walters. No puritanism in her. And Marjorie Williams relished her daughter's attitude: 'My daughter – she's a Conservative, too – doesn't mind sharing her bed with a man but she doesn't want to share the bathroom or the kitchen with them. And she'd expect him to be a good cook. Very good. But I don't expect she'll find one. I'll have to knit her one.'

Perhaps surprising, given the preconceptions about Conservative women as puritans, was some of the women's disappointed desire, regrets about their own sexual histories. A retired shopkeeper said:

It's good that sex is more open these days. It was probably the war that did it, because women just went off and had affairs – this was the beginning of the change, I think. My mother never talked about sex or contraception, so I was completely ignorant about everything. I was a virgin when I got married. My husband was very keen to take my virginity away. I even slept with him, but I wouldn't let him touch me. Quite frankly, the first time, it just didn't mean a thing to me, and I didn't get anything out of sex until I was pregnant. The point is you are giving in to the men and I ask myself why, why? You worried all the time about getting pregnant. And then when I got pregnant I had my first orgasm and I'm sure it was because I didn't have all the worry about pregnancy.

Hidden in her cynicism were strong feelings about her own desire, her own longings which weren't respected:

Men like to say no to you, they want to belittle you and keep
you as the little woman. Men just like to dominate and get
the better of you. The trouble is that a woman depends on a
man for sexual satisfaction. When you're in your twenties
you need him. After all, you've been uprooted from your own
family, you're alone and sex is terribly important – you only
want to please him. So you don't think of yourself, you don't
seek what you need, and they probably play on that. My
husband did. I was fit and well and wanted sex more than
he did actually. Not that he didn't want me, I know he did.
It probably required all his power to refuse me. But he
shunned me, so I was belittled. I was very strong though. But
you're hurt and when they next make up to you you're so
grateful.

It was the problem of power which made retired businesswoman Betty Zikel resistant to adolescent sexual affairs: 'I think
the girls today, if only they knew, they wouldn't be bothered, because it's just giving the men satisfaction, and I wonder why we
should.'
Former secretary Barbara Stone has teenage daughters of her
own and feels somewhat the same:

Girls get less pleasure. There are millions of women who don't
like it. Maybe I've got that blockage too. I know when my daughter
is doing it and I wish she wasn't, I don't like it. Now why is
that? Maybe I don't really like sex, or maybe it's about not
liking the sex we've been getting. It's to do with violation and
privacy being infringed, and thinking I have no rights over
my own body. It's about exploitation, that's where my pain for
my daughter comes from, because the chances are she's
being exploited.

Several women spoke of their own experience of thwarted
pleasure. 'I lived with someone who didn't cuddle,' said divorced
countrywoman, Susan Maynard. 'He didn't want to make love to
me and of course I felt it was my fault. It's because women must

nurture everyone else but you don't get any support yourself. Men can be very selfish.'

I cite these comments drawn from personal histories because they indicate Conservative women's commitment to pleasure, not only in the generalised, romantic terms we have come to expect from women like Barbara Cartland, but in ways that touch both optimism and pessimism which are the weave of women's common sense. There is not only flight, fear and distaste; there is passion and desire.

Additionally women are visiting their sense of sexual humiliation and disappointment upon their daughters. After all, they wonder, what's new, what's changed in men's treatment of women? It is, of course, an utterly pessimistic view of sexual relationships but nonetheless one that is grounded in real experience. Even where they argue that girls aren't mature enough to handle sexual relationships, there is another meaning: that sexual relationships require stamina that they don't demand from boys. The implication is that boys get what they want and girls don't.

Victoria Gillick

Victoria Gillick's campaign in the 1980s against girls' access to contraception without parental consent, and against the Department of Health and Social Security which sanctioned their access, was the stuff that Thatcherism was made of. Did it succeed where Norman Tebbit failed? Ironically, it exposed the fragility of Thatcherism as a moral coalition. Although Victoria Gillick's campaign echoed the language of Thatcherism, the government and elements of the Establishment (in defence of their own professional autonomy) opposed her. The case is stressed here because it is a paradigm of the contradictions within right-wing sexual populism. It is important because it revealed the state of support not only for the Gillick campaign but also for the moralism of Thatcherism.

Victoria Gillick's campaign called up the social purity movement of the nineteenth century and thus appeared to connect with a pro-woman culture of sexual dissent. The assertion of mother-power and of mothers' responsibility to save their daughters from sex and the state also appeared to connect her to an earlier anti-statist feminist tradition. But we shall see how her dissent was smothered by acquiescence in women's sexual subordination. Despite her claim to some continuity with feminist antecedents, her campaign also split her from both contemporary left-wing feminism and from what could be seen as a conservative feminism. From the comments of her supporters and opponents, we shall see how both derived their stance from diverse tributaries of women's common sense, a critical common sense which resists the domination of women by men: for some that is expressed as a quest for pleasure, a commitment to women as active sexual subjects; for others it takes the form of that weary complaint that men are beasts who are best denied. All those positions saw themselves as being in some sense pro-women – but does that make them feminist?

The Gillick case is an arresting example of the breach within Conservatism between the consciousness of the party women's organisation in the 1980s and the Tory women's tradition. It is often assumed that Tory women supported Victoria Gillick; in fact the women's organisation did not, and that distanced modern Conservative women from earlier traditions in which their consciousness was coded by the moral rearmers. In the Gillick case, Conservative women were in the mainstream and distanced themselves from the authoritarian right.

Finally, Victoria Gillick's campaign will be considered as a classic case of authoritarian populism, which (just) failed to become hegemonic in British politics.

Like the government she was criticising, Victoria Gillick built her case around potent symbols of power and powerlessness. And, like the government, she consecrated a new political subject, the *parent*. Parents were established as heroic, solitary and innocent individuals ranged against a collective enemy: *experts*. Experts were lined up, in her scenario, as a new Establishment, aided and abetted by a self-interested state. Instead of the state being threatened by anarchic libertines, as in the 1960s, she imagined a new power bloc: a libertarian civil society, the state and a new Establishment of experts, organised against the 'natural rights' of parents, who were thus, of course, represented as being outside political society.

Victoria Gillick began her career with 'Parents in Suffolk' and produced a particularly paranoid representation of the fate of parents, particularly mothers, as an organic community besieged on the one hand by their charges, children, and on the other by expert enemies. 'Experts and Caring Professionals' had finally 'harangued and bamboozled parents into taking a backseat in family life'.[29] Parenthood had been 'encroached upon by "interested" outsiders'.[30] Valiant mothers had vanquished the patriarchs of the nineteenth century only to find themselves under the paternal authority of the state:

> They used to laugh at, and deride the Victorian attitude that placed the Father in total authority over his wife, and his children also . . . They welcomed the emancipation of women and wives, and their equal responsibility for the welfare and happiness of their children. Yet by the 1970s they had happily embraced the notion that the State itself could once again take on that authoritarian mantle, and dictate to children how they should behave, even while they were under 16; thus once again reducing the status and role of mothers.[31]

She was alerted to historical precedent by the Salvation Army, which supported her campaign, and put her on to Josephine Butler's campaign against the Contagious Diseases Act over 100 years ago – which the Salvation Army had also supported then. Gillick writes herself into the historical continuum by comparing the state's attempts to curb venereal disease by regulating prostitutes in the late nineteenth century with the state's attempt to curb teenage pregnancies among girls under sixteen by permitting contraception: both are represented as coercion. (Except, of course, that the Contagious Diseases Act did attempt to regulate and control the behaviour only of women, while the DHSS regulations modestly facilitated young women's access to contraception.)

Commenting on a letter from a Christian mother who suggested that 'due to the evil that is in the world not all parents honour that responsibility and in those circumstances obviously provision must be made to ensure that children of such parents are properly protected', Gillick argued that 'unfortunately the State has moved on – if it ever was stationary – from the idea of "protecting" children in the way *that* kind mother suggested, to "controlling" them'.[32] The state, through the schools, had 'taken it upon themselves to be the vehicles for social change and policy. They preach health education and political principles every day in class: condemning smoking, drinking, drug-taking, nuclear warfare, unprotected sex and repressive parents.'[33] And since 'most parents, apparently, do *not* talk to their children about sex and most schools *do* and yet are now witnessing a "copulation explosion" then the conclusion must be "let the cap fit where it may"'.

Gillick argued that the DHSS regulations and sex education in schools together represented coercion, but more important, both constituted state interference in mothers' prerogatives to protect their daughters from the fall:

> Like Victorian women, mothers today know all too well that what we need in our present state of sexual delinquency is 'wiser teaching' – and wiser parents! Children need care and protection at any age and *in* any age. They do *not* need drugs, provided free at public expense, and dispensed in secret to them by the medical profession. Hard cases need *good* laws – not expedient medical remedies. Let the state put its own shaky house in order before it presumes to intrude upon the territory of others.[34]

Instead of the mother who knows best, children have been lumbered with 'the "Nanny-State"-knows-best dictum'.[35]

The argument against the state camouflaged Gillick's case against sex itself. She posed the bad state against the good mother – an inversion of the line used against her: the good state intervening against the bad mother. It is the good mother who stands alone, defending her territory against the state and the sex industry – and even fathers. Sexual abuse of children 'within families is said to be one of the horrible manifestations of the present generation of adult perversions'.[36] But these were not a problem of the patriarchal family; they are in her view a function of permissive politics. 'The fathers involved in such abuses were themselves young boys in the swinging Sixties.'[37]

The Gillick crusade echoed the tone of Thatcherism's relationship to parents: they were celebrated and chided in the same moment. Culpable for 'declining standards' they were also its victims; they were blamed and yet pitied. The gods, like the state, turned against them and visited the sins of the children upon the parents.

In all this, where were the children? It was parents who were the subjects of the crusade – it was their campaign after all – while the children were merely its object, seen, suspected, but speechless. Despite the centrality of children to the debate, it is never really

clear whether Gillick spoke for them or for herself – whether she
saw any distinction between the alleged asexuality of children and
herself as a woman, or whether the evidence of children's sexuality
rose up and confronted whatever was unresolved in that of the
woman. She declared, after losing round one of her bout against
the DHSS in the courts, that there was no one to protect her
children 'from themselves as well as from others'.[38]

Reflecting on the space given and yet simultaneously denied to
the child in Gillick's discourse, I was drawn into Jacqueline Rose's
inspired study of *Peter Pan* which asks where lies the origin of the
claim that the book 'represents the child, speaks to and for children,
addresses them as a group which is knowable and exists for the
book, much as the book (so the claim runs) exists for them'.[39] In
the glorification of childhood in *Peter Pan*, as 'a primitive or lost
state to which the child has special access',[40] there is not only 'a
refusal to acknowledge the difficulties and contradictions in relation
to childhood; it implies that we *use* the image of the child to deny
those same difficulties in relation to ourselves'.[41]

Rose points out that *Peter Pan* was written at the time of Freud,
who disrupted notions of childhood, the acquisition of language and
sexuality, and above all dislocated the idea of childhood as a lost
state of innocence, since it lives on in our unconscious and is
therefore a state which is not autonomous from adulthood. It is only
the beginning, part of the process, of becoming human.

Victoria Gillick and her allies are organised against these discover-
ies. For them the child has neither speech nor sexuality of its own.
It is the girl, of course, who is the primary object for the crusaders
obsessed with sex – like the predators from whose seductions they
seek to protect her. They're all obsessed with the body of the girl:
they watch her, they guard her, they talk about her all the time.
They all want to possess her. In the name of anti-statism Gillick
even went so far as to mobilise the authority of the state against
her own daughters' desires. Daughters, unlike sons, were to be
compelled to confess their desire, to make their private lives public
to their parents, and thus to be purged of their sin. No way was all
this about innocence – it spoke a sense of childhood steaming with
overwhelming sexual desire.

The Gillick campaign also visits upon the girl a premonition of
what will become her sexuality as a woman. In white western culture
it exists only insofar as she is desired. Having no self-determining

desire of her own, apparently, it is only when she is desired that she becomes a desiring woman, and therefore also dependent. Victoria Gillick's revolt is against this vortex of desire and destruction.

Having denied the sexuality of the child, it follows in the demonology of the Gillick campaign that sexual desire is what marks the break between the innocence of childhood and the corruption of adulthood. How does she describe this desire? Victoria Gillick has little to say about sex as such, but her view of its impact on the girl is devastating:

> It is certainly one of the saddest things, that so many amongst the Women's Liberation Movement have failed to understand this crucial point. That in every society that encourages, or condones, or expects its young females to be engaged in sexual relationships – whether inside marriage or out of it – the status and education of those girls falls behind the males. In our western society, where this retrograde step is compounded by promiscuity, not only do the girls suffer through loss of educational and social advantage, but the males . . . grow ever more irresponsible, and yes – violent towards the community in which they roam, uncontrolled.[42]

She believes that men have been doing women over since Adam.

While femininity is set up as the mirror of childhood, a state of innocence, a blank page, masculinity is represented as raw, corrupt, 'incontinent'. Wendy Hollway has reminded us that our ideas about the male sex drive, which we see as biological, primitive, promiscuous and dangerous, are so familiar that they have become hegemonic; they are the *dominant* discourse, everywhere in common sense and legitimated by experts'.[43]

Gillick is no madwoman in the attic. She echoes the commonsense culture of women as we have heard it expressed year after year in kitchens and at Conservative Party women's conferences, not to mention Women's Liberation consciousness-raising groups, that men and boys are bad. She also speaks the despair and disappointment of millions of women. Lest there be any doubt, Gillick goes further than this exposition of the disorder and disorientation sexuality spreads in the girl's life. For 100 years Parliament offered legal protection to the young, she says, and by and large these laws reflect the commonly held view that, for girls, the sexual act was a disaster in every way. She was physically not able to endure it and would be badly damaged by prolonged or brutal intercourse. Emotionally it would disorientate her; casting her both as woman and child at the same time.[44]

What is this dread of the child who is also a woman? Is not the woman also a child? Aren't we all? And is not the fate of the child the fate of the woman also? Why is the sexual act a disaster for one and destiny for the other? It is the moment of desire which marks the girl's transition to womanhood, and that Victoria Gillick seeks to defer: desire is seen as the moment of her creation as a woman and her destruction. Her destiny is her doom.

Does Victoria Gillick the woman feel that the sexual act is only 'prolonged or brutal intercourse'? I think she does. And her complaint is commonplace in the culture of women – we've all been there! That is why it is not enough to consign her to the loony right or to religious mania. For sure, it is not insignificant that Victoria Gillick is a Roman Catholic and that other moral rearmers are devout Christians, among whom the crisis of female sexuality is resolved, as it was among an earlier generation of feminists, in chastity and motherhood. Adult women's sexuality is a silence in the ideology of moral rearmament, it speaks only in maternity: the married woman is the angel in the house, the sexless saint, the mother with power only over her children.

All the significant popular studies of sexual activity in the twentieth century have discovered an epidemic of displeasure among women. The latest is *The Hite Report* which found that

intercourse by itself did not regularly lead to orgasms. What we thought was an individual problem is neither unusual nor a problem. In other words *not* to have orgasm from intercourse is the experience of the majority of women.[45]

Expressing a Women's Liberationist critique of the relationship between sexual pleasure and power, Hite argues that

the pattern of sexual relations predominant in our culture exploits and oppresses women, the sequence of 'foreplay',

'penetration' and 'intercourse' (defined as thrusting), followed
by male orgasm as the climax and end of the sequence gives
very little chance for female orgasm, is almost always under
the control of the man, frequently teases the woman
inhumanly and in short, has institutionalised out any expression
of women's sexual feelings except those that support male
needs.[46]

Victoria Gillick operates inside all that disappointment, which
Women's Liberation identifies as not so much a problem of ignorance or innocence but a problem of *power*. Gillick's campaign to
protect camouflages a *protest* on behalf of women against their own
sexual distress and powerlessness. Ultimately she is also into power
because she works with patriarchal power. Pessimistic and paranoid,
she is stuck inside the patriarchal paradigm.

Victoria Gillick covers her tracks − as long as her protest is on
behalf of the child she never has to speak her despair or her desire
as a woman. Implicit in her campaign to protect her daughters from
themselves is there not also an admission that women must protect
themselves from their own impossible desires? Doesn't the daughter
confront the mother with her own unresolved history? This collision
brings psychoanalysis into the conversation because it

directs its attention to what cannot be spoken in what is actually
being said. It starts from the assumption that there is a difficulty
in language, that in speaking to others we might be speaking
against ourselves, or at least against that part of ourselves
which would rather remain unspoken.[47]

Her protest is redirected against the sexuality of both girls and
women. Nowhere is there any sense of women having desire that is
not dependent and self-destructive; no sense that girls and women
may make love to themselves and to each other; that women might
design a different sexual culture among themselves and among men.
In other words, she does not contemplate the possibility that women
don't have to be *defeated* by desire. She sets herself against modern
feminism (although she is in a certain feminist tradition herself) for
throwing girls into the lions' den. But Women's Liberation, on the
contrary, sought not protection but political challenge; it sought
to re-think and re-make both masculinity and femininity. The

differences between the two mirror those between different femi-
nisms in the nineteenth century, and certainly between the Women's
Liberation Movement and the social purity movement 100 years
earlier. From the perspective of the modern women's movement,
Judith Walkowitz, who has written a classic study of prostitution and
the social purity campaigns, concludes that the latter's

> attack on patriarchy and male vice involved no positive assertion
> of female sexuality. It was still couched within the terms of
> a 'separate sphere' ideology and assumed that women were
> essentially moral, 'spiritual' creatures who needed to be
> protected from essentially animalistic, 'carnal' men.[48]

Today the conservative almost-but-not-quite feminism epitomised by Gillick is turned against the liberationist feminist critique.
However much they might share some sense of patriarchal power,
the conservative crusaders are imprisoned within it; for them it is
historically and biologically inevitable. Women's Liberation, however, adheres to Simone de Beauvoir's immortal thesis that there is
no biological *essence*; that 'woman is not born she is made', and that
therefore she may make her own history.

Protecting girls from men

The significance of Victoria Gillick lay partly in the pleasure for
some women of seeing another woman having a go, like Mary
Whitehouse or Brookside's Sheila Grant or Tina Turner – or
Margaret Thatcher. A Northern county councillor Frances Bowden,
with a teenage daughter, reckoned, 'She's terrific! She stood up for
what she believed in against all those bitchy men.' Another of
Victoria Gillick's admirers was a reluctant grandmother, a suave
woman in her sixties, her grey hair cropped in a sculptured 1980s
bob, her eyes restless, roaming for recognition that she is beautiful –
and she is – and yet evasive because that quest means she can't
concentrate. That's my guess anyway. She's a great talker. And she
can tango. But that takes two and like the late Dora Russell she
believes that the trouble is that men won't co-operate. She first slept
with a man when she was a teenager; she's had abortions; she's
desired men, and yet in her desire she's felt endangered – it gave
men power. And so,

> A girl should remain a virgin as long as she can rather than

giving men their satisfaction. Mrs Gillick is protecting girls from men, I truly feel it. I believe the pill is deadly. Why should a girl change the metabolism of her body just for men?

A Birmingham mother of sons, who knows they watch blue videos and says she doesn't mind, whose household buys the *Sun*, and who buys her husband the Pirelli calendar every year for his depot, says she is uncertain: 'Oh, I don't know. I don't really agree with her, but some terrible things happen, incest and such a lot of sexual abuse.'

'I know I probably look like a dissolute wreck; I was on the pill when I was sixteen – I probably had the last childhood,' said a Cumbrian civil servant in her early thirties, who has stayed resolutely single *and* sexually active:

> The trouble is that when you're on the pill there's no reason
> to say no to a bloke, it's terrible. You're sexually immature
> for a long time, and to be bullied and harried into sex is terrible.
> The girls probably do come off worst.

'I admire her for fighting for something she believes in and I also support her views because otherwise we are condoning an illegal act. We should keep it illegal to have sex under sixteen because girls are not mature enough to handle it,' said Frances Bowden. Did she think boys were too immature at that age for sex too?

> I just think it is very difficult for girls now. The pill has opened
> women up to all sorts of pressures from men to have sex. It
> is acceptable to a far greater degree now for people to have sex
> outside marriage and that's a good thing. But the sex act for
> women is a much more emotional thing than for most men.
> What boys and girls get out of it is different, and girls aren't
> mature enough to handle it. It's very difficult. I've tried to
> explain what I feel to my own daughter, but she says, why
> should she ask permission? It's my life, she says. I said it's
> dangerous to be on the pill, and emotionally they're not
> mature. I don't think anyone has the answer – these things
> have always been going on. It's the same with homosexuality:
> since they changed the law, more have gone that way. I
> understand it and I accept it, but since they've changed the law

some have gone that way who should have been straight. I'd understand it if a child of mine was homosexual, though I'd not be 100 per cent happy. But sex and girls – I don't think it gives them respect for their bodies.

Mature enough to handle what, though? Pleasure? Or pain? Why is lack of self-respect invoked here? Of course, we know that loss, theft, conquest are inscribed in the way common sense captures the meaning of the 'sexual act' for young women, and it is that, in part, which encourages many women to identify with Victoria Gillick. But their solidarity with her puritanism does not exhaust their sexual politics.

All the women quoted above were supporters of the Abortion Act – some have had abortions themselves – and of the concept of women's right to choose. There is no sense in which they could all be coralled into the conservative crusade on all the issues that matter to the moral right: marriage, abortion, homosexuality, reproductive technology. What animated their support for Gillick was not always to do with control, not much to do with the medical profession, but *everything* to do with their feelings about women and men and the sense that a strong *feminine* identity could be defeated by sex and men.

Self-respect is central to Angela Hills' sense of Conservative values. This prominent member of the Young Conservatives is an admirer of the political stance of the assassinated John F. Kennedy, if not of his personal life, and of the black South African revolutionary, Winnie Mandela: 'I don't agree with everything she says, but as a woman she's led an exemplary life. She's undergone a lot of hassle and harassment and kept her dignity through it all.' It is her commitment to self-respect which makes her support Victoria Gillick's campaign: 'People should have a more responsible attitude to sex, because it should be special, if you share your body with someone it should be someone you trust and respect and not just anybody. A lot of girls go into sexual relationships because they're pressurised to.'

But ultimately, Conservative women divided according to whether they felt Gillick was for women's *pleasure* as well as *protection*, and what they felt about the power of parents. What to many women seemed like maternal megalomania prompted them to disavow her.

'I saw Mrs Gillick on TV and I thought anyone who has so many children has something wrong – that's a punishment,' said London businesswoman with teenage children, Leah Hertz:

> Parents find it very difficult to cope with children, and once they've had sex you've lost them. An intelligent woman can't say she loves her child because it comes out of her vagina; she loves them because they're around. I feel responsible for mine, I'm their guardian, but you've got to be realistic. I'm concerned about their physical safety, and I always know where they are and who with, but when it comes to sex they're free agents. Show me a parent who's won any battle on sex. And even if you win, you've lost them.

Lorna Walters, a Cumbrian civil servant, single and close to her own mother who lives nearby, reckoned that Victoria Gillick 'seems to think her children are *hers*, but children aren't property'.

'Damnable woman', was how one London borough councillor described her. 'What bothers me is the way the biological fact of motherhood has such an influence on everything in a woman's life.'

Yorkshire magistrate Pam Smith went with a coterie of Conservative women active in the party's women's organisation to check out Victoria Gillick in person when she addressed a public meeting: 'She should sit through some sessions in one of my juvenile courts,' she muttered. 'I'm disappointed she's so blinkered – like a 125 train, she's obsessive. In my juvenile court you see the problems of the inner cities and you realise her approach is just not possible. Young people can't all relate to their parents, they've got to have a third person.'

For all the appearances of popular support, the organisations associated with Conservative women have found the Gillick campaign difficult. The Mothers Union, for example, the largest Christian women's movement in Britain, was deeply divided on the campaign and took no position on it when contrary resolutions were brought to its 1984 annual conference. Within the Conservative Party itself the women's organisation came out in opposition to the campaign. The Greater London women's committee, which takes policy-making seriously and regularly carries out its own research before formulating new policies, prepared a paper on Gillick, and the Conservative National Women's Committee set up a working party on the campaign which concluded after its success in the

Appeal Court but before its rejection by the Law Lords 'that a situation comparable to that of abortion before the 1967 Act was passed is developing'. The law on the age of consent 'is a very difficult law to impose if people wish to avoid it', and although they felt that society should dissuade children from breaking the law, the effect of the Appeal Court's ruling, in backing Gillick, was that in some areas contraceptives were available to under sixteens while in others they had not been. For the children under sixteen who did have sexual relationships, the working party believed that the medical profession should be free to give advice and practical help. But they went even further in recognising teenagers' privacy:

> Parents should consider their responsibilities to their under-age children and decide whether it is appropriate to provide their family doctor with a letter of consent to the provision of contraceptives.

Even though Victoria Gillick believed in her 'heart of hearts, that if the public were ever asked to vote on this, 90 per cent at least, would have given the thumbs down to the DHSS guidelines that had been causing all the devious and divisive problems for parents and children',[49] her heart was wrong. According to a Harris poll in 1984, the biggest category of parents – 45 per cent – felt that the guidelines should be retained. Margaret Thatcher was known to have been sympathetic to Victoria Gillick, Kenneth Clarke – the father of a teenage daughter at the time – was opposed, although a former Health Minister, Gerard Vaughan, was a firm supporter of the Responsible Society–Family and Youth Concern, the organisation which worked closely with Gillick. The judiciary was divided, but the professional bodies were all opposed, because the Gillick judgment interfered with their professional autonomy.

What the whole campaign exposed was the fragility of Thatcherism as a moral force, not least because in the end Thatcherism was too internally unstable fully to endorse it. And what it also revealed, therefore, was the well-hidden breach between the party's women's organisation and its own traditions – after all the women's associations had always been the keepers of the far right's moral conscience. By the 1980s they may still have seen themselves in this role, but this no longer positioned them on the far right.

Why it failed

Clearly, Victoria Gillick's campaign disturbed the right's relationship to women. But it was also resonant among women outside the right, so that support and opposition cannot be explained solely in the language of left and right. Nor would it be adequate to locate Gillick's motivations solely in her Roman Catholicism or her far-right connections. Searchlight, the intrepid monitor of the far right, reported the Gillicks to have been involved with the pro-Enoch Powell group Powellight, and this prompted speculation as to her possibly eugenicist and racist views about reproduction. However, I have also heard her protest that family planning is being used against poor working-class and Third World women. Nevertheless, she gathered around her a powerful coalition of dogged conservative crusaders who trespassed across class and gender thresholds in a way that made her a classic case of what Stuart Hall has designated 'authoritarian populism'. He draws on the work of Antonio Gramsci, who theorised the way in which ideology may not simply be read off from the economic conditions of exploitation, and who mapped the contours of common sense in ideology, 'the uncritical and largely unconscious way of understanding the world that is common in any epoch'.[50]

Because he was primarily interested in the ideological architecture of subordination, Gramsci was concerned with the way that a group 'may for reasons of submission' assimilate borrowed concepts buried in common sense, which is itself a 'product of historical processes which have deposited in you an infinity of traces, without leaving an inventory'. When your conception of the world is a cluster of commonsense values, not critical and coherent but 'disjointed and episodic', then you find yourself belonging ideologically to a multiplicity of groups, with a multiplicity of political allegiances.[51] Common sense may imply stoicism, patience, resignation, but it also gives 'a conception of necessity which gives direction to one's activity'.

Victoria Gillick clearly deploys common sense in some of these ways. This has prompted uneasy debate in the Women's Liberation Movement which has seen not only the re-emergence of a counter-revolution against feminism in its own time, but the renaissance of feminist puritanism, too, in the wake of the sexual liberation associated with the 1960s. Discussing 'what we believe to be a conservative sexual politics' within feminism, Ellen DuBois and Linda Gordon explain that

we use a label like 'conservative' cautiously. Such terms, like
'right' and 'left' come to us from class politics. When applied
to sex and gender they fit less comfortably. The oppressions
of women, the repressions of sex, are so many and so complex
by virtue of their location in the most intimate corners of life,
co-existing even with love, that it is not always obvious in
which direction a better world lies. We use the term
'conservative' to characterise strategies that accept existing power
relations. We are suggesting that even feminist reform
programs can be conservative in some respects if they accept
male dominance while trying to elevate women's 'status' within
it.[52]

Victoria Gillick assumes just such a body of values, affirmed by
religion, to give meaning to the conditions in which women have
lived out traditional motherhood – conditions which have often been
impoverished, but within which women have often not only survived
their subordination but also made it their only reservoir of strength.
Gillick has recuperated that role, but she has taken it to be self-
evident and universal exactly at a moment in history when it has
been destabilised and challenged, primarily by women themselves.
   Certainly, although her campaign was organised by the right it
did not belong to the right. Her conception of motherhood has a
long history in common sense, and yet it is a history against which
women also have a counter-culture of commonsense subterfuge and
resistance. Her campaign rang bells in the discontents of many
women, but its pessimism, its authoritarianism and its criticisms of
women themselves dissipated its unifying potential.
   Again it is useful to return to the Gramscian tradition within
Marxism, which has theorised the distinction between the 'popular'
and the 'populist' in politics. Stuart Hall distinguishes between
popular politics which *empowers* The People, clarifies and intensifies
the contradictions and conflicts of interest within their society and
enables them to withdraw their consent from the dominant forces
within their society and to create their own political resources.[53] It
is the project of *popular* politics to establish mass consent, to become
hegemonic, to become *the* culture: in other words to constitute The
People as The Power.
   Can a politics be *popular* without empowering The People? No,
for then it is *populist*, and while appealing to the powerless, the little

people, against the powerful classes in the language of common sense, it aligns them not to the forces of resistance but to the powers that be.[54] It is in this sense that the Gillick campaign was populist rather than popular.

Unlike Norman Tebbit's crusade against permissiveness, and Margaret Thatcher's inept invocation of Victorian values, Gillick's campaign was almost a paradigm of populism. The medical authorities and the DHSS, the 'lunatic element on the fringes of socialist politics' and birth control agencies, and the 'Agonised Aunties' (a reference to the campaign against her by the Agony Aunts of the popular women's press), had become

> a part of the Establishment, itself, and its secular humanist philosophy. It was we, *the people*, who were now making all the running. They tried to say it was all the work of something called the Moral Majority – or the Moral Minority – or the Moral Right – or the Moral Backlash. But what they *didn't* call it, because they daren't, was what it really and truly was: the Will of the People.[55]

Although appearing to challenge the new Establishment, the Gillick campaign appealed for protection from a prior Establishment and – the ultimate irony – from the state itself. It was as if she were saying: Stand up and be a man, be a real state! Although she appeared to defend motherhood against all-comers, she actually defended the social structures which rendered motherhood subordinate. In the end, whatever were the 'popular' elements of her campaign, they were incompatible with her 'authoritarian populism'. And yet, as we have seen, it was the popular dissent among women against sexual powerlessness and disappointment which sustained the authoritarian discourse. Stuart Hall has theorised 'authoritarian populism' as a response to real and incurable contradictions, and certainly Gillick's campaign touched the raw nerves of the permissive era and the hard edge of patriarchal sex. She intervened in the space of sexuality in which Women's Liberation, too, has built its politics.

But in contrast to Victoria Gillick, Women's Liberation attempted to expose the contradictions of patriarchy, and in so doing reconstruct women not as objects but as sexual subjects. The Gillick campaign was a classic case of what Hall describes as a movement which organises to conserve the status quo, operating not just defensively but formatively to create a new alliance of force. However, it must do more than that. It

> must not just reflect the crisis but operate as a positive response
> to it. Its success *depends* on the extent to which it can translate
> old doctrines into the language of common experience,
> common sense, for an alternative ethic. The right's
> discourses work on popular feelings and philosophies among
> *dominated* elements of the people, and because this common
> sense does not have a fixed class belonging, it appears to
> transcend class or political allegiances. But its effect is to
> draw The People into a 'populist subject' which is *with* rather
> than *against* the dominant power bloc.[56]

The crusade which is generated creates unity with the power bloc rather than a rupture. That is what the conservative crusaders and Victoria Gillick failed to do – they neither created rupture nor unity with the dominant bloc, nor did they revive an alternative ethic. Asset-stripped motherhood shorn of moral authority and social esteem might be regarded as a job hardly worth having. Mrs Gillick might seem to have reached the fears that other parts of liberal, progressive and enlightened conservative consensus did not. But for two decades now the moral rearmers have been outmanoeuvred by other forces among women, still largely without any expression in party politics, which have ensured that it is no longer only the right which appears to speak the authentic voice of ordinary women.

8

EQUAL IN THE SIGHT OF GOD

There is far less general desire for equality (as opposed to equity) in Britain than is often claimed . . . the pursuit of equality is a mirage – *Margaret Thatcher*, 1975

Quite frankly I don't think mothers have the same right to work as fathers. If the good Lord had intended us to have equal rights to go out to work he wouldn't have created man and woman. These are biological facts – *Patrick Jenkin*, 1979

Everyone is equal in the sight of God. If you don't start from that position then I'm not with you – *Emma Nicholson*, 1985

Poor Patrick Jenkin – if ever a minister were doomed it was he. He was the government's 'dirty jobs' man. After being the man everyone loved to hate over social security, rate-capping and abolition of the metropolitan authorities, during which he was immortalised in the phrase 'doing a Jenkin', he was dumped. But the jinxed Jenkin had already reached immortality in his endorsement of the good Lord. In the context of Thatcherism's generic anti-egalitarianism, he confirmed many women's worst fears that everything the Conservatives were saying and doing in the late 1970s pointed to a counter-revolution.

But that was to underestimate the impact on the Conservative Party of the world in which it lived. If the party had legislated according to the spirit of Jenkin's remarks it would have had to abolish the Equal Opportunities Commission, the Equal Pay Act, the Sex Discrimination Act and the Employment Protection Act; it would have found itself alone among its European allies, and it would have been compelled to cast itself, Canute-like, against the laws of the market. Finally, to include women in its general assault on equality would have brought calumny from the Surrey hills and the Solihull plains – Tory women wouldn't have worn it. In any case, Jenkin's colleagues didn't join the argument. He was neither repudiated nor endorsed – except in private among consenting adults, as we discovered when notes from the government's Family Policy Group were leaked in 1983. Certainly, he would have found few soulmates among the women's leaders within the party. 'If that's what he thinks then that's his problem,' said Emma Nicholson.

Once Thatcherism became a governmental reality rather than a threat – or a promise, depending on your disposition – it became obvious that the elements within its ideology were as diverse and even as contradictory as the above quotations from Thatcher, Jenkin and Nicholson imply – classical liberalism laced with misogyny and proto-feminism.

We shall see how many Conservative women believe in women's *equality* without having a theory of *inequality*, which often leaves them without a political strategy to deal with inequality. This prompts the question: Can Conservatives be feminists? The answer is yes, of course. Then what divides Conservative from radical or socialist feminists? Conservative women's feminism is rooted in liberalism and, in the British context, it therefore tends to end where contemporary feminism starts: with investigating and organising against the *social system* of sexual oppression, and mapping the connections between class and sex. Conservatism on the other hand is concerned with individuals rather than systems, and necessarily separates class from sex in its ideology. This explains the absence of key words – oppression, exploitation, discrimination – from the lexicon of Conservative feminism, and indeed from Conservative ideology: for them the problem is not power but nature.

These characteristics of Conservative ideology are expressed in the practice of Thatcherism, and will be discussed later in the context of the government's response to pressure from the European Commission to modernise British legislation on women in the workplace. We see that the government did not purge women – as women – from the workplace, but simply ratified the form of women's re-entry into the post-war labour market and encouraged the extra exploitation of working-class women as economically dependent employees. What it rejected was any claim on the social purse: the devaluation of women's skills was seen as a function of the market, and therefore immutable, and childcare was to remain the mothers' problem and therefore a private problem.

I'm equal

'My parents made no difference between us, my brother and I. There was no nonsense about not letting girls go on, as there is in Labour households,' said Councillor Delphine Roe, a retired public servant. In her modern Birmingham bungalow, among the books on travel and British birds, the occasional ornaments, good carpets and old armchairs, stood a clock with a plaque on it, presented in memory of service given by a deceased member of her family. Her life, like his, was guided by a higher purpose: the social good. Unlike his, however, hers had been devoted, in its own way, to the service of women. She wasn't animated by a sense of the wrongs done to women; in fact she said she hadn't much experience of that. 'I came from a very loving family, there was no bar on me. I can't say from my own experience that women are discriminated against.'

From her comfortable and committed family, she travelled to one of the few places England offered to the daughters of the middle class, the public professions. If free enterprise was closed to enterprising girls, their spirit found a space in the very institutions their spinster aunts and antecedents made for women – in paid public service, administration, running services, charities, hospitals, women's colleges and girls' schools.

Councillor Roe ran a women's college in the Midlands. 'It was a women's college, that's why I was so fascinated by it. I love women, and I like their company.' For most of her adult life she voted Conservative, though with a small lapse when she voted for Hugh Gaitskell in the 1950s, 'because I felt he had more humanity, and he was very courageous for standing against his wild boys. I always waver between the party and the person.' Until she became a councillor, after her retirement, she had not been a member of the Conservative Party, but was active for many years in the Soroptimists, 'it's like the Rotary Clubs, only it's about women's things'. (Their stated objectives are to 'maintain the highest standards in business and public service, human rights and to advance the status of women'.) Her particular group organised a survey of lavatories and advocated better signposting, raised money for old colonies, sponsored children from overseas, 'and we went round the shops to see how many could greet customers in their own languages. And we did a leaflet on rape – the Rape Crisis Centre says there's more rape than we know about. I don't know, probably a lot say it's rape when it isn't.'

When the Labour Party set up a women's committee on Birmingham Council following the model of the pioneering Greater London Council Women's Committee set up in 1982,

we decided to go on. That's what gives me most trouble in my council work. I was petrified – it's so unpredictable. Labour have some quite powerful women and I thought that if we attacked the women's committee, it could easily be seen as attacking women. So I worked out a speech on what the Conservatives do for women. I couldn't understand the women's committee at first. I find it hard to work out what makes them tick.

She has no anger because she doesn't find life as a woman difficult. As she trawled her memory, she caught a couple of memories: 'Yes, I have worked for two men who hated women.' But it wasn't what she'd call discrimination, perhaps because she couldn't imagine being daunted enough to give it the name. She believed that 'the root of the problem is the manual workers'. It was a problem of enlightenment and a problem of 'class funk'. Like many of her ilk, Councillor Roe believes in equality without recognising inequality. It is, then, not illogical in her terms to believe in the Equal Pay Act, for of course women should be paid equally for equal work, but not to believe in the Sex Discrimination Act. 'I ask myself if it's not counter-productive, because you can produce the wrong result by being strident about discrimination. My problem is that I've never experienced anything myself that would make me understand discrimination. If a woman is determined, she can make it.' That's what her own experience tells her.

Jean Brown is what one of her employers called 'the backbone of England. She's smashing. She doesn't feel bitter. We're equals.' Her employer is a woman, and Jean Brown does her cleaning. Her own home is on a modern private estate on the edge of Birmingham, where she reckons most of the wives work as school-dinner ladies nearby or, like herself, as cleaners. 'I work every day, for three different women. One put me in touch with the other, that's how it works. They're doctors and businesswomen, working in a larger field really, so they know a bit more of life than I do.' Her own home shows little sign of conspicuous consumption – a worn three-piece, a video and a handsome television housed in a reproduction cabinet – some evidence of home improvement, all the evidence of her labour, no dust, no flecks on the carpet, no papers or ashtrays, nothing that doesn't belong anywhere.

'No, I won't sit down,' she said as she sat on the edge of an armchair. 'I don't watch telly so I never sit down. I haven't sat in a chair properly since last Christmas!' Although it was the following winter, she wore a tee-shirt and a pinny over her skirt and kept hold of a teatowel. She was in her late thirties, the baby boom generation, had no wrinkles and the body of a keep-fit enthusiast. 'Actually I get up at five every morning to go to see to my horses. I've got two – that's my interest in life.' The Conservative Party had always received her vote, although she'd never been a member and didn't go to any political meetings, 'because I've never had time, except for occasional meetings at the school'. She was Conservative because 'they stand for everything we want, and the party offers it: our own place, our own luxuries and the work that we need'.

Although one of her grown-up sons was unemployed for three years, she wasn't offended by Norman Tebbit's advice to 'get on your bike': 'That's what I kept telling him. Work won't come to you, you've got to go out and find it, haven't you, really? You've got to keep on going out and trying for it. I have, I've always worked, except for a couple of years off when I had the children.' Things had changed for the better, for women, she believed, and

husbands are more willing to do part of women's jobs in the home. But then again, I go to some houses where the wives don't know how much the husband earns, or the men leave the wage packet at work so the wives don't know. It still goes on. *It's more the case with Labour people.* The women are more downtrodden, they don't speak their minds quite as openly. It's the 'women's place is in the kitchen' sort of attitude. It's surprising how many people are like that. My father, when Margaret Thatcher is on television, he's terrible. Partly it's because she's a woman and partly because he's strong Labour. But he's always been the same when women talk on television, he's very biased against women telling men what

to do. He can't stand that, he doesn't think a woman should
be running the country.

She believed in equal pay: 'Yes, if women are doing the same
work, although strong as I am, I'm not as strong as my sons, so
maybe not for heavy work that women can't do.' But she wasn't sure
about the Sex Discrimination Act: 'Yes, for some things and for
some things not. How can you get offended if somebody preferred
a male? I wouldn't be offended.' And if she found herself not getting
the same pay as a man doing the same work? 'I wouldn't go on
strike. I'm against strikes.'

Both of these women were proud. They believed in themselves.
Despite their differences they were anybody's equal. That was their
personal and their political starting point. Perhaps it is where the
modern Conservative woman starts from these days. But is there a
commitment to equality which women of the right share with the
women of the left? Yes. Is there a new consensus among women
that is unmoved by Thatcherism's break with post-war notions of
equality? Yes. But these women don't like notions of oppression and
discrimination which suggest structures and systems of power.

Councillor Roe and Jean Brown support equal pay but aren't
sure about the sex discrimination law. Discrimination implies an
organised power; equal opportunity need not, and in the Conservative consciousness it does not. Men's opposition is only a matter of
attitudes, and women's opportunity is a matter of *will*. While supporting women's will, they may not feel inclined to organise against
men's attitudes, or the structures which have produced women's
inequality, because they seem natural.

Conservative women tend to be both for equal opportunity and
against it. They are for it when it is about women, or rather enabling
women, but they baulk at the concept when it is about changing
social structures. A Conservative Parliamentary contender, Jackie
Lait, who says of herself not 'I'm not a feminist but . . .' but rather
'I'm a feminist and . . .', explains that

Conservative women don't think about structures! This is one
of the problems we have when, for example, the Chancellor
introduces something like the paper on taxation and
transferable allowances. The problem is that the Chancellor
would not be thinking about the way society is structured and

the way it is developing. He'd think that women go out to work because they have to rather than because they want to. There would be people in the party who would be thinking about the way society is structured and who'd say transferability wasn't the answer. But the Conservative Party regards the equality of women as peripheral in terms of policy effects. They're not really analysing society's structures in the way the socialists would, not philosophically.

So, much to the surprise of many in the women's movement and on the left, but no surprise to right-wing women, the Thatcher government has not prescribed women's return to the home. Indeed the problem has been working out exactly what the government has been up to.

The European crunch

One way of finding out what the Conservative government has been up to is to look at what it has tried *not* to do.

There was a precedent in the performance of the Heath government, elected in 1970 contrary to the pollsters' predictions. Labour MP Joyce Butler and Liberal peer Baroness Seear tried on many occasions to press ahead with Anti-Discrimination Bills to supplement the Equal Pay Act between 1968 and 1973. First Labour and then the Conservative government deferred Commons debates on twenty-six occasions, fourteen of them during the Conservative reign. Only after the Labour government undertook to present a Bill itself after the February 1974 general election did a Sex Discrimination Bill have a hope of getting on the statute book.

It took nearly a decade for Britain to comply, more or less, with a directive issued by the European Economic Community in 1976 requiring member states to operate the principle of equal pay for work of equal value, which had been long supported formally by the TUC but rarely deployed as a tactic in collective bargaining. This would have radically enhanced the limited 'equal pay for equal work' terms of the Equal Pay Act implemented in 1975. The limits of the Act when it came to dealing with the highly sex-segregated labour market were revealed in the sex differential which endured after 1975. Although the average hourly earnings of full-time women workers, excluding overtime, had risen from 63.1 per cent of men's in 1970 to 74 per cent in 1985, the average gross weekly earnings of full-time women were still only 65.7 per cent of men's in 1985.[1] Among married couples in which both men and women went out to work full-time, only 8 per cent of women earned as much or more than their husbands in 1980.[2] In any case, the percentages disguised the real sex differential, which was and is determined by men's and women's access to skill, collective bargaining and, most dramatically of all, to working time at home and out at work: nearly half the women in the labour market, 4 million, had part-time jobs.

After the Labour government failed to implement the equal value directive, the EEC began infringement proceedings in 1979 (the year Labour lost the general election) and offered Britain a deadline in 1982. The Conservative government didn't like the directive or the deadline and did nothing until it was ordered to by the European Court of Justice. A year later Employment Under-Secretary Alan Clark brought the government's reluctant compromise to tired and unsuspecting MPs in the Commons late one summer evening in a form unavailable for amendment. His performance was memorable for the offence it caused even among some Tory MPs – although not the Tory Member for Northampton North, Tony Marlowe, who wondered 'What have the regulations to do with trading? Why must we put up with this rubbish?' In a tussle with feminist Labour MP Clare Short, Clark seemed to admit that he didn't support even this compromise: 'a certain separation between expressed and implied beliefs is endemic among those who hold office,' he said. A row erupted over his sobriety, over the extensive exemptions and over the government's refusal to let the Commons modify the order.[3]

One of the government caveats to equal value was that market forces could constitute a 'material difference', and therefore exemption. But the purpose of the EEC's directive was precisely to intervene where the marketplace of collective bargaining by trade unions and employers negotiated unequal pay for women.

Many Conservative women supported the principle of equal value, but although the EEC deadline was looming it was not one of the themes at the 1981 women's conference, which focused on women in employment. Nor was it in the 1983 Parliamentary session on the regulation: apart from Elaine Kellett-Bowman's twenty-nine words in the Parliamentary debate, no women on the Conservative side spoke.

The EEC has turned out to be an unprecedented agency within western Europe for the promotion of women's employment rights.

Ann Wickham has traced the history of its remarkable interventions, showing how they have emerged from the convergence of the contingent interests of women workers on the one hand and the EEC as a transnational institution on the other. Her pioneering study[4] argues that the European Commission, made up of representatives of member states who were expected to represent the commission rather than their own states, and backed by the commission's own civil service, was competing for authority with the Council, made up directly of government representatives accountable to their own governments. Therefore the commission needed to develop its own constituency of citizens beyond the individual interests of member states, to which it could appeal for legitimacy. Within western liberalism political subjects had been constituted as individual citizens similar to the concept of free and equal economic agents with natural characteristics. This concept de-sexed individuals, seeing them in isolation from social relations, and it was this which was inscribed in the Treaty of Rome. But in the context of national citizenship, the commission had no effective way of reconstituting the citizen at a European level.

However, it came to see women as a political resource precisely because legally and culturally 'they have not been widely constituted as political subjects at a national level'.[5] And by investing in women, the commission engaged in a process of 'sexing the political subject' and so began 'moving away from the identification of the political subject with individual subjectivity'; in other words, it moved towards constructing 'women' as a collective category, rather than an aggregate of individuals, by allocating rights to women as sexed individuals. In so doing it established itself as a supranational and independent body.

Member states' readiness to endorse the commission interventions on behalf of women as a sex derived initially from a fear of other states' economic competitiveness and later, in the late 1960s and early 1970s, from pressure both within the EEC to expand beyond the economic into the field of social action, and within member states from the women's and labour movements. All these produced the social action programme in 1974, and its first directive was on behalf of women – the equal pay directive in 1976 which formed the basis of legal action against a majority of states. One of the effects of this process was to challenge the historic effects of cultural, political and legal practices on the definition of 'woman'.

Wickham argues that there is no inherent essence which is 'woman'; it is a socially constructed category, and by legislating for the employment rights of 'women' the EEC participated in the process of changing the social meaning of 'women' as political subjects. What she theorises is the symbiotic relationship in the 1970s between the commission needful of its own social base and 'women' as a new political subject with rights allocated by the commission.

From Ann Wickham's chronicle we can understand how subsequent clashes between the British government and the commission over women's rights were occasioned by this symbiotic relationship. The commission's aura made itself felt upon Conservative women Members of the European Parliament (MEPs), who began to take matters into their own hands. Sheelagh Roberts and Gloria Hooper in 1981 tabled an amendment to proposals put to the European Parliament on equal opportunities, asking the commission to come forward with proposals for parental leave. Sheelagh Roberts later told the House of Lords Select Committee on Parental Leave that unlike her own government, 'certainly I was in favour of the principle of it'. In 1983 the EEC published its proposals and these were examined by the Lords Select Committee before they went back to the European Council of Ministers in June 1985. The British government was alone in opposing parental leave.

The EEC proposed minimum paid leave of three months per worker per child, and with the agreement of employers, this could be taken part-time and extended over a longer period. The proposal was a device to extend equal opportunities to men – recognising that they could be parents too, and that since women's presence changed the profile of the labour market and by implication domestic labour, men's rights and responsibilities as fathers needed to be inscribed in employment practice. The beginnings of men's equal responsibilities as fathers was vital if the terms of women's employment were to be equivalent to men's.[6] A survey of member states showed Britain to be out on a limb, without any statutory paid or unpaid parental leave entitlement for men – even though Britain had one of the highest levels in Europe of participation in the labour market by women.

What was at stake in the parental leave proposals was institutional recognition of the revolution in men's and women's relationship to waged work, and an attempt to make nation states match the changes in men's and women's real lives. In the case of parental leave the

Conservative government was hoist on the petard of the family – its political programme didn't mean *helping* the family, it meant the *family helping itself.* The rest was merely rhetoric.

Furthermore, the government had to meet diverse political pressures within the party: it had to satisfy its own 'men are men and women are mothers' lobby; it relied on the on-your-bike school to fend off its own feminists, and it had to satisfy the anti-statists and the business community. Against that there was no united front among the party's women, as there was undoubtedly over child benefit, which was why the government caved in on child benefit and family credit. Outside the party and Parliament, the advocates of parental leave were the EOC, the women's movement and the TUC. The EOC was on parole after the 1979 election – survival was conditional on good behaviour. It stuck its neck out on the issues of contention between the EEC and the government – and all issues were contentious – but since it was never a campaigning body it had not created an alliance with the women's movement which could popularise its struggle with the government and mobilise political action. The TUC proved to be no problem – it had not activated parental leave as an operational demand of employers within collective bargaining and so undermined the employers' complacency.

Although both the TUC and the EOC gave enthusiastic support to parental leave when they appeared before the Lords Select Committee, it must be admitted that their enthusiasm was encouraged not so much by pressure from their own social base as from the initiative of the EEC itself, and it represented a significant shift in their traditional ideology of 'equal opportunities' and the priorities of the 'equal opportunities industry'. It was the kind of shift which some feminists advocated as necessary and inevitable once the Equal Pay Act's initiative was exhausted and the real depth of the sex differential could be addressed. The sex differential was always a *time and money* differential. In the culture of workplace politics, men's parental responsibilities had been acknowledged only as economic. Their own exile from the world of women and children, and their support for the exile of women from equal access to wage labour, had secured men's money-time privilege in relation to women, enshrined in the concept of the male breadwinner's family wage and the full-time working week.[7]

Parental leave introduced the politics of time to the industrial agenda in ways towards which employers had always been opposed and trade unions had, at best, been indifferent: it involved a collective economic contribution to the costs of parenthood; it faced employers with parents' right to time off, and it implied a redistribution of the work of parenthood as a political claim by women on men's time and labour.

The Lords' report makes salutary reading.[8] Evidence against the proposals was brought to the Lords Select Committee by the Department of Employment, the CBI and by Boots, a respectable company employing 45,000 women. Boots said, 'We experience no demand' but offered neither evidence that the women had been asked nor figures on potential need. The CBI said it was 'strongly opposed' to the idea, and likewise claimed there was no demand: 'Certainly there is no real pressure coming up from the workforce.' It asserted that the proposals would add 'substantial operating costs' but offered no figures as evidence. By 1986, however, the CBI had shifted slightly – it was taking part in seminars on parental leave and although it remained opposed to statutory requirements was encouraging member companies to consider voluntary parental leave schemes. The Department of Employment told the Lords that the government believed the draft directive would 'threaten the prosperity which is essential to the stability of the family'. Asked by the Lords for evidence, the department admitted that they hadn't any and that maternity leave – often cited by business as a disincentive to employing women – 'didn't affect employer costs'.

'So you're guessing,' commented Lord Chitnis. Lord McGregor suggested that there might be a large number of women who needed parental leave who did not have representatives to negotiate it for them. A Tory, Baroness Faithful, wondered whether the CBI 'really know what is the wish of the workforce'. On the other side, the Equal Opportunities Commission produced pages of meticulously researched evidence supporting parental leave, backed up by Baroness Platt, its chairwoman, a Tory county councillor with no previous experience of the EOC or the women's movement before her surprising appointment to the EOC. She was no radical feminist. Which made her intervention all the more significant. The debate drew attention, she said, to 'the distance opened up between the reality of family life in Britain today as contrasted with the conventional picture'. Drawing on statistics extracted from the Department of Employment by feminists within the trade union movement, she pointed out that only 6 per cent of households conformed to the picture of a working father with a dependent mother at home with two and a half children:

> What we have come to recognise is the direction in which social change has occurred as a result of millions of individual choices by men and women. Given that people have chosen to move in this direction, the Commission believes that its duty is to propose those reasonable institutional changes which will accompany and correspond to the social changes which have already occurred.

Unlike the government, the EOC then costed the EEC's proposal – and found that three months' parental leave would increase the UK wages bill by less than 0.01 per cent.[9]

The Conservative government was threatened by these ideas, but is it enough to say that it was morally and politically opposed to women's, and particularly mothers', presence in the labour market? The government, for a start, reinforced a nationalist and anti-European relationship to the EEC and thus resisted the Europeanisation of Britain implied by the initial campaign for membership of the EEC. But it nevertheless had to operate within a national equal opportunities framework already minimally established in British law and culture, and its inducements to employers, in fact, did not prescribe a male waged workforce with women coralled within the home. But neither did that mean that the Conservative government ever did, or ever would want to *promote* equal opportunities. It neither promoted the expulsion of women, as women, from waged work, nor did it promote equal opportunity, equal terms and conditions. What it did do was cement the sexual division of labour and women's economic subordination by promoting low-paid and part-time jobs and the erosion of part-timers' earnings and employment rights.

When government spokespersons, including Margaret Thatcher, were challenged about unemployment throughout the 1980s, they celebrated the creation of many part-time jobs. (Although many part-timers' jobs also disappeared, virtually all the net increase in jobs was part-time.) And when we witnessed many of the government's media interrogators almost, but usually not quite, replying that these were not *real* jobs, the government insisted rather disingenuously that of course they were real jobs and women were real workers.

Parental leave provided the clues to what the government was up to. Defending the government's opposition to parental leave, Employment Under-Secretary Peter Bottomley, one of the younger generation of Tory ministers who was not insensitive to the world of women (and who, therefore, must have felt a little uncomfortable) laid out the argument in the House of Commons debate on 26 November 1985: this was 'not the time' to give extra rights to people in jobs; it would add to employers' costs (though he offered no figures to show this, because there weren't any); the government was already encouraging women's employment through its proposals for part-time work and job-splitting incentives to employers; parental leave should be left to agreements between employers and workers.

The result would have been self-fulfilling prophecy. According to the *Industrial Relations Review and Report* at the time, only 7 per cent of agreements included some parental leave. This was hardly likely to improve if left to collective agreements, since the CBI's line on leave was: no surrender! And the CBI found plenty of allies in the House of Commons. 'The Minister need not take too much trouble to persuade Conservative Members that the directive is a load of rubbish that should be thrown out,' Teddy Taylor told Peter Bottomley. Taylor was nothing if not consistent and expressed the mood of the men on his back-benches.

Another problem about parental leave was that it was about men and it was about the social relationship between parents, employers, the state and children. The Conservative women MPs deserted their *compagnas* in the House of Lords, the EOC and the world at large. Led largely by Edwina Currie, who made her cavalier views about her own sex characteristically clear, she said of the EOC: 'I despair of that ragbag of a body which finds it so easy to waste time and public money fiddling around with stuff like this. It merely encourages women to think that equality grows out of a law book, which it does not.' A conclusion most women might feel compelled to concede. However, she added an abrasive on-your-bike view of equality: 'It comes from women taking the opportunities open to them and making the best of them. It comes when women face the demands of a responsible job and, like the men, ensure that they have made the arrangements accordingly.' Which could only mean that women, like men, should solve their problems by taking a wife.

The EOC's enthusiastic deputy chairwoman Jane Finlay, a Conservative, whose sudden and untimely death in 1985 shocked and saddened women associated with the EOC – many didn't share her party politics but loved her commitment to women – took on all comers in the cause of parental leave. In a radio debate she repudiated the Institute of Directors' oft-repeated objection that parental leave would backfire on women themselves because employers wouldn't hire them:

> Well you know this is just the kind of thing that was said when maternity provisions were brought in, it is not what has happened . . . Every time we have taken a step forward, whether it was sex discrimination or equal pay, we've had to have legislation, and after all this government is supposed to care about the family and it's supposed to care about children. The provisions are not provisions to give men or women a rest, they're meant to provide for the proper care of children. We have to remember that not all employers are good employers . . .

Among Conservatives, it was left to the Tory leaders of the EOC alone to defend women against their own party and their own government. If the government didn't dare abolish the EOC when it came into office (not that it didn't think about it) then it did the next best thing – ignore it. None of the women Parliamentarians seemed to have a reference point beyond Westminster to make them risk the wrath of their men – and there is none greater – in the name of women.

Working mothers have had to reclaim work and wages on the condition that they make no demands on employers and on men and on the collective purse. Britain has amongst the lowest levels of public childcare provision in Europe. This aspect of the welfare state, above all the one in which women have such a stake and which has been supported by women across the political spectrum for decades, remains in a state of underdevelopment. What is remarkable about Britain is that although it has one of the highest rates of mothers' participation in the European labour market, this has been at no one's expense but their own. They have paid for it with their own time and money – either they work part-time, and so shoulder the responsibilities of children and their household virtually alone, or else they pay for their replacements with their own incomes. They have changed their own lives without anyone else being required to change theirs. Not least the trade union movement, the only organised resource available to working women. Employers have been implacably opposed to parental leave, but they have also been able to argue that in practice there has been no demand for parental leave, because, of course, women are not the architects of trade union demands. Men are. There was little force behind the TUC's elegant endorsement of the EEC proposals on parental leave when it appeared before the Lords because although the proportion of women belonging to trade unions is almost the same as it is among men, the trade union movement has hardly taken responsibility for the world of women.

Thatcherism had seen the ideology of equal opportunities for what it was becoming: it was challenging the idealist ideology of the free economic agent and, therefore, the meaning of 'man' and 'woman'; it was about collective rather than individual solutions, and it threatened Britain's nationalist stance in the EEC. That is why it was impossible. The government's fears were voiced by Peter Bottomley and the populist right-wing MP Ann Winterton. Bottomley complained that parental leave was about 'social engineering'. And Ann Winterton insisted on 'Woman's Hour' on 3 December 1983 that: 'I do not see that this kind of policy is anything to do with Europe. I think we ought to be masters in our own households . . . matters like this are matters for the individual families concerned and the employers concerned . . . arrangements can be made quite happily between employers and employees.' This notwithstanding the employers' emphatic NO. Throughout the debate 'Europe', like 'expert' and 'social worker', became a key word in the Tory vocabulary, and Ann Winterton wondered whether, like them, Europe lived in an ivory tower and 'never actually lived in the real world'.

The new model army of labour
Unprecedented during such a deep economic crisis, women's presence in the labour market was central to the government's employment strategy in the 1980s. Although the ideology of equal opportunities, as we have seen, challenged the whole of the government's strategy for the family, for women and men, the state and employment, it nevertheless wanted women *in* the labour market.

But as we shall see it did not want to disturb the sexual division of labour. In practice it perpetuated a sex-segregated labour market defined by that old time/money differential: the men full-time/ women part-time division solved the problem of childcare, it solved the problem of women's wish for waged work, and also mollified the men-must-be-breadwinners neanderthals. But most important of all it fitted the government's low-wage jobs strategy.

It is tempting to underestimate the cultural revolution in which Thatcherism found itself after 1979. Thatcherism's familial ideology was a throwback to the 1950s, the formative decade in the creation not only of the stereotype of the Tory woman, but also of the Tory photofit of 'woman' as a political subject, her contours defined both by what she was and was not: she was in the home, and she was out of work. But 'woman' in late twentieth-century Britain could no longer be defined by what she was not: women were workers, they could even be Prime Ministers. Margaret Thatcher herself consummated women's long march through history. Thatcherism's economic liberalism provided the accommodation to the 'working woman': she was to work for a wage she couldn't live on.

The economic liberalism of Thatcherism left it with limited room for economic manoeuvre: tax cuts and lowering wages. It could not lower wages by enforcing an incomes policy, because it had been pledged to support collective bargaining (the trade-off with organised, skilled working men whose support had proved vital to Thatcher's electoral success). Instead it imposed an indirect incomes policy through spending limits on the public sector, a large employer of women; abolition of the wages councils which set minimum wages, particularly for the young and for women; job splitting; low-wage job creation schemes, like the Youth Opportunities Programme and the Community Programme; the Young Workers Scheme which paid a premium to employers providing they recruited young workers for wages of £50 or less, and finally 'available for work' tests introduced in 1986 which enabled social security supervisors to suspend claimants' benefit if they could not work unsocial hours or make immediate arrangements for the care of dependent children and elderly or disabled relatives, a test which implicitly discriminated against women.[10]

The government's *only* jobs strategy has been the promotion of wages below the subsistence level. At the very moment when the equation between the breadwinner and masculinity was destabilised in the labour market, which was recognised by the European Commission's proposal to give part-time workers parity in pay, terms and conditions, the British government reinstated 'economic man' by promoting pin-money for the young workers and women. Women were to be employed in a more strictly sex-segregated labour market; poor teenagers were supposed to defy the rhetoric and *not* get on their bikes because that meant qualifying for supplementary benefit – they were to stay at home with their parents and take jobs with employers who were being subsidised to pay a wage that you couldn't live on. So, the government's support for part-time work was part of its attack on the individual and the social wage. It enabled Thatcherism to appear to support women *without* supporting them.

That has been the whole history of Conservatism. Part-time work by women, while men were full-timers, allowed the government to endorse women's presence in the labour market without offering any challenge to the sexual division of labour.

It was in the context of enduring and rising unemployment that by the mid-1980s those who had been regarded as headbangers in the small business lobby came in from the cold and began to be listened to. In 1985 the government published *Burdens on Business*, which included surveys of 200 firms' views on the impact of government regulations, and later that year it published *Lifting the Burden*, a White Paper using the *Burdens on Business* research to support its case that business was hampered by the regulations. It was a fragile case at best. VAT provoked the majority of complaints, but no firms complained unprompted about anti-sex and race discrimination legislation, and only 5 per cent or fewer complained about employment protection and minimum pay levels, a figure which rose to 29 per cent when prompted. The researchers concluded that employment protection was a burden for *few* firms. Undaunted, Employment Secretary Lord Young urged Europe to abandon a long list of regulations and singled out Europe's directives on part-time and temporary work and the draft directive on parental leave as 'particularly unhelpful'. The British Tories also opposed a recommendation put to the November 1986 European Parliament by an alliance of right-wing and left-wing women MEPs for a minimum wage.

Maternity rights in particular seemed to ignite the ire of Conservatives after the Labour government in 1976 introduced a mother's right to return to work if she worked for more than sixteen hours a week and had been with her employer for two years. However,

what seemed to Conservatives to be an outrageous extension of
employment protection was more restrictive than in the rest of
Europe, and in any case applied to only 46 per cent of all pregnant
employed women.[11] The government had already stiffened the
criteria applying to part-time workers, and further restrictions were
proposed in the 1986 White Paper. But the most significant study
of the impact of maternity leave – a survey of 300 companies in the
private sector by W. W. Daniels – found that 84 per cent said they
had no problems at all, and contrary to conventional Conservative
wisdom, small firms reported fewer problems than others.

Cause or cure

So deregulation of the part-timer was the key to Thatcherism's
novel relationship to sexual difference in economic crisis. We were
perhaps misled by the statements of right-wing recidivists into
thinking that Thatcherism's programme involved the forced retreat
of women. It did not. But this did not make it an era of reform for
women. To purge women was simply not available as a political
solution: the party was the prisoner of the changing consensus about
women and waged work.

There were rare voices from the recidivist ranks, however. The
right-wing economist P. E. Hart complained that the government's
policies encouraged mass unemployment among young workers
through the workings of taxation and National Insurance. Part-time
women workers were thus doing the kind of jobs which would once
have been left to the young:

> The competitors of young people are not adults in full-time
> jobs earning over £130 a week (when the full employers'
> NIC rate is payable) but married women part-time workers,
> particularly those earning less than £35.50 a week when
> neither employers' nor employees' NIC is payable.[12]

The conclusion was clear: 'Such an incentive to increase the supply
of labour from married women cannot be justified in times of heavy
unemployment.'

In contrast, some on the right represented the woman part-timer
as the economy's new model army because she was both a model
mother and would stoop to the jobs spurned by the louts on the
dole. With characteristic bravado, Edwina Currie spoke

Thatcherism's mind: the part-time woman worker was not the *cause* of unemployment but its *cure*. She reminded the House of Commons in 1985 that of the 153,000 new jobs in 1983–84, 152,000 went to women working part time:

> Part-time workers are now doing roughly half the average working week of the men and are picking up one third of the male full-time earnings. Half the work for a third of the money is a bargain, so it is no wonder that they have got the jobs. The message is clear for any employer: lay your hands on as many women as possible and employ them.[13]

Scorning the notion of women as 'second class', she said: 'In fact, most employers consider that we are first-class workers, and we are certainly the employees of first choice.' The main reason was, of course, cost: 'Women are cheap and plentiful and there is no evidence that the supply is drying up.' But

> Labour Members would increase the costs of employing people, whereas we must decrease them . . . They want equality, and that means encouraging women to leave the home and look for a pay packet. On behalf of the women I say, 'We have done it chaps and look where it has got you.'

If Currie spoke the mind of Thatcherism did she also speak the mind of Tory women?

'Equality is a funny sort of word'

Conservative women were faced with the problem of squaring up the conjuncture between Thatcherism's economic liberalism and familial ideology with the equal opportunities ideology already taking root in contemporary politics. Women who were wets, moral authoritarians or new-right libertarians didn't always feel their own aspirations echoed in their government's Victorian values, anti-egalitarianism or anti-statism when it came to women's opportunities in the economy. Despite the apparent unanimity of the government benches in Parliament, some women MPs still adhered to an egalitarian agenda. 'I believe passionately in equal opportunities,' said one woman MP, 'because women are in an evolving role.' Although she was cautious about state intervention on the side of

women workers, she admitted that perhaps 'there is room for the
state to show leadership. I do believe in the anti-discrimination
legislation.'

Councillor Shreela Flather, an educated Asian, was critical of the
labour movement's failures.

> We've had equal pay legislation, but what are the unions doing
> about it? I support social legislation of this kind. I trained as a
> lawyer, and most social legislation follows need. We'd never
> have had race and sex laws if they weren't needed.

Out in the shires, where many Tory fortresses are staffed by
women councillors of the old school who took up local government
when their children were grown up, many women seemed both to
share the government's emphasis on motherhood and support equal
opportunities, albeit rather hesitantly. One county councillor in the
North-East, a grandmother in her sixties who believed firmly that
women's work as mothers and wives 'must come first', also thought
it was no bad thing for men to become more actively involved in
fatherhood – 'Changing the nappies – if he wants to, let him' – but
she also repudiated Norman Tebbit's opinion, expressed in the
Family Policy Group, that unemployment would be relieved if
women left their jobs and went back home: 'No, women shouldn't
go back to cleaning the silver.' Another county councillor in her
forties rejected the recidivists: 'They're out of touch with reality.'

But this is not to say that they all supported equal opportunities.
Often their feelings for women were muted by a fear that equality
undermined their own personal efforts.

Freda Cocks is former Lord Mayor of Birmingham City, a JP,
and a widow now who lives alone in a neat, cream-painted flat. With
her own portrait on the wall, you sit there in the presence of two of
her, both a little larger than life, one wearing the plush armour
of office and the other in the armchair, rosy and robust. Her
anti-egalitarianism is testament to her own history: 'Whatever I've
got I've earned it.' It could be the motto of her city, both its employers
and its workers, of which she is mightily proud – she is the first
Tory woman to be given the freedom of the city.

> Equality is a funny sort of word. You can't make everybody
> equal, well, there'd be no society at all if everybody was equal. I

get very insulted when I hear all the time about these women's committees. If women want the opportunities then they've got to work for them. No profession should be barred to women, but women shouldn't expect just to get things. Women staying at home shouldn't be sneered at, because that's an important job, but if she works she should be paid equally – if it's the same job.

Despite her dislike of women's committees and all this talk about equality, she nevertheless felt she'd done her bit on the council to campaign for civic services to help women:
We were always good friends with the Labour women. We felt

nursery education was very important so we ganged up on the men. We ganged up to get child minders registered. We realised even in the 1940s and 1950s that women were going out to work and women needed their children to be looked after properly.
Equality is truly a funny word, not only for many right-wing

women but for many women in the feminist and socialist movements, too, because it was only ever an idea. Men and women aren't conkers or shells to be weighed and measured for their equivalence. Women may reconnoitre the world and nowhere find something called equality. It is a word that often gets in the way of understanding not only what many right-wing women think they themselves are, and what they think 'women' are, but also what they think they might become, since their fantasies orbit around their experience of the real. Equality seems to flash dangerously only in the imagination, like a bat which disturbs the peace of darkness; is it bad or is it beautiful, is it a mouse or is it a rat, and if it will fly why won't it walk? It's a mystery. And when Margaret Thatcher says that equality is a mirage, her supporters know what she means because there is nothing in their experience that could tell them otherwise. Equality, like freedom, was often, of course, a word deployed by those more free and equal than others. 'Equal under the law does not apply to the economic inequalities it is there to mask ... Equality always denies the inequality inherent in its birth as a concept,' argues the feminist theorist Juliet Mitchell.[14]

Nellie Newman was a skilled sewing machinist in Birmingham before the Second World War, proud of her own crafts – 'What do I like doing? Everything. I take pride in everything I do' – and resigned to the realities of class:

> They'd let you work for nothing if you let them. But if you stuck up for yourself they'd increase the rates. But I wasn't aggressive. We didn't have unions before the war. Was I exploited? No, not really, we didn't know any better.

So did anything make a difference? 'The war. I got chocolates for my Christmas box. That was marvellous. We got flat rate during the war – things really improved! It's sad that it takes a war to make things a lot better.'

There's nothing in politics that makes Lucy Robson think 'I like that!' 'I'm just boring. There's nothing in the news would affect me because I'm just here, it's not as if I'm working and worrying about taxes.' She lives on a farm, the wife of a stockman, but her account of herself as 'just here' neglects to mention that she not only works at home and around the farm but also as a school-dinner lady. She was brought up a Conservative and so she says she is 'against unions. I'd have to pay out so much a week for nothing and if they came out on strike I'd lose.' She does believe in equal opportunities, though, and she knows exactly what would make a difference for women: 'Someone else to do the shopping for me! They say there's equal opportunities, but there's not as much as they make out. There are more equal opportunities because women have stuck their necks out.' But she doesn't see herself as one of them. 'I'm just here' seemed to say that her own experience eluded her consciousness and that anyway politics was somewhere else and about someone else.

Many old Conservative stalwarts, whose youth was lived in the aura of suffragism or its aftermath, never abandoned their pride in being women, their commitment to the company of women or their politics of emancipation. There is a different feeling among middle-aged women, whose formative years were spent in the post-war anti-feminist desert. Making it meant making out in a men's world, by being the women men wanted them to be. Among the daughters of the 1944 Education Act who have spent their adult lives in the era of women's liberation, both of these tendencies are evident. Some seem to share more with the spirit of suffrage; some seem to feel that femininity, as one suburban councillor put it, 'is an unfortunate interference'. Others spurn the stereotype of the Tory wife and share the aspirations of the professional women of their time. They're the generation who want everything, and as women their politics are shaped by forces outside Conservatism as much as forces within. Jackie Lait always expected to have her own job and to share the domestic jobs when she married. She was formed politically both by the Thatcher era and by the era of feminism and equal opportunities, which she readily invokes as a challenge to her own party. 'I'd have had the equal value clause in the equal pay legislation in 1970,' she said. 'Now it's all piecemeal and very unsatisfactory, but that's the only way left open to us.'

Capitalist feminism – a contradiction in terms?

For women who are wets, the notion of state intervention is by no means anathema. The role of the state in supporting women feels perfectly consistent with their commitment to consensus and a caring society. More surprisingly, women who espouse the economic liberalism and moral libertarianism of the new right find that it fits their emancipatory consciousness. Just as they want a cultural revolution in the economy, so they want a cultural revolution *on the side of women* in politics. To many of them, economic liberalism means an *idea* of equality, state intervention the *means*. The theory of the limited state does not prevent them from wishing that its limits be extended to include not only themselves but also women for whom they feel they have responsibilities: Conservative ideology can be infinitely accommodating. Emma Nicholson suggests:

I value quite a lot of what the radical right are trying to do. The thrust that goes back to the liberalism of the 1850s and 1860s, old-style genuine liberalism, that's what the radical right have created. Although they're breaking new ground, they're picking up a big current of political thinking in Britain that reaches into aspects of free thinking which our political ancestors would recognise more as liberalism. It's that trend that I identify myself with. Where I think we have to be careful in the radical right is that in freeing people more one has to be careful not to damage the people who are vulnerable.

If you can get that balance right then I think we're away to a good future.

Emma Nicholson is a dynastic Tory, a grandee – men in her family have been in Parliament since it was formed in the thirteenth century. So she is not typical of her generation; indeed her style and her assimilation into the party leadership in the early 1980s aroused strong antipathies among some women of all political tendencies in the party. But she is in some ways emblematic of the new Tory woman, the young 'high flyers'. They represent a kind of capitalist feminism which is commonplace in the more commodious culture of the United States but which after fifteen years barely existed as a formation within British feminism. She has spent her life working in industry. She's been a management consultant, a computer consultant and a charities consultant. Her style and circumstances provide clues to her definition. Her history of deafness gives her eyes the habit of seeing all in order to hear everything. She arrests your attention because she herself can't afford to let her own wander. She's tall, dark and handsome. She wears full frocks with big, bold shoulders and big, bold bows. Her home is wallpapered as if by those appointed to the gentry, its design a statement of femininity, its order a statement of her control – not a dish to be seen draining, not a newspaper or magazine littering the coffee table. She has 'help', of course, but it's her home, no one else's; there is none of the compromise of co-habitation.

What's in the radical right for women like her?

In the crudest sense it means freedom of choice; it means that a woman should have genuine freedom of choice, no legal pressure, no social pressures to choose whether she's a housewife, someone who is unwaged and spends her time caring for other people within a family setting, or going out to work, or doing both. Now there are various ways in which society doesn't recognise those choices, although it says it does. Invalid care allowance has only been going to single people or married men, why not to married women? That would free married women who give care – 80 per cent of elderly people and disabled people are cared for at home, the bulk of them by married women. Without state recognition of the way that diminishes that woman's choices, she can't get out and can't pay someone to take over so that she can get out for an hour or two. The state has to make a positive gesture sometimes to make sure the freedom of choice some of us have is extended to everybody. Our philosophy is freedom of choice, and sometimes that comes into conflict with our philosophy – which is absolutely genuine – of stand on your own two feet. In my terms that means helping everybody develop their own potential. So you've got to be careful that you're not just mouthing a slogan of freedom of choice if it means stand on your own two feet when you can't. So I think we have to put our money where our mouth is.

What does she feel about subsidising employers to pay wages below subsistence level? Nicholson says she has a different objective. In her conversations with ministers, she says she has expounded her view of the state: it is not so much about minimising its role as clarifying it, and using the state to distribute protection instead of discrimination:

The state is a safety net. Now that unhooks us from the issue of how much the state consumes, because at times it might have to be very thickly woven, and that might be expensive for the rest of us. At other times, when things are going well, it could be a much looser mesh. So I don't think that the amount the state actually spends in caring for its citizens is the judgemental factor – in recent years that is the factor people have been using. It's an accountant's way. The question is whether it fulfils the philosophical overview you have for it. Sometimes a safety net is very expensive.

That sounds suspiciously like the pre-Thatcherite consensus about the role of the state. How, then, does she feel about the role of Europe, with its interventions in the national member states' legislatures and ultimately in collective bargaining on the side of women?

It's a very good thing. To me it's about the re-establishment of natural justice. It's been very interesting working with Conservative women, because I've thought much more about women than I have done before. I believe people must have equal opportunity. If we hadn't finished tidying up our laws, then yes, something had to be done. There is still tidying up to be done.

Nicholson is an equal value enthusiast: 'I think it's a super idea.'

I have another bee in my bonnet. I can't see my way through it, but I have a very strong belief that somehow or other we have got to get protection for part-timers. I'm talking about extending the standard things that people who are waged expect and get from being employed to part-timers. I think we ought to do more to help the mother at work. For example, we should take the tax off workplace nurseries, for both full- and part-timers. It's about extending to part-timers the rights of full-timers, in some degree. This is something we should take on board and start thinking about. It would be very important for part-timers. Over and above all that, I believe it would help significantly a lot of young mothers who don't want to work but who work full time because full-time jobs make it worth their while. And that would have the nice effect of releasing more work – though that's not the reason I want to do it.

These things *are* already the agenda of women in the labour movement, and of organisations like the Child Poverty Action Group and One Parent Families, but Nicholson and Tory women in general show little sense of debt to, or connection with, those movements.

She is quick to disagree with Edwina Currie's 'nab 'em 'cos they're cheap' ethos: 'It's unbelievable. We've gone way past paying a man more because he's a family man. It's the rate for the job. I don't personally think human beings are exploitable resources.' And how does she feel about those Conservatives who want women to return to the home, to turn the clock back? 'No, and it won't happen, because nobody wants to turn the clock back in the Conservative Party. You have to go with the grain. You couldn't, even if you wanted to, go backwards.'

Nicholson's sense of the *duty* of government belongs less to Thatcherism than to the moral framework of the old grandees, but then she's not the only traditional Tory to have accommodated herself to the new regime. Yet even where women like Nicholson have embraced the radical right and, for example, its emphasis on small businesses, they have their limits. 'I believe strongly in small businesses, they are the key to growth,' she says, and so she supports the government's campaign to exempt them from employees' rights:

> You want to create an entrepreneurial environment, but what I'm desperately concerned that what we don't do is exploit people to do that, so somewhere along that line I part company with the people who want deregulation to create slave labour. So, as much deregulation as possible, but protecting employees. Workers from whatever group are very vulnerable. Because they're not the boss. I remember when I started as a computer programmer at ICL. I felt, and was, totally powerless, we were just ants on the floor. But it mattered just as much what happened to ICL as to those at the top.

Conservative women in the public sector, who have already enjoyed the results of trade union and political pressure for terms and conditions, seem inclined towards support for the European directives. In any case, the long history of women's participation in the public sector has already transformed their expectations. One active Tory woman employed in local government, where she is a member of the local government officers' union NALGO, reckoned after hearing Norman Tebbit speak at a women's conference that 'one of these days we're going to boo him'. And 'Yuck' was the response of a para-medic, Kay Wood, who got within a whisker of winning Wrexham for the Tories, to Patrick Jenkin's views on equality:

> Yes, I support the Equal Pay Act and the Sex Discrimination Act, though I think we've got to be careful on that one, because there's always the risk of a backlash if you push too hard. Yes, I think most of us would agree with the European directives, although I'm not sure about parental leave for dads.

Her reservations were rooted in a preference for addressing women's needs:

> I'd probably want less time for fathers than Europe, but there should be something for fathers, or rather partners I should say

in this day and age, because at least it would help mothers sort themselves out. And the mother bonding is probably more necessary. It's psychological, because mothers do feel it's their role. I don't know about the men, we know our own after all.

As a part-time worker herself, she supported the extension of full-timers' rights. 'We should have the same rights, especially so now because we have to think forward to the sharing of jobs.'

The free marketeers

Unlike contemporary feminism, which has delved deep into theory to pose challenging questions of Marxist, liberal and psychoanalytic theory and practice, there was until the mid-1980s no equivalent school of women involved in the theoretical renaissance of the radical right to insert gender as a problematic or to generate a capitalist-feminism which would challenge the anti-capitalist hegemony within British feminist politics.

Among women, theoretical initiative has lain with the left. One of the few attempts to modernise the separate spheres concept in the new right's economic theory was a paper by Dr Ivy Papps, *For Love or Money*,[15] which deployed market theory to the sexual division of labour within the home and in the market economy. Papps assumes that since the market value of women's paid work is lower than men's, 'men will expect to specialise in market work and women will expect to specialise in household work'.[16] Papps produces an essentially economistic case for the origins of these specialisations: there is no account, for example, of the intervention of the culture and of politics in the market to devalue the price of women's work, nor any account of why and how, since the capitalist market was allegedly gender neutral, women came to be excluded from large sectors of the market economy. She does not explain why capital refused to employ women equally or why organised labour operated both a marriage bar and a bar on women in many industries. Unequal pay is simply assumed to be a function of specialisation, apparently freely chosen. In other words, there is no analysis of political or ideological struggle over sexual difference.

The re-entry of married women into the wage economy after the Second World War on unequal terms clearly poses a problem for free market economic theory, one which is assumed to be accounted for in the theory of specialisation. When she seeks a position on the sex discrimination legislation, Papps argues that 'they are not really aimed at discrimination as such. On the contrary they prevent employers from taking into account all information which may be relevant to the productivity of the potential employee.' Therefore, the laws

> *artificially* alter the relative price of both men's and women's
> time spent in the household relative to that spent in market work.
> They will cause women to specialise less and men to specialise
> more in household production. Such a result is inefficient
> for society as a whole because time is being used inefficiently
> in an activity in which it is less productive.[17]

But Papps offers no empirical evidence to demonstrate this inefficiency effect.

The only significant information to which she refers is the unreliability differential: 'Women with children tend to be relatively unreliable in time keeping because of children's illness and family crisis.' Certainly, this statement is part of commonsense culture – which is apparently enough for Papps. But it isn't true. According to the *General Household Survey* for 1983, published in 1985, the average absentee rates (which excludes holidays and, of course, unemployment, but includes all other kinds of absence) were 7 per cent, a drop of 2 per cent on the figure for 1979. Absenteeism among the self-employed was slightly higher than for the employed. Among men, the absenteeism rate was 6 per cent and among women 7 per cent – a 1 per cent difference which, according to a Department of Employment spokesperson, was in any case statistically unreliable and 'so small as to be meaningless'.

Men's and women's absenteeism should also be considered alongside the estimated domestic responsibilities undertaken by men and women. According to *British Social Attitudes 1985*,[18] in 61 per cent of households with full-time working women, evening meals and household cleaning were performed mainly by women, and this rose to 81 per cent when it came to washing and ironing. In 79 per cent of households in which women worked part-time, the evening meal was prepared mainly by the woman. In 83 per cent mainly women did the cleaning and in 95 per cent women did the washing and ironing. Given that division of labour, women have allowed the weight of their domestic responsibilities *not* to impinge on their waged work to a remarkable degree. In fact, women could be seen as extraordinarily efficient workers.

A spirited coterie of small businesswomen prominent in the Conservative Party women's organisation tussles with the apparent contradiction between their interests as employers and their interests as women.

'I'm on women's side, I get on with women – and I employ a lot of women,' said Theresa Gorman, an iconoclastic, ruggedly right-wing former councillor in Westminster:

> Equality – I don't think in those terms, I'd like a system that accorded women more rights over themselves. That's an attitude of mind. I'd introduce a lot more liberal reforms – I'm not sure equal pay 'forced' is good for women. In teaching and nursing it's harmed women. You should kick up hell if you want something, but I don't like forcing people. If men and women are the same price, you indulge people's prejudices – there's a big case for that because we are in danger of seeing women squeezed out. You want to change the world, but it'll only change slowly.

Gorman's feminist head tussles with her libertarian heart. Her libertarian anti-statism is vindicated in her conviction that state regulation of women's work has operated against rather than for women:

> Nearly all the legislation has made things worse because it is being used by men. In many spheres where women had the edge, women are being pushed out. The Equal Opportunities Commission says this, too, but they never stop to ask why. The reason is that women had a semi-protected market.

Or maybe it was a ghetto. And anyway, Gorman is exaggerating. Either way, there is a problem – employers mobilised to circumvent the equality legislation, and the Tory government has opposed the EEC's equality initiatives. All this is a contradiction for a feminist free marketeer. Can you be a free marketeer and a feminist? Yes – for them, the market's theory of free choice sustains their feminism. The problem for libertarian feminists on the right, however, is the practice. It's not only the perfidy of the law but the problem of exploitation and power. Capitalist feminism forces its adherents to reconcile conflicting interests which in Britain have *never* been reconciled.

The dilemma was revealed in the following discussion between a troika of young women, Joanna Faust, Marjorie Brady and Karen Cooksley, who in 1986 set up the British Association of Libertarian Feminists, the first free-market feminist axis in Britain which is autonomous from the tendentially 'wet' Conservative Party women's organisation.

KC: Differentials in pay are because women leave their careers earlier than men, so legislation won't help them. Women are being encouraged by market forces, women expect to go into the new industries and women are prepared to learn new skills. I suspect in a decade or so we'll be wondering if society really is male dominated.

MB: The legislation assumes differences between men and women.

JF: Where you have equality legislation it's made things worse.

MB: Legislation on maternity leave is to the detriment of business and women. Why should the employer have to take a woman back if she's had a baby? It's her choice so it's her responsibility.

KC: I'm more into the idea that you can contract with your employer as you want, and you should be able to contract with employers on this. But it won't happen until employers realise it's important. If a woman is no good she'll get the sack anyway, and if she's good the employer will want to keep her. People are realising that it's worth doing that. As women get more economic power, the demand will be created for more crèches and childminders.

MB: You could say that should apply to a woman working in Tesco!

KC: Well, it should. What if she's a single parent or her husband doesn't give her any money?

MB: Why should the employer be under any obligation?

Leah Hertz runs her business from her Finchley home and writes extensively on small businesses and on women. She, like some of her small business sisters, was disappointed in the performance of the EOC, though for slightly different reasons: 'It's doing nothing – it should be a watchdog, but it isn't, it should be like Ralph Nader's boys in the United States.' If she wanted more from the EOC because she was a woman, then she wanted less from that other source of pressure, the trade unions, through which women might *organise*, because she was an employer. She readily acknowledged that her own investment was not only profit but power: 'We resisted unions in our business – I'm in business because I want to be the leader. I don't want to be a dirty capitalist, but I don't want to negotiate – I can't take that because it takes time, it's very tiresome, it keeps everyone on edge.' What did she think, then, about the conflicts of interest in the relationship between the market and the needs of women? 'Well there *are* two conflicting interests: you need cheap labour to compete, and then there's the needs of women, we all agree women are underpaid. It's a Catch-22.' The solution to discrimination was that 'Women should all go into business, because it's the great equaliser of all the minority groups. Who goes into business? The socially marginal. And if it's good for them it's good for women.' But *all* don't have capital. 'Yes, it's not a panacea, but I'm only speaking about the women who are already half-way there.'

Christine Chapman wears designer spectacles, works in television, and is a scholarly adherent of the libertarian school:

There are two Tory traditions. I firmly put myself in one and I'm extremely hostile to the other – and there's a lot of women like that. One is old values, law and order, decency and people acting in families – what most people think of as Conservatism. The other is the nineteenth-century idea of individual freedom, that society is best not being organised, the individual being allowed to act on their own with the least restraint necessary: it's formally called the liberal tradition. There is a very deep contradiction within the Conservative Party between those two strands, and the two sets of people are quite hostile to each other.

You can't have the ideas like law and order, decency and Norman Tebbit's speeches on permissiveness if you also believe the individual should choose. How can you be responsible for your own actions if you haven't made the choice yourself? The libertarian is an optimistic view of human nature, that if people are allowed to choose they will naturally perform acts that don't harm other people. The other tradition that believes in church, the family, the right of parents to tell children what to do, the right of the Establishment to set rules, is a pessimistic view of human nature.

How, then, does libertarian Conservatism assimilate women's freedom of choice? How does it deal with the problems of class and power, the weight of culture and tradition?

If the question means how does it deal with the problem that women can't enter the marketplace equally because of people's attitudes to women, well the answer is that it can't, I'm sorry to be pessimistic but it can't, no more than it can deal with ethnic minorities or environmentalism – these are difficulties for libertarianism. The difference between a libertarian and a Conservative is that a libertarian would do nothing to change or enforce tradition, wouldn't pass an Equal Pay Act, for example, but on the other hand wouldn't pass pro-family legislation, would go for fiscal neutrality. As a woman member of the Conservative Party and a libertarian I'd prefer it if my party were working on the Inland Revenue and shove the EOC out of the door. But even if the women's organisation did that nobody would listen to them. I'm yet to be convinced about the EEC directives. You're caught – the libertarian instinct is that you shouldn't force change, but because the directives tend to undermine male dominance in social security, employment law and all the rest you could say, pragmatically, that it's to be welcomed. On the other hand when you try to define certain areas in which people should have rights then it all becomes incredibly difficult. I'd prefer the EEC not to intervene in social legislation, I'd prefer women to work on their own governments to remove *any* legislation.

So, what's in the libertarian tradition for women? 'Nothing, it doesn't recognise women as a separate issue.'

The new right remain a minority tradition amongst Tories, but it is with them in the 1980s that the ideological initiative lies. They push the logic of the new right's libertarian ideology to its limits, and challenge the Thatcherite mix of economic liberalism and moral authoritarianism. But all the Tory traditions, whether wet or dry, authoritarian or enlightened, have a problem. None of them 'recognises' freedom of choice for women.

9

TO BE OR NOT TO BE A WOMAN

One of the things that both Margaret Thatcher's friends and enemies have been known to say about her is that she is just *like* a man. Yet she is unmistakably a woman. Uniquely among politicians, in the public mind she belongs to one sex but could be either.

Margaret Thatcher reacts cautiously to this gender-bending. She wants to be seen as a woman, but as more than a woman. She is not like a man; she is more than a man – she is a prime minister, a warrior, *and* a housewife. Men are prime ministers and warriors but they are not housewives. The undomesticated woman, especially the undomesticated bourgeois woman, is always still a woman. But the domesticated man is somehow unmanned (though wouldn't every wife wish she had one). Part of many women's pleasure in Thatcher's power is everything to do with her gender: Thatcher is more powerful than all the men around her, she bosses them around. But what does all this reveal about femininity and its changing forms?

We have already seen how gender was an early component of the coalition that became Thatcherism. We shall see that Thatcher's gender was critical to the development of Thatcherism as a populist ideology. 'Mrs Thatcher has given the "swing to the right" a powerful impetus and a distinctive personal stamp, but the deeper movement which finds in her its personification has – when properly analysed – a much longer trajectory,' wrote Stuart Hall when he inaugurated a path-breaking debate within the left about the meaning of Thatcherism.[1] He sees Thatcherism as not only a reflection of the crisis in British politics towards the end of the 1970s, but also as a *response* to it, as a new alignment on the right against both Labourist social democracy and 'moderate' Tory social democracy. That two-pronged assault drives a wedge in the contradictions of social democracy, and that is what gives Thatcherism its potency in popular culture. This chapter is concerned with how Thatcher gives back to women an image of woman, how that image is deployed in Thatcherite ideology, and explores the limits of Thatcherite woman in the Tory Party's 'longer trajectory'.

It takes a housewife

Margaret Thatcher's first opportunity as leader of the Tory Party to speak about women to other women came with the annual women's conference in May 1975. There she outlined the rudiments of what was to become Thatcherism's ideology – self-reliance, anti-statism, property ownership, the exercise of personal rather than public obligations to the family and to the community – and this prompted her only engagement on that occasion with the world of women. 'Many of you do voluntary work,' she said, and in a swipe at the then Labour government's 'social contract' with the trade unions, she said the Tory women's voluntary tradition was the 'spirit of a real social contract'.[2] Like the men who preceded her in power, she acclaimed the traditional and subordinate feminine role of her audience, giving them once again a place in the sun. But it was International Women's Year, and she was not a subordinate female: she was the most powerful woman in the country. What that speech revealed, then, was that her relationship to them was the *same* as that of the men before her: she told them they were important, but she did not invite them to become, like her, powerful.

Insofar as she referred to the experiences of women during her first years as leader of the party, it was in their hallowed role as housewives. Using that immortal phrase 'as every housewife knows . . .', her speeches in 1975 and thereafter conscripted the intuitions of the housewife to attack the state of the national economy and to describe her approach to economic revival: 'Perhaps it takes a housewife to see that Britain's national housekeeping is appalling . . .'[3]

Her deployment of the domestic economy as a model for the national economy has been scorned by many of her critics, whose case is summed up by Roy Jenkins:

It's good populist stuff, it sounds simple, it sounds good and irrefutable, but I think it is nonsense . . . on the whole a family cannot increase its income by increasing its spending. Whereas a nation, a government, by increasing its spending . . . can substantially increase the total of national income.[4]

But Peter Shore, the former Labour Cabinet minister (and one of the few among his party colleagues not to scoff that being a woman she'd lose the election for the Tories), reckoned that Thatcher had deployed her domestic economy to brilliant effect:

> She is undoubtedly a formidable communicator. She has the ability to take hold of complex issues and, if you like, simplify them, moralise them, according to her own bourgeois values and get them across . . . I think she has articulated right-wing moral convictions more than any leader of the right in post-war Britain.[5]

Margaret Thatcher's populism did not necessarily persuade all her own colleagues, but few would challenge its success as polemic: she appeared to have succeeded in peeling off the mystery of monetarism by the domestic analogy. But what does that mean for women? Certainly, it has inserted women into the discourse of national political economy, but on what terms?

Margaret Thatcher talks to women only about what she thinks they are and ought to be. In the first Dame Margery Ashby memorial lecture on 26 July 1982, she said: 'What are these special talents and experiences which women have to bring to public life – are they different from those of men? Yes – because women bear children and create and run the home.' This was a speech in memory of a Liberal suffrage activist, and caused offence privately amongst veteran Liberal feminists. Margaret Thatcher's 'tribute' to her did not celebrate the suffrage struggle but the protagonists' domesticity:

> Like Dame Margery they had the inestimable privilege of being wives and mothers and they pursued their public work against the background of full and happy domestic lives. They neglected no detail of those lives . . . The home should be the centre but not the boundary of a woman's life.

So, once again she was given the opportunity to engage with the political history of women and spurned it. For that would have involved acknowledging that first of all it was a *struggle*, secondly a struggle to reach beyond the boundaries of domesticity so that women could embrace power in the public sphere as well as responsibility for the private; thirdly it would have posed the question: what was her own commitment to the political struggles of women in her own time? All of that was impossible for Thatcher. The structure of her speech is illuminating, because it must be seen as an opportunity to *declare herself* in relation not only to women's wisdom, but to women's work and to the history of women's quest for political power. She poses the question 'What's the government going to do about it?' Her reply invokes President Kennedy's inaugural address: 'Ask not what your country can do for you. Ask what you can do for your country.' Having dispensed with her responsibility for women's cause, she urges 'a dispassionate look at what has happened to the structure of society across the century'. What she sees is an increase in illegitimate births, a rise in juvenile delinquency and marriage breakdown. The message is clear: there has been too much emphasis on 'individual rights, less on our duties to each other', and the implication is that women have indulged their rights at the expense of their duties. Returning to her familial theme, she insists that 'when children are young, however busy we may be with practical duties inside or outside the home, the most important thing of all is to devote enough time and care to their problems'.

The question she asked herself about the role of government was further foreclosed when she declared: 'The battle for women's rights has largely been won. The days when they were demanded and discussed in strident tones should be gone forever. I hate those strident tones we hear from some Women's Libbers.'

These statements typify Margaret Thatcher's approach during the rest of her career. She brings women into the political conversation only as housewives. It was no doubt affirming for many housewives to be so positioned, to have their expertise called up as a measure of management, and there can be no doubt that only a woman could have done it: 'Much of her rhetoric is suffused by appeals, arguments and propositions that could only be made by a woman, and to which only a woman could lend authority.'[6] But Margaret Thatcher invokes only the *idea* of the housewife, not the *lived experience*; she does not refer to her work, her isolation, her sacrifice, her other longings. In other words, she does not refer to the contradictions in women's experience.

Margaret Thatcher has made the domestic visible – she has made it *the* experience of women. But in making it visible she has also rendered invisible the housewife who is also in waged work and she has blurred the contradictions experienced by the wageless housewife. She has been silent about the solitude of mothers, about women's unemployment, and about the effect of deregulation in increasing the exploitation of women. That's not surprising because of course, like equality, exploitation is not in her vocabulary. But she also uses this silence around the conditions of mothers and housewives to mobilise her idealisation of women for her populist project.

State support *for* poor families is reconstituted in her ideology as an inducement to sloth (a disease the rich believe is endemic to the poor) and state interference by bureaucrats and busybodies. Women's powerlessness as a sex is suppressed in her division of society into two classes, 'the powerful and the powerless': the powerful are state bureaucratic élites and the powerless are 'the manipulated masses'.[7] On other occasions the masses are manipulated by trade union 'barons' and 'bully boys'. Significantly, trade unionism is constantly represented in Tory women's discourse as the unacceptable face of masculinity. '*We*' never went on demonstrations or went on strike, she told Miriam Stoppard in her 1986 Yorkshire Television 'Woman to Woman' interview. And her own experience is echoed in the real experience of many women, particularly of housewives, if not always for the same reasons as her own.

Thatcher's petty bourgeois background put her decisively outside the experience of mass trade unionism. But she has been able to convert her cultural isolation from that mainstream – it is after all a *mass voluntary movement* – by connecting with many women's real experience of exclusion from what appears to them to be a 'men's movement'. The housewife is worked into Thatcher's representation of the 'national interest': she is seen as an isolated, free-standing citizen, with no affiliations or responsibilities other than her own family. Her subordination to the male breadwinner (the trade unionist) has for generations enabled Tory ideology to represent her as the disenfranchised member of her class, the victim of men's industrial action, with her own stake in the society held to ransom by 'sectional interests'.

Herself talking about herself

The housewife is *the* model Tory woman, so Margaret Thatcher is careful not to distance herself by asserting her difference. Some women need extra responsibility, she told *Woman's Own*,[8] but 'it is not right to impose it on others'. So she suppresses the complexity not only of their experience but of her own. She presents herself to other women as a wife and mother, but as a mother with other *needs*; these are as instinctive as destiny, because they are individual needs not collective or conscious decisions, and the latter would involve her naming not only the personal but also the political consequences for all women and the whole of society. And so far Thatcher has implied that women's economic self-determination is a cost, not a benefit, to society. The implication is that women like her are a bad thing.

But Thatcher exempts herself from the right's criticism of her own and subsequent generations of women who work outside as well as inside the home. The most famous working mother of all explains her will to work for a living not as typical of contemporary women but as exceptional. She still refers to herself primarily as a mother with an exceptional urge towards . . . what, exactly? Not just a job, for that would bind her to the collectivity of women. No, she divorces herself from the shared experience of women by her urge towards *greatness*.

Although Margaret Thatcher has been uniquely able to introduce the *personal* into politics, her idealisation of the everyday and the familial hides more than it reveals. She trades on our collective recognition of the *truth* of personal experience, and yet does not reveal the truth of her own experience. Charlotte Brunsden[9] illustrates the function of the personal in a different context, the women's liberation movement, and shows how that movement 'began to piece together a way of understanding the world from the *point of view of women* which *necessarily* drew on individual experience'. She also shows, however, that the making of feminist consciousness must recognise the limits of individual experience as well as class and race differences between women – it is not a *world* view. Thatcher is able to idealise the experience of the housewife only because she universalises it.

Where feminism trawled the personal to disclose women's problems, their strength as well as their subordination, Thatcher's idealisation suppresses the problematic: she presents herself as an ordinary housewife and yet she *never* was an ordinary housewife, it's almost as if Margaret Thatcher the woman subsequently became the victim of Thatcherism the ideology.

Thatcher became a lawyer and then an MP when her children were very small in the 1950s. She had married a businessman and in 1953 gave birth to twins: 'Right there and then in her hospital bed she determined to put her name down for the Bar Finals.'[10]

During Miriam Stoppard's 1986 TV interview with her, she described her thoughts as she looked at her new-born twins: 'I'm not going to be overcome by this.' Convinced that 'I really ought to be able to combine both' she resolved to do something about it and wrote off for the papers for her bar exams. She publicly defended her hope at the time that 'we shall see more and more women combining marriage *and* a career'. But what about combining children and a career? 'It is possible to carry on working, taking a short leave of absence when families arrive and returning later. The idea that the family suffers is, I believe, quite mistaken.'[11]

It all depended on Dennis Thatcher's money – they had a live-in nanny-cum-housekeeper until the children went off to boarding school. While the children were toddlers in middle-class Farnborough, tea was cooked by the nanny who 'took over management of both children and house' while Margaret Thatcher travelled in to chambers at Lincolns Inn. And after the children went to boarding school the nanny returned during the school holidays, 'providing the twins with much of the warmth and physical affection that, fond though they were of their children, neither Dennis nor Margaret found easy to communicate'.[12] Penny Junor's detailed and sympathetic study of the Thatchers shows that they were *formal* parents in more ways than one. By the time Margaret Thatcher was selected for the safe Finchley Parliamentary seat she was ever more the absent mother.

Her decision to carry on with law and with seeking a Parliamentary seat was not only courageous but *rebellious*. She rebelled in practice though never in theory against the dominant ideology of her own party, and her rebellion remains at odds with her own rhetoric. That means there's something corrosive at the heart of the Iron Lady: all these years she's been faking it.

Her iron will no doubt derived from her own family background: that was the gift she received from her parents, Beatrice and Alfred Roberts. One of her most important memories of childhood, which evoked both austerity and willpower, was of her parents chiding her not to be influenced by the things other children had. Like many strong women she feels she inherited her access to 'the world' from her father. It was he who talked with her about politics; it was his books she enjoyed collecting from the public library every Saturday morning, and it was through his career as a councillor and an alderman that she derived her ideas about 'public service'. When she was asked by Stoppard about her mother, she said that no, her mother had not taken part in her political education, that 'mummy backed up daddy'; and then she resumed her reminiscences about him. Her face and voice became grave as she recalled how 'they threw him off' the council when the office of alderman was abolished, and he lay down his robe saying, 'In honour I took up this gown and in honour I lay it down.' Seconds later Thatcher drew a hankie from her pocket and wiped the tears from her eyes. She wept for her father, grieved for his grief, but there were no tears for her mother and her stern subordination to her father.

Beatrice Roberts helped Alfred run their corner shop in Grantham where she 'lived very much under her husband's thumb'. A reserved woman, she 'never appeared to those who knew her as a woman who enjoyed life very much. She worked all the hours that God sent, and was seldom seen about town'.[13] Thatcher told Stoppard that, 'My mother was very busy . . . we all were!', and when talking about wanting things she couldn't have, she said, 'I can still hear my mother saying: we're not situated like that.' Buying new covers for the furniture, 'always a great event', produced a conflict: 'You'd choose something light with flowers' but her mother would reply, 'That's not serviceable.' The picture this gives is of a strong but oppressed mother, a childhood that was not poor but frugal: Thatcher's account of its material austerity seems like a metaphor for its emotional poverty, with a mother who was – as mothers were – too busy, exhausted, unrewarded and self-denying. A cruelty lurks behind Thatcher's account of all that petty-bourgeois self-reliance against which she seems to have defended herself: her mother could not give her time, nor could she give her joy; she did give her a commitment to work, though. But she was no model for her daughter, this mother. The bereft daughter turns to her father who gives her back a vision of herself that works: he offers her a way of being a human being, the possibility of success.

The daughter honoured her father and she repudiated her

mother. That's not in the rules: she is supposed to honour her father and *become* her mother. So, Margaret Thatcher is not her mother's daughter and yet she doesn't recognise her own rebellion.

The codes of Conservative ideology make all that difficult – though not impossible – because as Thatcher constantly reminds us, the family is the centre of the universe and the home the centre of a woman's life. The evidence of her own family, however, clarifies a contradiction in Margaret Thatcher: her family gave her ambition and her ambition was her route out. The Roberts household was patriarchal; its middle-class and Methodist Rotary Club culture also wasn't much fun; Beatrice Roberts wasn't given to displays of affection[14] and Alfred Roberts seems to have inspired awe in his daughters. The family rarely ate together, and 'this lack of a family life, while still being a closely-knit unit, is a pattern which Margaret came to repeat with her own family, when she too was a working wife and mother'.[15] But is it the *lack* of a family that Margaret Thatcher reproduces, or is it that she created a family in which, unlike her mother's family, she as a mother was *not* subordinate? And in producing her family thus, she saved herself, as perhaps her own mother failed to do, from her fate. The difference is that her own mother was always there, and Margaret Thatcher wasn't.

The sentimental and idealised family rhetoric of Thatcherism has enabled the Tories and Thatcher herself never to call up the truth of their own experience. Thatcher has never brought to bear her own experience as a critique of the patriarchal family and of the conditions of most women's existence. She hasn't taken her own mother's side and she hasn't taken other women's side. If anything, she has annihilated her mother from her own biography, as if assimilating her mother would have meant having to assimilate her mother's and every mother's pain and anger. By identifying with her father she not only edits out the picture of a subordinate woman, but she also extinguishes a daughter's disappointment with a defeated mother.

Thatcher's politics are patriarchal, but that still doesn't make her a man. She shows, however, how much femininity is a production: femininity is what she wears, masculinity is what she admires. She wants to be a woman who does what men do. That means that her femininity is expressed both in her sexuality and in her strength. Her sexuality is hidden, not because we only see her clothed, nor because she wears the conservative chic of a woman in control. Her body language is 'womanly' – as she speaks into the glass screens scrolling up her speeches at party conferences, she tilts her head in that gesture which is placatory but superior, her stride is stiff from the waist down, she makes her point in the nuanced tilt of her shoulders and her bosom, which manoeuvres her sexuality into vision. Her gender is unmistakable, her power is manifest, but her sexuality . . . ? Is this a function of age – that a middle-aged suburban woman is not represented as sexual in white Anglo-Saxon culture? Is it because she is a married woman and a mother, facts which both express sexuality and make it inaccessible. Is it because the arsenal of criticism fired at Margaret Thatcher, surely one of the most personally disliked politicians since the war, de-eroticises her – 'she's not a real woman'?

Margaret Thatcher is one of the most seen women in the world. We all look at her, but in the power of our gaze we have no control over her – she does not protest at this mass observation, because she is not an object. We have seen how there is in her both a flight from femininity and from the world of women, and yet an absolute adherence to its appearances. Perhaps it has been through her consciousness of being watched that she has rearranged her 'feminine persona', putting both her femininity as well as her power on display.

However, it is not femininity but buccaneering masculinity which is evoked in her celebration of Victorian values, of the prime ministers who came before her, of 'merchant venturers'. Having deployed the housewife against socialism, so she deploys piratical 'action man' against socialist planning. Where Labour allegedly fears the future,

We rise to the challenge of the adventure. But then *ours* is the British way. This is a nation built on the success of the merchant venturers. Men who sailed into the unknown to carry our trade and bring back wealth to our people.[16]

So Margaret Thatcher seeks after something not given to women – valour. She has been able to borrow it, as she did during the miners' strike and the Falklands war, and by virtue of her resistance to detente she has been endowed with something akin to valour – although it was expressed as a criticism by the Soviet Union, which named her the Iron Lady. She presented herself to her constituency in 1976 thus:

Ladies and gentlemen I stand before you tonight in my [green chiffon] evening gown, my face softly made up, my fair hair gently waved . . . The Iron Lady of the Western World! Me? A Cold Warrior? Well, yes – if that is how *they* wish to interpret my defence of values and freedoms fundamental to our way of life.[17]

And so she became a lady and a warrior.

The values fundamental to *our* way of life are assumed to be shared in the way she talks of 'we' and 'our people': 'Look, we were patriotic, we all were,' she told Miriam Stoppard. She universalises her own biography in the way she recalls her own childhood, its emptiness filled by work and the radio, her private memories infused with public events. The Roberts family were 'Home Service' citizens whose connection to national power and patriotism was transmitted via broadcasts of the war, the Jubilee, the Mayor of London at the Guildhall . . .

For powerful women there is always a decision to be made – will they go with women or without them. For feminists the question is even more stringent: in what ways can they be *accountable* to women? Margaret Thatcher has declined to ask the question 'what is my relationship to women?' Furthermore, she has declined to acquaint herself with the mood among women. One of her admirers and former colleagues, the Tory journalist Patrick Cosgrave, who has made one of the few attempts by a right winger to work out the meaning of Margaret Thatcher the woman, recalls that he always thought it important to build on the fact that Thatcher was a woman. He rejected the view that her gender was irrelevant, and concluded that there were women out there among the voters to whom she could make a specific appeal – particularly younger women married to 'Labour voters with old-fashioned views on the place of women'. He suspected that 'these ladies had been touched by the Women's Movement to the extent of feeling some discontent with their lives' while not being radical feminists. He felt that Thatcher, as a career woman with traditional views about family life, 'might strike a particular chord with them' and suggested some opinion polling to explore their aspirations. 'Since, however, my draft idea for a poll depended on an emphasis on her sexual identity, she turned the scheme down flat.'[18]

Thatcher may have lacked curiosity about other women, but they have not returned the compliment.

The women's verdict
Because she is a woman, Margaret Thatcher excites strong opinions in most people. If she were a man that would be that, but because she is a woman, she engages the thoughts of women in a particular way – there is an expectation that her power will bring something to the feminine condition and *vice versa*. Among Conservative women she has always had a lot going for her – a kind of gender solidarity. So how has she squared up to their expectations?

Among Conservative women who like her there may not be love but there is certainly admiration:

> I feel an enormous sense of admiration for her, greater than I expected – *Tory MP Virginia Bottomley*

> She's so strong! And her policies in many ways are right; there's a wrong and a right way to live. I'm pleased she's a woman because women are stronger than men – *Betty Zikel*

> She's so everyday, down to earth. And she's helped women an awful lot. A man wouldn't help women because men are jealous of women – *Dorothy Love*

> I admire her because she's strong. I think 'great mate!' Especially because she doesn't look as old as all the men – *Carol McKurniss*

> She's the only leader we've got today, no complaints about that. I know she's a caring person, but she comes over as hard, cold, unfeeling. But I give her credit for the fact that she always listens – *Freda Cocks*

> Deep down I'm a Conservative because of my mum and dad, but to be really truthful and honest it's because she's a woman. Women can think of two things at once, men can't. I know men are wonderful and they tell us that. But she runs a home, she's had babies, emotions and upsets. Men don't have that – *Birmingham voter*

> I admire her determination because there's never been anything like it in man, woman or beast. She's a one-off, she's what we need. I like to see her hitting her marks and looking good – I admire her brains, her ruthlessness and ambition. The

ruthlessness, it's nothing to do with being a woman. She's an aberration, one day the waters will close over her and no one will ever know. She's surrounded herself with weak men and not grooming a successor – *Lorna Walters*

But among the women I interviewed there was a stronger current of criticism. Lorna Walters, although one of her admirers, also had her worries:

Having said all that, she's a very stereotyped woman. What got her started was getting married. She wasn't in the vanguard for women's liberation. I'm annoyed by her heartlessness; her policies have done nothing but harm, and no, she doesn't support women.

Something's going wrong. I don't understand what she's doing. Perhaps she's listening to the wrong people – *Birmingham voter*

She's not really interested in women. She doesn't look at gender but ability. I think she could support women more, some people feel she doesn't want other women to be powerful – *Freda Cocks*

When it comes to women I'm a bit cross with her. She could have done so much for women. I've voted for her all my life because she's a woman and that's all there is to it – *Finchley voter*

Thatcher didn't make a difference to women in the Conservative Party. It didn't affect the issue – *former Central Office full-time official*

Thatcher is the backlash. What I worry about is the thousands of people who've been told to stand on their own two feet despite having had a double amputation the day before. She's done for manufacturing and for the welfare state. It's the folksy bit that gets me – it depends on a degree of unreality for its magic. In an asbestos sense she's totally remarkable, but she's heedless of any new data getting on to the computer. God I'm jealous of it because she mustn't have lost any sleep. If you don't let any vibrations touch you then you sleep well. I bet she's thoroughly organised – *former Central Office official*

> She doesn't listen to people, and she won't take advice – that
> worries me – *Elsie Ward*
>
> I know why I don't like her, but it's difficult to put into
> words . . . she fawns, but then she doesn't really because
> she's so arrogant – *Nellie Newman*

It seems that women's conclusions were guided, in part, by
whether she is a good thing for women: and here Conservative
women were divided. For some, Thatcher's 'just being there' was a
testament to women's will; others felt disappointment, because 'just
being there' wasn't enough. They wanted her to feminise politics
and to create space for other women.

For sure, Thatcherism and Thatcher shifted the centre of political
gravity to the right, and no political force seeking to challenge its
effects can resurrect the old Labourist mores and live in hope that
she'll defeat herself, not least because Thatcherism engaged with
real feelings of pessimism and powerlessness. But the question in
many Tory women's minds remains unanswered: why did Thatcher
and Thatcherism not increase the power of women? Many of her
Conservative sisters believe that she has done the opposite, and
some, particularly women active in the party, have forgiven her for
that. She couldn't be seen to be doing women any favours, they say.
But all this begs the question: what does Thatcherism mean for
Tory women?

Curiously, Thatcher is the triumph of an old tradition, albeit a
tradition which she herself has transformed. What Margaret
Thatcher has not done is follow feminine archetypes in the Tory
tradition, she prefers instead the protoypical patriarch, Churchill.
So she is a model neither of traditional femininity nor feminism,
but something else altogether – she embodies female power which
unites patriarchal and feminine discourses. She has brought qualities
of ruggedness and ruthlessness to femininity which perhaps only
men hadn't noticed before in women. She has not feminised politics,
however, but she has offered feminine endorsement to patriarchal
power and principles.

She is a woman of her own time, even though she could only
triumph in another time. Her triumph was also the triumph of a
long march through the institutions of the Conservative Party by
traditionalist women. Under the aegis of Thatcherism the women's
heterodoxy of the 1950s and 1960s became the orthodoxy of the

1970s and 1980s. But that was less the expression of a united front among Conservative women than a tactical realignment within the party. The Tory Party is better than any other in hiding dissent, and despite Thatcherism's palpable success in re-uniting the Conservative Party, it is an unstable coalition. Thatcherism's moral authoritarianism and familial ideology warmed the broken hearts of many traditionalist women. That left others cold who were reassured by the free market ideology of nineteenth-century liberalism: their stake in the new right was that it appeared to offer women freedom of choice. But the triumph of the traditionalist women's agenda arrived too late, when it was past its prime and represented a declining force within the party. Or as a Yuppie libertarian Christine Chapman put it: 'The Conservatives have an appalling dilemma, because genetically the traditional Conservative woman is dying out.' In any case, as we have seen, things are afoot among Tory women because they, like many other women, have been touched by the aspirations of the modern women's movements.

The traditionalist women's agenda was always a moral minority in the Tory Party. Its ascendancy depended on an alliance with racism, anti-statism and monetarism to provide the hegemonic orbit within which it could circulate. Thatcher has raised women's expectations by her very existence, and yet Thatcherism has disappointed them. Nonetheless the impact of both means that no political party can venture into the future without women – and win.

What and who is the typical Tory woman candidate? Is there such a thing? The answer, of course, is that increasingly there isn't. But she has to contend with the notion that there is such a thing – or should be – nowhere more than in her own party.

There is a premium on keeping quiet about the hazards women have to survive en route to Parliamentary power. Failure is likely, but to complain is to make it certain. Some veterans tell us their own stories about how they survive failure and success:

Kay Wood has two passions, her son and her Parliamentary ambitions. Her son goes to a private school and she reckons she spends £5,000 a year trying to get a seat.

> Certain decisions I've made mean I'm less free to do other things. I live on a very tight personal budget, there's my son's education and politics. When people talk about MPs being paid they don't realise how much you invest in it. It costs me £5,000 a year, travelling, speaking at meetings, the wear and tear on clothes, shoes – all that expenditure is down to me. I remember going on a training weekend: it cost me £4 for lunch, a taxi home to pick up my child. I have to buy a couple of outfits I wouldn't necessarily buy otherwise, because you've got to look presentable, another lunch, the cost of overnight stay. You're never reimbursed, because it's your decision to stand. Then there's the party conference – you've got to go, and be seen. There's the train fare, £60 for a nanny, £30 for bed and breakfast, drinks and a meal out with constituency representatives if you've got a constituency – you could spend a couple of hundred pounds without thinking about it. Then

there's interviews, and when and if you get a seat you're
spending every weekend away, so you have to have a second
home. There's the drinks – you've got to stand the rounds of
gin and tonics, and the parties in the constituency. There's
no level at which the party pays. You've either got to be very
well resourced or very careful.

Kay Wood is very careful. She lives at a good address, a small
conversion on a one-way thoroughfare. She does her own housework. You might find her doing the washing on a Sunday afternoon
or Thursday midnight, and she saves on food by not paying out for
pre-packaging. She is also a single parent, a modern woman. Not
that she'd put herself in the vanguard – she hasn't read any modern
feminist books; she doesn't read women's magazines, and she's not
interested in the 300 Group, an all-party campaign to make 50 per
cent of the Commons' MPs female and to promote women for
public appointments. Her peers are the class of '68, although age
and stamina are all she appears to share with them . . . No, there is
more. Her personal priorities are theirs, too. She wanted work and
have a wage and a child: 'I had a training and I expected to use it.
I never expected anyone else to be my meal ticket.' Her political
career began through her profession as a para-medic within the
National Health Service: 'We needed to be stronger financially and
we needed to present ourselves better.' She's proud, and the quest
for social recognition of the profession as a whole drew her into
political campaigning.

Anyway I was very unhappy with the way the country was going:
either I had to emigrate or do something. What worried me
was the creeping socialism. Dictatorship can take two forms:
an individual dictator, which tends to be right wing, or
committee dictatorship, which tends to be left wing. That's the
danger that takes away any chance to grow and be different.
If the state takes over more and more of your life, then your
choices are reduced and your life planned for you. That's
the approach I was taught not to take, and that approach makes
you more and more dependent. I was encouraged to stand
on my own feet, that you had to create your own chances. The
biggest infringement of your rights is the erosion of your

right to be an individual. I always felt you'd no right to grumble unless you were prepared to change things.

And so she wrote to a minister who she'd met through the campaign: 'I said to him that I wanted to be an MP.' Her divorce put her politics on the line,

because you suffer from a handicap being a woman, and being divorced even more so. There's plenty of divorced men, and men who have just walked out on their commitments, and nobody bothers, but if you are a divorced woman it's a different issue. It counts against you.

Obstacles are not to be contemplated; they are to be got through:

I remember being on a committee with four men. You were constantly reminding them that you weren't the secretary, and covering for them, but a woman would never get away with it. I was once in a house where an MP had forgotten an appointment. The female secretary moves into action, the wife is rung – they covered for him. A woman doesn't get covered, that's the iniquity of it. I can recall going to canvass in a by-election and the candidate didn't turn up because it was raining and he was doing a television interview – he didn't want his hair to go frizzy. A comment like that from a woman would be political death. A woman can't afford to make the same mistakes as a man. You've got to back yourself up all along the line.

All the women I talked to believed that the Conservatives were better than Labour in promoting women for Parliament. There's something in Labour's bluff, butch image which seems to give that impression. Margaret Thatcher's election to the leadership of the Conservative Party seemed to vindicate Conservatives' view of their party as the women's party.

'In the Labour Party women have to cope with the trade union sponsorship problem, so that's a minus to start with. You see remarkably few women in Labour seats, they've got a harder battle than Conservatives,' said one hopeful.

Conservative Party vice-chairman Emma Nicholson reckoned that

Parliament is 'a male preserve. I see that as wrong, out of date, out of touch with real life, not my style anyway, but it's also out of touch with the reality in Britain. The Conservatives do slightly better than the other parties in the House of Commons, but we're only a nose ahead, no better.'

History makes liars of us all. There is a popular myth that the campaign for women's suffrage was crowned in an irony of history – the election of a Tory as the first woman MP, Lady Astor. Actually, the first woman ever *elected* to the House of Commons was Ireland's veteran suffragette and a revolutionary republican, Countess Markiewicz. But because she was imprisoned in Holloway at the time she could not take her seat, even if she'd felt inclined to. Lady Astor nevertheless did make history: she was the first woman to *sit* in the House of Commons.

However, Labour fielded more women than the Conservatives in *every* general election between 1918 and 1979. And in nearly half of those elections, even the declining Liberals fielded more women. Women have only ever comprised 5 per cent of MPs, and of them more Labour women than Conservatives have actually made it to the Commons in more than half of the Parliaments. In only five general elections were the same number or more Tory than Labour women elected, and in another two Parliaments Tory women topped Labour after by-elections. Tory women MPs outnumbered Labour women in 1983 for the first time since 1970, although this is attributed to Labour's devastating losses overall.

The record of all parties is terrible, and the Tories' is worst. Even during the 1950s, when the Conservatives were securely installed in government and the party's women's organisation began heavily promoting women candidates, the maximum they ever fielded was thirty-three, a figure equalled again only in 1974. It was during the late 1970s, and certainly the early 1980s, that the women began to *organise* to get more women candidates. Angela Hooper and Janet Young worked closely together to put yeast into the project, which was to increase the number of women candidates and to consolidate women as a political force within the party.

'We set area quotas for names of people to be candidates. They did very well at first,' recalls Hooper, 'but that went off the boil after a bit because they weren't chosen, which was a bit exasperating.' Hooper was also a member of the all-party equal opportunities committee concerned with public appointments, and so the women nationally were alerted to that too: 'At each meeting of the national committee we'd ask how many women had been submitted for the candidates' list and how many were being put forward for public appointments.' They also challenged the way selectors' criteria were weighted against women candidates:

> What people do not realise is that women do not form the majority on a selection committee. So one of the key things is to have a choice of more than one woman, so that one woman can't be rejected because she's got the wrong shoes. One woman wore Hush Puppies in an interview for an urban seat! And another wore a *black* suit – no way! It did happen that women were rejected because of their clothes. I know of some. Dress is identifiable much more easily if there's only one woman. So I thought that if silly things like that were having influence, then surely one out of five would have the right dress and hairdo. Things certainly improved and the variety of choice got better.

Hopefuls were also encouraged to modify their attitude to themselves:

> Women couldn't be expected to have been Young Conservatives, to have served on a local committee for ten years, and done everything else, as well as bringing up a family and having a career. They don't expect men who have been successful businessmen to have sat on local ward committees for donkeys' years, but somehow or other quite a lot of people did expect women to have done it. It was unfair. We also encouraged women on selection committees to ensure fair play, because among the frequent questions asked of women were things like: 'You've got three children, Mrs Smith, what arrangements have you made?' And she'd then have to spend ten minutes explaining that she'd got things organised and that was why she was wanting to stand, and political questions quite often weren't put to them. But they didn't ask that of Mr Jones the businessman, also the father of three children.

And Euro-MP Sheelagh Roberts reckons that women are either expected to be married – if they're not, they're not normal – or, if they are married, to be at home with their families.

Angela Hooper challenged the conventional wisdom that women on selection committees are women's worst enemies:

> That's an easy excuse for men to use, to be honest. When you've seen the number of selection committees that I have and the prejudices they start off with, you realise that it's not just against women: it's religion, it's shape, it's everything. This is why I've always felt one could understand how the minority groups feel. Having worked in women's organisations all my life I've always felt we were treated in the same way.

She remembered that Lady Janet Young 'never hesitated at meetings to ask about the number of women candidates. I must say, I don't think that was liked. But unless the question was put, the position wouldn't be recognised.'

Hooper and Young made their big push at the beginning of the 1980s when, with a couple of exceptions, the number getting safe passage to Parliament had remained under a dozen for three decades. In the 1979 election, thirty-three women had stood, most of them languishing in no-hopers: only eight were elected. That was even fewer than the defeated Labour Party's eleven women.[1] Plymouth Drake stands out as the only constituency which has always returned a woman since it was first represented by Lady Astor. It is now represented by Janet Fookes, a well-liked former history teacher – described even on the Labour side as 'a very *nice* woman' – who couldn't be more unlike the razor-witted Lady Astor, except perhaps for a mutual regard for women.

In the 1983 general election, twenty-three women were elected in total. The Tories stood forty women, the Alliance seventy-five and Labour seventy-nine, and a few more women stood for the smaller parties. That's out of a total of 2,577 candidates. According to David Butler and Dennis Kavannagh, the social characteristics of those candidates 'showed little change' and despite 'some concern in the Labour Party and the SDP about the under-representation of certain categories, attempts to raise the number of women MPs and to elect the first black MP were unsuccessful'. They concluded that 'too few women were adopted for winnable seats, or rather for seats which the parties were able to win on June 9'.[2] In the reselections after 1983, 10 per cent of Tories were women and 11 per cent of Labour candidates were women.

The Tories have been conspicuously unsuccessful in securing black votes in Britain. Research by the Commission for Racial Equality after the 1983 general election showed the scale of the Tories' failure among Britain's ethnic minorities: 81 per cent of ethnic minority electors said they voted Labour, rising to 86 per cent among Afro-Caribbeans and 80 per cent among Asians. The Tories have been unable to match the Labour Party's adoption of a dozen or so black prospective Parliamentary candidates in Labour strongholds in the post-1983 reselection process. After the May 1986 local elections, black Tories won only six seats, while black Labour candidates won 120.[3] There is a growing black presence in the party, however, and at the party's 1985 conference it heard the voice of a new kind of black party activist, Brent's Ambrozine Neil and Harrow's Lurline Champaignie, a nurse who lives in a wealthy white suburb, Harrow. She brought the conference representatives to their feet with pleasure when she reassured them that 'I'm Conservative, black and British and I'm proud of all three.' She acknowledges that 'I live in a country that has racism in it', but insists that she doesn't find it in the Conservative Party. And that is despite Margaret Thatcher's echo of Powellism when she talked in 1979 of whites feeling afraid of being 'swamped' by black immigrants. Champaignie is suspicious of black people's campaign within the Labour Party for black sections, which she doesn't see as a power base for black members. But then black Tories don't have a power base of their own, only a polite National Association of Conservative West Indians. 'We're not organised in a group, but we meet to tell the party what we need. They have to listen to us more, but it's not easy for the indigenous group to bend, we have different values and it's these things we want recognised.'

A rather more forthright black member of the party, Shreela Flather, is a Tory councillor in the wealthy Royal Borough of Windsor, where she became the first Asian woman mayor in Britain in 1986. An assured and serene woman who worked as a teacher and then spent some years organising among women and children in her community, she roots her Conservative values in her own class background – upper middle class and educated – unlike that of most of her Asian compatriots, many of whom come from a village milieu which she acknowledges to have been beyond her ken. She has advised Thames Valley Police in a programme to recruit more ethnic minority police officers, and attracted some calumny from fellow Tories when she commented that 'the problem is that police culture is sexist and racist, not at all welcoming'. Flather's approach, like that of a number of her black contemporaries in the party, is to dispose of the complacent 'we're colour-blind in the Tory party' ethic: 'I'm not sure that any party really cares about us. It will be up to us to make sure that they are not able to exploit us.'

In the tradition of her antecedents, Emma Nicholson gave the promotion of women, including black women, to Parliament a high profile, but the party itself seems not so sure. 'No, it's not a thing we're interested in,' insisted a Central Office staffer:

> A candidate is a candidate is a candidate. Of course, we're keen on having more women candidates, but the fact remains that the party looks on candidates as candidates.

Norman Tebbit referred to the campaign to get more women into Parliament when as party chairman he addressed the 1986 women's conference:

> Of course women's world is not confined to the home and the family. Increasingly women are competing with us men in all those spheres we thought were safely ours – good luck. You have been steadily taking more responsibility, but not yet enough as office holders or candidates.

Some of those in his audience who were seeking seats were appalled. 'The cheek!' said one, 'we can't get the bloody seats.' After a similar speech at a 1986 'High Flyers' conference, another said: 'Imagine saying that to *us*. It's just a damned insult. The in-crowd just thought, "Get stuffed, Sunshine." The cynicism is just awful.'

The stakes are very high – 1,000 contenders looking for a clutch of safe seats. The victors are mainly men: 'Look there's 400 of them in there already. It looks like the party churns them out.'

Women's quest for a seat is like the holy grail – a trail of tests. They rarely get safe seats, so they end up in marginals or no-hopers where at least, it is felt, the women will give the constituency a run for their money because they're desperate to prove themselves. 'The seats that interview most women are the unwinnables. They'll take more chances selecting a woman, because they get a better deal,' said one veteran of the marginals:

It's because women dedicate themselves to it more, and that's because they've got more to prove. Women will be remembered more in a selection process, because there are so few women, and they impinge more visually on the memory. More women are beginning to be selected for by-elections. Before Angela Rumbold's by-election victory women didn't get a look in. The trouble is that women are automatically seen as being in a supporting role, running constituency things, raising money, etc. Although that's no longer true, because they're making themselves felt on all the major issues.

Nevertheless, the odds are stacked heavily against women, particularly in by-elections and safe seats. More than one hopeful complained after the Ryedale selection in 1986 that they felt they might as well give up – especially because they'd heard that as the Alliance had chosen a woman there was no way the Tories would. 'So they chose another clone instead! They deserved to lose,' said one veteran seat-seeker. Before the 1986 Fulham by-election, another said, 'I'll scream if they select another bloody merchant banker.' They did – and she did. In the selection for a safe southern seat three women reached the final six, but one was knocked out for the last round after a bitter wrangle, because some selectors said there was no way they would consider three women.

The redoubtable Emma Nicholson admits that she's experienced herself as powerless in the quest for a seat:

When I got on the list I was about the eighth woman on a list of 700 people. I was terribly lucky, because by that time people felt they ought to be interviewing women. So I got more interviews by the square yard than the men did, and I hit the most extraordinary comments, like 'Do keep going, dear, the committee think you ought to be in Parliament, but not here because you're a woman.' It is a very odd feeling; it must be what it's like being black, something you're born with, can't do anything about – it's very odd indeed. But it just gives me a determination that one will win. I fought a seat in the 1979 election and I failed to get a seat in the 1983 election – miserable for me, but that's life. I came second in a couple of seats and didn't get selected, which was a bit sad. Why didn't I get selected? Perhaps I wasn't good enough.

Conservative women seem to have a great deal staked on protecting themselves against the humiliation by denying it. So some blame themselves. 'I don't get angry,' said a thwarted seat-seeker:

> No, I didn't get angry the time I heard that they didn't want me because I was a woman. Although I was probably upset – but then I thought if they didn't want me, it was probably my fault. That's what I always think, it's better to think it's my fault and that I've got to do better.

Other contenders watch her and wonder: she's rich and she's beautiful, her face seems fixed in a state of grace, the effortless equilibrium of the upper classes. Hard to imagine her blaming, appealing, weeping. But she must have.

Unlike on the left, where the women's pressure for power is accompanied by naming the pain, both in public and private life, the Conservative women tend to put a brave face on it. They concentrate on success because they say it discourages people to name the defeats. But that means that within the party they can't name – and blame – the system. So, when they're successful politicians they say they're lucky, and if they're married they say they're lucky, too, to be married to super supportive guys.

Privately, one woman shares her secrets:

> My husband used to get very angry with me – I mean, he was quite blatantly and openly jealous. He said, 'You've moved into a man's world.' He thought it was all right while I was working with women, 'but now you're with men and I don't like it.' It was overt. At the back of his mind there was the thought: maybe she's going to be tremendously successful and how am I going to relate to that? It's a hell of a shock if your partner has been sitting at home doing nothing and suddenly overtakes you in the public eye, which is exactly what happened, and it's what happened to Margaret Thatcher. The comparison is exactly the same, and it must happen to every husband whose wife does this. So every wife has to fight for the relationship, because the relationship is at stake, and you fight like mad if you want it. It is my experience that in all these situations, there's a danger that you'll lose the relationship. The men are angry and jealous, and the women

have to protect it and take responsibility for its survival, no question about that. It's nothing to do with sex, it's to do with the man–woman relationship. You need a kind of chemistry, aggravation, constant push. I'm sure it exists, watching the women here in the House.

Like many women politicians, she needed economic support behind her political career, and like many Conservative women she worked in a family business: 'I worked with my husband and helped build up the business for him.' *For him?*

Oh yes, it was all for him, it wasn't for me. It generated a lot of aggravation already, because by that time my husband was getting distinctly ratty about the time all this was taking. I was no longer there just for him. He got very fed up and said, 'If you're going to do things like that, why don't you go out and earn some money, because this is very boring, it is costing the family.' He always used my expertise in the business and had given me a retaining salary, though a very low one, to keep me just below the taxable rate – very male, if you like. But I don't blame him, that was the time, that was his generation, a classic public-school product, and he's had a hell of a time learning to change. I went into a women's world and loved it actually, I liked working with women. I feel very comfortable with women, I always feel you can be totally honest with another woman, I don't know what it is. I've never had any difficulty with women, far less than I have with men. It's that I don't feel I can totally rely on male friendship. It's funny to say that, it's the first time I've ever said it, but it's true. Anyway, I couldn't sit at home, and even my husband recognised that and knew there was no hope of keeping me in the kitchen. But, again, the awful admission that I couldn't get up and apply for a job – lack of confidence in my ability to convince the outside world that I had something to offer. What a pity to have wasted all those years. I'm probably also underestimating the difficulties we all faced in breaking through.

I wanted to push out for individualism, so it was natural then to be a card-carrying member. My husband had been an active Conservative, so I was a kind of wife in the party. I had the chance to become a practising politician and went on the council. I'd never been in the women's bits of the party, and I wasn't interested. When I got on the council I just couldn't believe that this group of incompetent people were running a town. A huge great budget, and there was very little in the way of sensible management skills. It was like a large pudding rolling around the kitchen picking up dust, and every so often you'd pick it up and put it under the tap. So the bossy bits in me came out and I thought, we must organise this. So I did. That was the beginning. Becoming forty – that was the beginning for me.

But the party is now only looking for Parliamentary candidates who are under forty-five. Women in their prime are often past it.

'This is my last fling, because I'm getting too old. If I don't get it now I'll have been around too long.' That was the thought at the front of the mind of a councillor looking for a Parliamentary seat in the mid-1980s when she was in her late thirties.

The town hall seemed an obvious nursery for women with ambitions for the big house, but not any more. Many Tories *believe* in local government and their own government's confrontations with councils over rate-capping and abolition during the eighties made a number of them dissidents. Dissidents don't get seats. 'I expect the toadies who've arselicked and who've been pro-government get on the Central Office list,' said a scarred combatant.

Once on the Parliamentary list, aspiring candidates go through an induction weekend. Some enjoyed it, learned a lot, and felt strengthened; others seemed to see it as a mandatory ordeal: 'For a week I was in tears, I couldn't sleep either,' said one. The prelude to the induction weekend was a Central Office interview after her last Parliamentary contest in which she'd topped the highest poll for a Tory in a no-hope constituency. She expected it to be routine: 'I thought it would be nice, but it was cruel.' She was faced with a man holding a file containing letters and cuttings from the constituency. 'He said somebody had complained I should be thrown out of the party.' This was allegedly because of a press release quoting her as criticising the government:

And people were complaining about my appearance. I said, would they say that about a man? And he just shrugged. I wonder if they do ever say that to some of the rotund little toadies I've been interviewed with. I was so hurt. Anyway, I didn't believe what he said, I didn't know whether it was a try-on to intimidate me or what. Central Office will always deny it, but there's no doubt that they interfere. There was a by-election in my own county and I didn't even get an interview – now you tell me why not! If you go for a by-election, they put up these little wet fellows, don't they? I think they lean on associations and say, 'Watch out for these names.' But you'd never find a piece of paper which actually said that.

This councillor is a veteran of the municipal beargarden. You'd see her at the Town Hall throwing abuse across the benches and kisses across the bar: 'Darling, what was that rubbish you were on about!' Nothing personal, no hard feelings, she's the human face of the Tory Party, the cuddly right, a fearless but generous protagonist, and yet she found the induction weekend awesome:

I knew it was going to be male dominated, although that doesn't actually frighten me. I've been on an assertiveness training course and it helps you not feel intimidated by things like men accusing you of being unfeminine. But I was already feeling so threatened. So I thought to myself: Sod you, you wimps.

So she swotted hard, shopped around for some new frocks, but was a frightened woman. 'It was like a Sandhurst thing, because the guy who runs it was some military man who based it on the selection of officers.'

Out of nearly fifty people at the induction weekend, only 10 per cent were women. They divided into small groups, which usually meant that women were alone, although recently the policy seems to have been to put a couple of women together. Agents would drop in and out of group discussions and each group had its own MP. Hers was a big, bluff man, 'overweight, dirty and dishevelled'. The proceedings began with an address from the chairman in charge of candidates. He reassured them it was not a competition – 'which is crap quite frankly, because only fifteen got through – so you've got to shine. Also, all the adjudicators were men, the group leader was a man, the agents stalking around were all men and the MP was a man, so it's quite a threatening atmosphere.' But there was a surprising shaft of enlightenment:

> Actually it was very interesting. The MP allocated to me asked if I was in the 300 Group, and I said I wasn't. So he said, 'You ought to, and get into the ethos of wanting things for yourselves. Men have clubs, men have everything. If you had something like that, then that's where you'd get your power from.' I told him I'd expected not to get through because of my appearance – 'But then look at you,' I said to him. At least he took that on board.

Then came the most gruelling test – the evening dinner:

> You felt that if you ate or drank too much you were being watched. You see it's this whole thing about a residential weekend – it's like a management course. And to many of the men, that would have been second nature. Then there's clothes – that was one of my biggest problems. A man only needs to take two suits. I admire Margaret Thatcher for that, because she's got to dress for every day, and she's worked out a uniform. I took four or five different lots of clothing. It's all an unseen pressure.

The different trajectories of women and men produce different crises for Parliamentary contenders. The women are either professionals who make out on their own account in the world at large. Or they're women who are provided for, kept women. 'I don't know any woman yet who's got a seat by being a political adviser or working in the research department,' said this aspiring candidate. Men are political advisers and women, like Sara Keays, are secretaries. Political advisers get seats, but secretaries, like Sara Keays, don't.

'Often women buy their way in and flash the minks around. I might have been pandering to that when I got mine – but without a husband I have got to put the image across that I'm capable.' Actually, this woman is a manager who earns her own living.

> I can show them that I'm capable in a number of ways. One is to show that I'm comfortably off – a car registered this year and

a mink coat. I haven't got a lot to offer, I haven't got a rich husband, or a rich backer, but it would affect an association to see a woman who doesn't seem to be affected by not having a husband. They'd feel more confident. Marriage is always an issue, but I can, in effect, say what do I want a husband for while I'm swinging the mink over my shoulders.

I think it's appalling, and I'd do it another way if I could. But if they see a woman who looks affluent and copes on her own they might think they could give me a chance. It's all psychological. The mink, it's like the Queen Mother, it's my props. I hate myself for pandering to it, but there isn't an answer is there? The time to be outrageous is when I get in.

Virginia Bottomley, MP reckoned that the selection process faced women with social tasks that went against the grain of their entire upbringing: 'Women are brought up not to ask anyone to marry you, or to dance, so it puts you in the classic position of not taking initiatives or risking making yourself vulnerable to humiliation.' As a moderate feminist she, not surprisingly, believes that 'if half the electorate are women, and Parliament should be a microcosm of the population, then that there are so few women is worrying. People say the hostility and fear is from women. But no, I've been impressed by women saying, "I wish I'd done it." There's a sense of pride and less jealousy than you're led to think.' But apart from the campaigns by the women's organisation to encourage women, the Tory Party has offered no structural challenge to men swamping the House of Commons, unlike Labour and the Alliance.

Nor is it easy for women to challenge the protocols of the House which set up women as strangers, as other. 'This is the first time I've worked in a setting where not a day goes past without the fact that you're a woman is commented upon. It's all the excessive chivalry and gallantry, I find it offensive. They'll say, "good morning gentlemen – and lady!" It makes me sick.' Do her fellow MPs share their grumbles? 'Women here don't talk about it. Maybe it doesn't irritate them as much,' said Virginia Bottomley. But it does. And still they don't discuss it.

Another Conservative woman MP reckoned:

it is all kept secret because if you exposed it that would expose the immense vulnerability of men in emotional relationships, the tendency for men to be much less stable. They're not involved in the fabric of relationships anyway: women have always undertaken to make the bedrocks of relationships. I still think we have a society in which the men are so frightened of the competition that they'll put up every obstacle that they possibly can. Insofar as we talk about it among the women here, it is very coded, because in Parliament everybody is competing with everybody else. It's probably one of the most competitive places in the world. So in everything you do, you are jealous of the next person, to the ridiculous level of how many letters you get. The girls who are most threatened are the most ambitious. I think I can understand how they feel, because in some ways you've got to seek your own salvation.

You can share that knowledge, but probably not with other women politicians. I can share it with other women, two or three very close women friends. I'm closer to the mothers here: we do talk a bit more and share the difficulties. I don't really know why we don't talk about the pain – maybe in the Conservative Party if it was expressed it would be regarded as much too close to lesbianism, to an admission that you were a great feminist protagonist – there is an absolute demarcation line. What is so fascinating about it is this: it's perfectly okay for the men to be gay, we've got loads of them. So they've broken down that barrier, or maybe it never existed for the men, because they did it when they were kids. Nobody talks about it but we all recognise it. But for women to have emotional feelings about each other, for women to have any kind of sexual inclinations, or feelings that they could form a better and closer relationship with another woman, is just not done. Women have got to be strictly for marriage, for all the things which are respected in this society, for men. Absolutely. That's my interpretation of it. That makes life exceedingly difficult.

It's almost as if the party has put a ring around you. I think this partly explains Margaret Thatcher's difficulty. Because she's ten or more years older than many of us, she's had to go through it ten years longer, and so she's isolated and she's attached herself to men. Completely! And I can see exactly why she's done it. There's no question that she still has the feelings, even though she doesn't act on them. Given a different era and a different opportunity, things would have been different. But she's been so long competing and she's had so much going against her – my God, don't underestimate what it's done to her inside. She's just like the rest of us, with all the same female instincts. She really has gone through all kinds of hell.

So who does this MP confide in? 'Not the women here. Not in many people. It's terribly important to get this out into the open.'

SEX AND POWER

The Conservative Party is about nothing if not about power: the power of men. Their power has been nursed by the most powerful courts, clubs and corporations in Britain – and by women; it is through the work of women that men have secured their popular base. Like the women of the labour movement, the history of Conservative Party women is about the problem of power, and the engagement of the powerless with the powerful. It is after all the party which claims an identity of interest with England's institutions and traditions, and so Conservative women's history is uniquely about their relationship with the most powerful men in British politics.

The party is, therefore, one of the critical institutions in which the ideologies of sex and class are organised. The party does not just reflect values, it produces them, and so its internal organisation both reflects the balance of power between men and women in society, and participates in producing a social relationship between the sexes. The existence of power based on sexual difference and subordination is diffused throughout the organisation; in fact the party is defined by sexual difference.

The contradiction at the centre of British Conservatism is that the party provides a space inhabited by a strong feminine presence and yet it is one of the institutions which structures women's subordination as a sex and supports the class and gender power of men. We know that women have a strong presence in the party, but that cannot exhaust our discussion; the question is, how is that presence organised and does it produce power for women? Does it produce a women's politics? And in any case, what would that mean: does it produce 'feminine' or 'feminist' politics? It could be, historically, that in a political world in which the patriarchal imperative was hegemonic, Conservatism most successfully among all the political parties profiled the acceptable face of femininity. But patriarchal values are no longer hegemonic, and so the question also must be: can Conservatism withstand the challenge, or find some accommodation with it?

Parading power

How does power present itself in the party? Watching the appearance of government ministers in the midst of Conservative women is to watch power on parade, suggested subtly by the nuances of style and sexuality.

When Michael Heseltine was Secretary of State for Defence he was billed at a Conservative conference for younger women in Birmingham in 1985. He was escorted in by a coterie of courtiers in frocks. Conservative women do not go in for the ambiguous androgyny of their contemporaries – their femininity is reasserted in the frock. Actually he's wearing the uniform of the ruling class, tailored in Jermyn Street. The lapels are sharp, the back flaps are deep, discreetly drawing attention to one of the modern man's erogenous zones. He is ceremoniously ushered forward with the chivalry usually reserved for women. But this isn't role reversal; it is the etiquette of deference and, it must be said, good manners. He didn't smile, he didn't look at the waiting women watching his body as he walked down the aisle. He didn't need to meet their eyes, because that would have denoted equality, or at least complicity in a relationship. He was already the centre of attention – he was the subject. For the women, it was their big day. For him, it was all in a day's work.

Tory women were worried about defence. Or rather, they'd say they were worried about the people who make other people worried about defence. Nevertheless there was a voice of protest that Heseltine hadn't addressed people's worries out there – Conservative women are often the conduit from '*out there*' to '*up there*' – particularly about Star Wars and Britain's subordination to the US. 'I have many private meetings with NATO ministers,' he told them, and they shouldn't be under any illusions that all he tells NATO is 'thank you'. But of course, he said, he couldn't divulge what he said without letting on to the Russians. By implying 'trust me' he wasn't sharing a secret with them, but keeping his secret from them. The politicians' prerogative allowed him to recover his authority. He appears to take them seriously and yet he withhoids himself from them. His narcissism is consummate and covert.

When his speech was over he was thanked with effusive ambiguity. The chairman rose and smiled at him, and as her head tilted towards him, she spoke for his audience: Thank you for addressing us in such a 'strong, reassuring and caring manner and bringing this morning's proceedings to such a super climax'. Is it gratitude or gratification? These encounters are inevitably suffused with the idiom of desire: the desire for such men is desire for their power. Fantasy may be the only control women can exercise over superstars.

Shortly after Jeffrey Archer was appointed deputy chairman of the party – and he was appointed, not elected, a salutary fact about the party which has stolen the vocabulary of democracy from the left – he toured the constituencies to cheer them up, rather in the genre of a stand-up comic or after-dinner entertainer. (He was forced to resign after first denying and then admitting that he'd paid off a prostitute who, he said he'd never met.) Addressing an audience of Conservative women in the North-East at their annual meeting, much in the same manner as the rest of his 'turns' around the constituencies, he told a few self-deprecating jokes and then reminded them of the achievements of their Prime Minister.

'Cuts! I'll tell you about cuts. Margaret Thatcher cut Arthur Scargill down to size . . . Have we forgotten how much freedom we have gained?' he asked, offering quips to questions without answering the women's anxieties. Everyone had a tendency to belittle public service, he said, speaking to the great strength of Conservative women. He, too, was glad to be of service when six weeks earlier 'Margaret Thatcher rang and asked me to be deputy chairman.' None of his audience may have experienced such personal and powerful patronage, but nevertheless he proclaimed that he was enrolling all of them into public service by his side. He transcended their powerlessness by the directness of his personal appeal and by his equation between public service and service to the party, making the party synonymous with the nation. 'With the authority of the Prime Minister behind me, I appoint every one of you deputy deputy chairman of the Conservative Party.'

Kiddies' stuff, we might think, insulting even, but this and the Heseltine story signify, in their different ways, the performance of power. The architecture of the party conference constructs the delegates as audience, in which their participation only punctuates main acts such as these. 'The delegates do not come to hear their rulers but to see them', wrote Christopher Hollis of the conference in 1960.[1] The women's conferences are exemplars of this spectacle; the agendas and participants are tightly controlled, no doubt as a matter of habit but also, it must be said, to silence the Tory mob who constitute the rabid stereotype of the Conservative woman. Even at their *own* conference the women are still a mere audience whose anonymity and passivity is mediated only by the activity of admiration and collective fantasy.

Conservative women's conferences are not really about women at all, but are events in which women's place in the party is registered; by all sorts of devices the boundaries of their rights and, more importantly, their responsibilities are carefully defined. What they do not do is talk about themselves, and so they do not make themselves their own political subject. Instead, the hierarchical structure which operates throughout the party intrudes on their own women's space, as a hierarchy of sexual difference.

Party organisation

A word is needed here about the party structure. The women's base is the constituency women's association or the women's committee of a ward branch, either of which is represented on the constituency women's committee. The women's work is mainly to organise events like the Christmas get-together, a political luncheon a couple of times a year, to get the MP or a minister down to talk to the women in the constituency. Most importantly, they resource the party machine locally and, according to one woman active amongst Conservative women, the women's meetings 'are not regarded as political gatherings'; they are 'where the real money is raised to pay the agent. If it wasn't for the women, the agent wouldn't get paid.'

Within constituencies, the politics are most likely to be galvanised by a branch of the Conservative Political Centre, where people really interested in politics meet. If the women feel strongly about something they can raise it at their monthly constituency women's advisory committee meetings and the chairman, who will probably be a vice-chairman of her constituency association, too, might bring it to the constituency, which might then relay it to the MP or the appropriate minister.

The women's committees have representatives on the area

women's committee, which is represented on the Conservative National Women's Committee (CNWC) which meets five times a year, usually at Central Office and, like the constituency committees, usually during the day. The timing is important, for it prescribes the kind of Tory women able to operate at that level: she is either a woman without a job (and in Tory circles that doesn't mean she's on the dole) or she is more or less a boss in her workplace. The CNWC is in turn represented on the Executive Committee of the National Union (the party). The constituency committee may send resolutions for the women's conference to Central Office, where the agenda for the conference is arranged; and, as a member of the national women's committee put it, 'they work out as anodyne an agenda as possible'. Another view would be that the resolutions selected express the consensus among members. That agenda is pretty immovable; people might criticise and have words in other people's ears, but to challenge it publicly would be disloyal. And that's a sin in the Tory Party. 'You're powerless to change the agenda,' explained a member of the CNWC:

> There's no committee you can go to to discuss rearranging
> things; you can talk about it behind the scenes, but you don't
> do it up front and let people see you, because you'd be marked
> down while everyone else is smiling sweetly. Actually, it's
> sick. And if you want a Parliamentary seat, you've got to be
> seen not to be disloyal. You fawn over ministers, because of
> their rank.

So, the women's conferences are not arenas in which politics are argued over or where ideas are interrogated. They are theatres in which the women are entertained by some of the most powerful men in the party and in British politics. The women are their witness.

The agenda is arranged around the ministers who pay their visits. The debates are seen to be the moment when the powerless *see* the powerful, and have the ear of the powerful. For many women, particularly those whose political life is spent in the warrens of fund-raising activities, this is a proud, privileged moment of access to the men who really run things. But to a few the whole thing epitomises not only the marginalisation of the women, but also the party's lack of democracy and an almost religious relationship between leaders and led. According to one woman:

These men are deified, they're treated like gods. You give a lot of reverence to his job, and you feel like saying, 'Gosh, somebody has deigned to visit us.' I'm a Catholic and it reminds me of the church – the nuns wheel in the priest and fawn all over him, and stand back in awe, treating him like god. The nuns are excellent creatures, they're usually intelligent, educated women, and the priests will be narrow-minded and limited. That's how I see the women in the party.

The eroticism of power

The women of the party minister to the men who possess the power. It makes them the mothers or the wives or the mistresses of the party – they're all categories which are invested with the power to give life, to nurture it, to keep secrets, but which have no social power. Women's role in the party is associated with the self-denying qualities of femininity which support the power of others. That's one way that the women are able to veil the realities of the power structure, because they *confer* power upon the men. And because the men's power appears to be *given* by the women, they consent to it. That makes women *necessary*. But it makes power-sharing unnecessary.

The party structures and the personal relationships between men and women within them reaffirm the way in which the problem of power is blurred by being eroticised. One woman councillor recalls her first encounter with politics as symbolising the situation of women in the party:

There was an older woman, a friend of my mother's, she was very rich, she had the biggest diamond ring you ever saw, and she was a brilliant fund-raiser; she bullied everybody! We all went one day to visit the Westminster flat of our MP, and this woman said to the MP's wife, 'May I see where he sleeps . . .' Can you imagine? That's why some of these women won't have women candidates, because there's something between the men and these women, and it epitomises the way our party carries on. A woman wouldn't have the same glamour. Imagine it, you go to a political supper and this dazzling man walks in, and the women feel young again, they feel free. The power is all mixed up with sex. It's like pop stars and groupies.

These men and women trade signals, signs and tokens which re-make their relationship. The women are caressed with chaste conceits. Their prizes are the baubles of antique chivalry – all those exquisite courtesies that enfeeble women in their moment of glory.

The annual women's conference is a gracious event, and between the ministers and the organisers the rather over-the-top ceremonies are reciprocal, except that the fetish of the vote of thanks often makes the women excessive: 'So grateful that you could come, minister . . .' But the point is that they *are* grateful. When it comes to who has the power, everything is covert and yet perfectly clear, such are the codes of diplomacy. The minister doesn't tell the women that he's glad they could come; he reassures them that their work is important – except, of course, that it is like cleaning the toilet: it is the work that only women do.

'Basically,' reckoned one young Conservative woman,

the women's conference is there to support the government, and the government looks upon it as its token representing women, to show that they've got women on their side. That's what's so sad: it's a bit of a con. Maybe it's a trade-off and not a con, because the women don't have much power, but on the other hand they get to meet ministers, and ministers recognise that the women can't really carry public opinion with them, but they're a resource to be drawn on. In any constituency where there's a Conservative women's organisation, any party official can always guarantee that the women will organise something for them. They are very, very loyal.

In general men's quest for power and admiration is unquestioned. That comes from common sense, from the idea that masculinity is self-evidently into power and control, that these are natural drives, almost biologically inscribed in the genes.[2] So the party's structures become amphitheatres in which masculinity and power are at play. What could be seen as men's megalomania is perceived as the *nature* of masculinity, and men are seen as social beings because they are not private beings: their identity is assumed not to be achieved through their private relationships.[3] The *idea* is that men and women naturally cluster in their separate spheres and skills, but the *reality* is that the party has a centrifugal effect: it brings men and women together and then throws them apart into their separate spheres.

What is hidden, though, is the work of others that supports men and their ambition and reinforces their need for attention. Their personal dependence on women – their public production of themselves, their *social* impact – relies on the services of women, on someone else taking care of their day-to-day reproduction, and so it is in politics and political parties. A friend of mine once described the modern male executive's promiscuous dependencies as being like a Yuppie version of a harem: they have their wives at home and surrogate wives at work, and no one is surprised when *all* their relationships with women are sexualised.

Sara Keays' relationship with former Cabinet Minister Cecil Parkinson, MP was perhaps the classic case of the traditional personal-political contract between men and women in which the man's dependence was clandestine, it was camouflaged by their differential power. The fact that he had social power and she did not, that he was always coming and going while she was always there meant that his power was manifest and his dependency was entirely covert.

Sara Keays – the problem of power

The trauma for the Conservative Party of the Parkinson affair was, of course, nothing to do with the personal trauma for the individuals involved, nor was it actually anything to do with morality. Cabinet ministers have been having affairs with their secretaries, or whoever, since whenever, and irony of ironies the Thatcher government has been besieged by the public revelation of prominent men's multiple sexual dependencies. Insofar as it survived the scandals it was because the contemporary culture had moved on from the 'traditional values' ideology promulgated with increasing desperation by the party.

Sara Keays' refusal to be the scapegoat kaleidoscoped the full panorama of sexual politics in the Conservative Party. She declined to remain in the proper obscurity of her role as a secretary and thwarted the Prime Minister's desire to restore Cecil Parkinson to what she believed was his proper place. She refused to be the only one left to pick up the pieces. Here was a woman from the Tory hinterland whose desire to be a politician only brought her into the service of other politicians. 'It was a classic situation,' said a woman close to the party leadership; 'she fell in love with her boss.' No doubt like many other Conservative women, she happened to have fallen in love with Cecil Parkinson. And no doubt like many other Conservative men, Cecil Parkinson – unlike Sara Keays – being a *public* man, was not expected to be responsible for his private life. That, apparently, was the responsibility of his women. 'The contradiction [of the double standard] is resolved for men by visiting it upon women,' argues Hollway.[4] Men are 'expected to be incontinent and out of control – "it's only natural"'.

At the 1985 party conference when the *Daily Mirror* published extracts from her book, *A Question of Judgement*, *all* of the women whose opinions I sought on the 'scandal', said, 'She must have known what she was doing.' Did they think that he, too, must have known what he was doing? 'Well, men! They don't, do they?' replied one of them, echoing the sentiments of all. In the party of personal responsibility, Parkinson didn't have to take responsibility. They forgave him as mothers forgive children. Still the party mourns the loss of Cecil. It is as if not only Sara and Cecil grieve for their loss, but the women of the party grieve, for their own fantasies about Parkinson have been ruined by reality. Parkinson's demise is discussed in terms of the party's loss of a charismatic and efficient manager and the personal loss of a political career, although it is expressed with a passion that also eroticises his fall.

Here was a man who enjoyed mass desire. The fantasised desire for Parkinson became a need to protect him, to save him from his descent, and to *blame Sara Keays*. But for what? In a curious reversal of roles, they blamed her for ruining him, when he had patently only ruined himself. Or was she also blamed for *having* him? For having what they wanted? And even worse, in her own fate had she not revealed the realpolitik of unequal romance? How many women who damned her had done what she refused to do, to hide herself in the abortion clinic?

He continued to be mourned, this Icarus, although of course he was never really a 'fallen man': men may err but they don't fall. He was never equivalent to Sara Keays, nor were any similar feelings of loss ever extended to her. She was exiled from the world of Conservative politics, not least, of course, because her political world was his. She was never an activist in her own right.

I was content to subordinate my own career to his. The events of October 1983 ended my career. The party refused to have anything to do with me and have never given me any reason for taking me off the candidates' list. Gummer [party chairman] insisted I see them. They've never put anything in writing. They've never said why I've been removed. Cecil's position in the government could only be secured by minimising the scandal, which was done by belittling his involvement with me and concealing that he'd consistently lied to us. Various Tory supporters in the media have written about him as my victim, he's paid the price and served his sentence. It was acceptable for my career to be destroyed, there was no comment on why I'm not fit to be a candidate.

If I'd been an MP my position would have been secure. But because I wasn't people had very little to go on – perhaps they didn't think I'd lost anything.

But of course Parkinson had prevented her from becoming an MP. According to her book, he intervened – unbeknown to Keays – with the chairwoman of Bermondsey constituency party to get Keays removed from the shortlist for the seat before the 1983 by-election.

The crucial factor in Sara Keays' case was the fact that she had important and confidential knowledge gained by her role as companion and confidante. According to Keays, she included very selective references to Cabinet matters in her book because she wanted to establish that she *knew*, to corroborate her case against Margaret Thatcher's handling of the Parkinson crisis. In effect she showed that there was a continuous relationship with Parkinson, because she knew state secrets. She says she did not want to 'kiss and tell' and I believe her: she has plenty to tell, and she hasn't told it. I think she wanted to establish herself as a considerable person, a person who had been respected, nay loved, by Parkinson, and who, therefore, deserved to be treated respectfully by the party.

But the leadership panicked when the *Daily Mirror* serialised excerpts from her book during the 1985 party conference, a crucial event in Margaret Thatcher's calendar for Parkinson's rehabilitation. Keays' references included the Falklands War Cabinet and Thatcher's repudiation of critics as 'fainthearts' because 'I knew the Prime Minister would remember the exact circumstances of that meeting, as I did.'

'That's when she [Keays] had the government in her power,' said one woman prominent in party circles. Margaret Thatcher had been unwavering in her insistence that this was a personal matter, which was rubbish in the context of Thatcherism's new moralism. Only when the leadership felt that Keays could tell *political secrets* was it clear that this line couldn't hold. For Sara Keays, however, the issue was how to defend her own honour, and what became represented as the wrath of a wronged woman was, for her, only a wronged woman's refusal to be the victim.

What was also extraordinary about the whole thing was that Sara Keays' strength derived from her deeply middle-class respectability. She believed in herself, and yet she was able publicly to defend herself as a single parent because the culture in which she and the Conservative Party existed had already been transformed by forces beyond them, forces for sexual change and equality which the Conservative leadership repudiated.

Women's quarters

The party has always enjoyed an enormous reservoir of women's good will, time and labour. But the traditional allocations of political space are experiencing a crisis of form. Younger professional women don't fit into it, and ambitious women avoid the women's structures like they avoid gonorrhoea because, like the Primrose League before them, the associations are contradictory: they are freedom and prison. Edwina Currie, MP not only didn't get tangled in the women's web of the party, preferring the 'political part', but pronounced the negative definition with the immortal words: 'I'm not a woman, I'm a Conservative.'

Women's associations have been an acceptable space for women to enter the social life of their community, and yet for many women their codes of conduct also prescribed subordination. 'I was brought up to do as I was told and men were definitely superior,' remembers an active member of the National Federation of Women's Institutes, Susan Maynard, who spent some years in the local Conservative Association:

My father was involved in the constituency Conservative club and you were because your father was. The trouble with a lot of the middle class is that convention is very important, sometimes overriding, because you're not sure what you are. Women

put themselves second. I didn't like strong women. I got
involved in the local Conservative Association because I did
it with my husband. It was about being involved in the village
and it was all about fund-raising. All the women got involved
in dogsbody things. Then I was asked to go to one of their
dreadful advisaries – they weren't my sort of woman, they
were very hard and very strong. I wasn't very self-confident. It
was just about belonging to the right social thing, the golf
club, etc. There was very limited contact between the women:
our main function was raising funds and elections. When I
joined the Women's Institute that had some effect – it made
me a feminist. I was married then to a man who went to a
public school and regarded women as doormats – it took me
twenty years to realise I wasn't one. I felt I had no rights. I
was reading things like *Cosmopolitan* and *New Society* because
I'm terribly curious – I didn't realise I was rebelling, because
nobody was interested in what I was doing. There isn't any
class distinction in the WI. You can go to a meeting and
someone can stand up, plump, in crimplene with an accent you
don't understand and she's a brilliant chairwoman. You go
and you are you, not anybody's wife or mother. I was successful
– for the first time people thought I was good at something.
I learned I was good at organising and working with other
people. I didn't know I could be firm.

The Conservative Association offered women the peripheral
jobs and that's what I felt, that women were being
marginalised. Women are very Conservative because they are
told not to be assertive, they don't like being unpopular, they
need everybody to like them and they don't like change. But
when you get in the WI people talking about social issues
like subsidy for buses or family planning they are very socialist
principles. I don't find Labour attractive because it's so
masculine, somebody like Scargill and the men come over very
heavy and macho. And I think women would think that.

Another countrywoman, Barbara Stone, became the chairman of
her association, but echoes the view of the women's sections and
indeed much of the rest of the party as apolitical:

I was frightfully bossy. The church and politics are very good ways of getting into the community. What did we talk about? The next party and canvassing. In its small way it was riveting, a little cameo of village life. It was the newcomers who needed it: the older ones would come to the parties as onlookers but the organisers were the dormitory types. It was all to raise money. It was such fun. At the meetings there would be about ten people, slightly more women than men. The men would complain, I felt because they didn't want the women taking over. The local big landowner was always the treasurer – he'll be the treasurer until he drops or somebody shoots him. It's just like the BBC or the church. One man actually went to something that discussed politics and he asked me if I wanted to meet a politician. I wasn't interested in politics and couldn't have cared less. As committee members the women had more time, they had more to do and were more active. All sorts of people from the community came to the parties. The MP would come and I'd say, 'This is a party and we're not having him speaking.'

It was a farce – all those wasted years. I used to work for the Tories in a very uncommitted way, it was like going to church. I don't do that much now. But I canvassed like mad – I enjoyed that because you could get through quite a lot on the doorstep. It never occurred to me to think about the issues, it was like a spirit, like your family: you didn't look too closely at them.

This speaks of the way women are both a presence and an absence – their presence is vital to the Conservatives' operations as a mass party, and yet there is no tradition of strategic work among the women. Their interventions are *ad hoc* and often dependent on an agenda set elsewhere. Their own conferences have been reticent about the politics of women. The line-up of speakers is determined by who is available from Central Office to address them, rather than by the women's own potential policy imperatives. There is thus little place for the women *en masse* to formulate their own objectives.

Women's women

Women's associations in the party represent for some a deliberate choice of women as their political companions, and an affirmation of women's political skills and strengths, their culture and their causes. It is a way of being *in* politics independently of men, without challenging men, and quite simply it is a way of having an unchaperoned social life.

The women's associations are also about *being women*, a way of being not like men. But until recently they were about *not* having or wanting power. 'To move into the women's structures of the party would have been death,' says one woman MP who is, for all that, passionate about her commitment to working with women. Tory women don't want to be like men, and generally they don't have a feminist critique of certain forms of femininity being in some way associated with their subordination – they cling to the *form*, if not the *content* of femininity.

A certain ideological promiscuity – they might call it pragmatism – enables them to share the feminist project insofar as it is about power – they acknowledge a sense of debt owed to the suffrage movement – at the same time as adhering to forms of femininity which in another context might appear as a caricature, as effeminacy.

To problematise femininity for many Conservative women is difficult, not least because so much of their social discourse is structured around it. But it also poses a difficult dilemma: does it mean being like men? Reflecting on the post-war dilemmas of the educated woman, Wendy Hollway writes about how one form of modern feminism represented women as equal because they were the same as men. 'This fitted my pre-feminist assumptions that men were more powerful, interesting, etc. I was attracted to men partly because I wanted to be like them.' But this produced a crisis. 'Being one of the lads necessitated a negative definition of myself as a woman . . . women were a group I put myself outside of.'[5] Many Conservative women live out the same contradiction. For some the women's organisation is a desert deprived of gutsy politicking, power and men. But, as within the culture of Women's Liberation, there is also a counter-tendency – an engagement with femininity as part of the process of belonging to the community of women, and as part of the process of redefining women as strong but as *not men.*

There is a sense in which the notion of equality is, to some Tory women, problematic: if it means being like men then they don't want it. In a situation in which objectively women are denied power as a group, the experience of powerlessness appears to be dissolved in the assertion of sexual difference. So, although the women's organisation appears to sanction men's power, it has also historically given women a space. And rather like the corners and kitchens which are women's space, it felt comfortable. It was not coveted, perhaps, but for many women it was preferable to being ignored in the parlour.

What women think of men

Gender and power are the most obvious things Conservative women see – they see it everywhere – but they make it into something with which they can cope and which doesn't injure their sense of self-respect. Behind women's subordination in the party and in society is their knowledge that although they do not have power they do take responsibility, and just as men's narcissism is forgiven, so the women cope with men's domination by infantilising them.

'Men – I love 'em, but they can be very stupid and very prejudiced. Stick with women, they get things done. Men talk about it,' says Freda Cocks, a former Lord Mayor of Birmingham who has a strong sense of the community of women and the hostile manoeuvres of men. 'I live alone and without the support of my women friends I'd be a very lonely woman. And men are far more bitchy than women. They talk about other men, and they gossip about women to suit their own ends.'

A widow, Dorothy Love, for whom the world seemed divided by gender as much as anything, reckoned that:

Men dominate. My husband would go on at me if I disagreed. I had three brothers who kept me down and pushed me into a corner. I had to fight that. In some ways women should have more power. Women are more courageous than men, maybe it's our generation. The war taught us that we had a lot to give, to fight for Britain and to make it good.

Retired businesswoman Betty Zikel believes that:

Without a doubt women are stronger than men. Women are harder workers from my experience. Men pooh-pooh it, but in their heart of hearts they know it. They have the masterly approach. If a woman worms her way around a man it's deceitful – I say what I think and it comes right in the end. They like to say no to you, they want to belittle you.

For many Conservative women men's dominance shrouds their dependence. A respectable Christian, Elsie Ward, is dedicated to the appearance of her own marriage as a sharing arrangement, but admits among her friends that underneath the appearances

> they [men] forget that it's a sharing thing. Mine is good, but he's rotten at giving up anything. Men never really grow up – there's that element in them. It's the mothering instinct we have. They want to be mothered, that's men. I always feel that he leaves a lot to me.

She tells him to put his coat on when he goes out, she nurses him when he falls ill, which usually happens when there are big decisions to make, and it is she who is the architect of their social life, bowls and coffee mornings, trips to concerts, evening meals with their friends.

'The husbands have a social life that's built around the women friends,' said her daughter-in-law. 'If the men have a social life it's based on work, so they never have to actually organise it. These older women *find friends*, they organise things and they make life function. Even if it's the men's network it's the women who are the enablers.' For her mother-in-law a politics which names women's oppression is anathema – because it doesn't describe how she feels about herself. But it also constrains her from extending her critique from the particular to the general, and from feeling that she herself can make change: 'I never felt unequal, though I gave up things and he didn't. Although I've felt pretty lucky all my life, I wouldn't want to get married again.'

All these are typical cameos of common sense to be found among women inside and outside the party. Their domestic strategies are not dissimilar to political strategies within the party, behind all of which is a calculation of the forces they are up against, a fear of the backlash. 'I rather worry about militancy among the Labour women. If they were more gentle and devious they could achieve more,' says an active Conservative rank and filer in Cumbria. 'Never go overboard,' counsels Wendy Mitchell, a recent chairwoman of the Conservative women in Greater London. 'If you go overboard you lose things.'

The positioning of men and women within the party effectively regulates women's role in such a way as to mirror women's room for manoeuvre in society at large. The party has its ways of doing things. Political manners, however, are never neutral, and just as they prescribe people's proper place in the hierarchy, so they prescribe behaviour proper to femininity.

Lady Olga Maitland has risked disapproval for taking her populist anti-CND crusade out of the institutionalised format of the party and into the streets:

> Grassroots politics is unusual for Conservatives. I'm an unusual person actually. I know people will laugh: 'Ho ho, we know she is', but I'm not actually a Central Office clone and that gives me greater freedom of thought. That means I don't get held back by that terrible term 'one doesn't . . . that's not the way we do it'. I've never been cloned and conditioned by Central Office habits. But Families for Defence was a different way of doing things. I took the left on on their own terms. Some people say that's not the right thing to do. I think it is.

Many Tory women have samizdat stories to tell of discrimination which derives from the party's political manners, and that, of course, made their dissent not only an offence against men, but against the proper ways of doing things. A London councillor in a Tory-controlled borough recalled an incident in 1975, International Women's Year:

> It was early in my life as a councillor, we'd been invited by the mayor to a dinner at the city hall. We had a wonderful meal, I was being abstemious because I was driving and I was really looking forward to the port, which I knew would be splendid. When the moment arrived, the mayor said would the ladies move out! I toyed with the idea of not moving and taking the port, but I went to the loo instead and slammed the door! All the other ladies there were spouses – I was the only female councillor present – so I got no support from them. Anyway, I had an argument with the mayor, and got nowhere, so I said I'd ask a question in council. He went purple and said, 'You'll do no such thing.' I said how come in International Women's Year the council was so antediluvian that women had to leave before the passing of the port. Anyway, I did put a question but it was intercepted by a secretary. One of the Labour members said, 'Trust the Tories to resolve it like that!'

For ambitious women going places politically, a party is the obvious and necessary conduit to power, but the amoebic architecture of the Conservative Party may not mean that they go there particularly fast, especially if, as with Lady Olga Maitland, they attempt to create their own base. Getting a reputation may end up meaning 'getting a reputation'.

A businesswoman attracted by the thought of a political career decided to get involved with the women's organisation of the party in her borough:

In all political parties policy is made at the top. The political structure is like an octopus, you don't know where the tentacles are. I say to myself, look for allies, otherwise people will annihilate you. I have none. Politics is the last thing they're interested in here. We have a political committee in every constituency which meets once a month, everybody shouts their mouth off. It's very foolish to start at the bottom – if you study power you see it doesn't come from the grass roots. In the Conservative Party they have a lot of parties and since we're in a Labour ward I thought it would be a good thing to have a political meeting. Everybody warned me we'd only get ten people. So I wrote hundreds of letters and we got sixty. It was basically PR, but the agent told me I'd offended people, that that wasn't how we do things.

Getting to the party women's conference was hell – it's an art form. I heard about it and didn't know anything about it, although I'm well informed and I've got a full-time secretary. So my secretary asked the agent and he said only the women's committees go. I said, 'I'm here two years, I want to be an MP, you know I'm interested, so why didn't I know about it?' Nobody expects the women's committee to do anything except have parties, but they get tickets to go. So how do you get on the women's committee? I started pestering head office, it took me about twenty-five phone calls. I had a black friend and she'd never heard of it either, and she's poor, she doesn't have the money to make these phone calls. I thought I'd tell them: 'Be smart, have at least one black face.' So I got her a ticket. I'm doing all these things and one day I hope it will all come together. To make what? To get you out of anonymity. I'm killing myself to do things for the party. A little while ago my secretary had rung head office. My agent knew about it. He'd wanted me to go through him. He said I was getting known. 'Known' means you're making a lot of noise, which is not 100 per cent positive.

Getting results

In all the major political parties, women's organisation has existed in a kind of quarantine, a contradictory source of both power and powerlessness. The questions we have to ask of all women's sections within political parties are: are women constituted as subjects in their own right; are they the centre of their own conversation, and does the party empower women politically? There has always been conflict about the efficacy of women's structures and whether they are the best way to encourage women's participation in politics. 'Some people probably felt that it was better for women to be in the mainstream,' said Angela Hooper,

> but on the other hand you don't get the results that can attract women to the organisation. A lot of people think you can achieve more by putting everything in the melting pot, but I don't because it gets reduced, melted down. A lot of people think you can achieve more the other way, but on the other hand the strength isn't there.

Edwina Currie admits that 'in the Conservative Party women are very important, they run it', but she didn't want to be involved in their structures: 'Most of them are not interested in making policy.' She was, however, and so she was involved in Birmingham Conservative Political Centre, 'which was for the people who didn't like the chasing around, got bored with fund-raising and who wanted to talk politics'. Did they ever talk about the politics of women, though? 'Not that I can recall.'

One of the participants in the women's organisation felt that the problem was not so much that the women weren't political but that they weren't taken seriously. 'I've always felt one could understand how the minority groups feel, having worked in women's organisations all my life. I've felt we were treated in the same way. Certainly the women had always been seen to be useful, doing all the envelopes and all the background work . . .'

The dominant modes for women making their views known are informal lobbying, writing to an MP, having a word in an ear. This generates a feeling within the party that ordinary members and local associations have access to power, that they have the right to expect a reply, and some action. But this does not challenge the distribution of power in favour of men. The system confirms the rulers' right to rule. 'Accountability' and 'mandate' are not words in the Tory vocabulary. The informal route is always contingent on good behaviour and constitutes women as the supplicant sex. They have a whispering power, the power to influence, but rarely to effect change.

By the mid-seventies, however, things were on the move: the women's organisation was moving into the mainstream, sharing some of the ambitions of the women's movement at large. The reserved style of Janet Young and Angela Hooper was very different from Sara Morrison's flamboyant iconoclasm, but they were no less committed to the cause. 'What we wanted to do was identify clearly for the women and for the outside world that Conservative women were a political organ in the party,' says Angela Hooper. 'When you sort of blew the trumpet outside the party to the press and they bit on something, that was very good from the public point of view.' Angela Hooper felt that

> there were moments initially internally when you thought, oh dear, they think we're trying to direct operations, identifying that other parts of the party weren't as political as they might be and showing them up if you like, so you had to take it slowly. But we were lucky in that we had Lord Thorneycroft as chairman, who actually said quite frequently that the real political arm of the party were women. That was because we followed things through.

There have been occasions when this enabled women to transgress their own traditions and risk official disapproval by clearly challenging the party leadership or the government. A classic case was child benefit. The very existence of the women's organisation provided women with the means of organising to defend it – and winning.

Hooper and Young not only introduced the habit of the women's organisation making its impact felt on the Budget-makers, but they also changed the format of the women's conference to politicise the women themselves. They began to spread responsibility for serious political thinking to the areas through working parties which prepared papers for discussion at the annual women's conference: 'That had been unusual, certainly for the women,' says Hooper, 'and if you take the National Union, apart from the constituencies producing resolutions, they didn't do anything, not in the way of working parties or, if you like, lobbying. Maybe they prefer it that way.'

Plus ça change. The National Union has remained subordinate to Central Office since the struggle by Gorst in the late nineteenth century to transform the relationship between the party leaders, the National Union and Central Office. Then, as now, the role of the National Union was to present no alternative centre of power which could challenge Central Office.

'The National Union wasn't producing initiatives, it was much more of a talking shop. But we gave themes to the women's conference and we had papers as opposed to resolutions to present to ministers, which hadn't happened before,' said Hooper. The switch to working parties and papers was radical. Each area would take on a theme, research it and write a paper:

> We wanted to do it that way because if you don't you lose grassroots opinion. That was regarded as a bold initiative at the time. The majority appreciated it and thought it was very important.
>
> The women had always been undervalued and this was one of the factors we wanted to open up, to identify what the women were doing – and it showed what I was convinced of, that the women were the most political arm of the party. They felt strongly about employment, housing; some of them were interested in working conditions, prospects for younger people, prospects for themselves coming back into the labour market in their forties. That marked a change, because in the past the majority hadn't had jobs. Certainly over the past ten years there were more women working, which reflected the changes in society at large. Women and tax, we've always felt strongly about that – independent taxation. We lobbied on that for quite a few years and produced two study booklets on it. And the environment, they were always very keen on that because there are so many different types in a women's

organisation. There were quite a group who were out for heritage and preservation, then there were others who wanted less lead in petrol.

What we found was that it was a *learning* process as well. We had representatives who were on all sorts of organisations, and although the women's organisation didn't instruct them what they had to do, they had an opportunity to report back to the national women's committee and quite often we were alerted to things we could do. For example, the women's hospitals, the Elizabeth Garret Anderson Hospital, which we fought very hard to save. Part of it was they felt very strongly about services for women. They didn't necessarily think that there should only be women-only hospitals, but they felt in that case that it was a monument that represented a lot to women and that if we lose these things we are losing part of our past. We also took up mixed wards – we didn't want them.

It was all about women identifying their ideas and showing the Parliamentary party that they were a political force – and source. The other thing I did one year was to invite the ministers who were going to respond to see if there were any areas of their departmental responsibility that they'd like questions on. What I tried to do was go full circle, which had never happened before. I think it made a lot more work for the women to do, but on the whole they were always pleased that it was a professional performance, it showed what they'd done and most people like that to be recognised. It was a good time.

The women's organisation also began to systematise its relationship to the areas. Area chairmen were asked to report on issues important locally and they would be reported to ministers. The women's committee capitalised on its special relationship to the government, both representing the women's grievances and providing a conduit for women to the highest powers in the party. They often lobbied ministers on their worries about political problems as they emerged – rates, small businesses, immigration: the Conservative women opposed discrimination against immigrant women who were not given the same facilities for marriage as men.

Tension was certainly felt, then, in the relationship between the party leadership and the women's organisation, and between the men and the women. The form the politicisation of the women took was to accentuate their interests as women, and to campaign within the party on behalf of women. However incomplete the process, however tentative the women's initiatives, something was afoot – and it was seen to be.

Hooper and Young had attempted to address what would have become a crisis in the women's organisation – its decline and isolation. Not only were the Tory women ageing, but the era of the woman with time on her hands was also running out. To attract younger women, and particularly working women, the party women's organisation had to be more political – the party also had to be as sensitive to those women's consciousness as they'd expect elsewhere. But although Thatcherism may not have had a problem about being seen to encourage women to come into politics (although it has not been seen to *do* anything) it would not feel so easy about the party's women's organisation moving into women's politics.

Thatcherism did not mean a stroppy women's movement. Shifts in personnel at the top came to be identified with subtle shifts in orientation. After 1983, when John Selwyn Gummer became party chairman, the work of women slipped from its place near the centre. 'I don't know what Gummer's views were. He never asked for the views of the women, whereas Lord Thorneycroft did, very regularly,' said one of the prominent women involved then. Another felt that

some people thought the women were getting too political. It struck me that it was probably true at the end of Cecil Parkinson's reign that some people thought that we were becoming too politically intense and they wanted someone younger and less political, in the sense of being involved in the women's organisation, and who was lighter-weight, that's the neatest way of putting it.

Janet Young was replaced by Emma Nicholson, and Angela Hooper, who was moved to work on the European elections, wasn't replaced, even though the women felt they'd been led to understand that she would be. She herself resisted the dilution of her department because it meant that the women were losing resources at a point when their work was expanding, as well as a professional full-time post in the women's career structure within the party. Some women didn't believe the assurances that there would be no decline in services to the women. They felt that they were offered no serious explanation, except the usual one – finance. Certainly, party funds were causing concern in the 1980s but many women felt that to amputate women's posts in this period was only subliminally a financial matter. Resistance died; the problem was that the women's national committee was ultimately powerless. 'The women's national committee was concerned, but their leadership didn't react. Basically the committee accepted the line they were sold. It didn't make sense. They probably didn't feel they had any option,' said one of its members.

Another participant recalled restiveness elsewhere in the party which suggested that the financial manoeuvre was a cover for a political manoeuvre:

> I've heard it from some of the men, officers in the party, that we were becoming far too political, and some thought it was wrong that we had a vice-chairman for the women and a chief woman executive, too. They'd say, 'Oh the men don't get that.' But it's not much. And they've got the chairman of the National Union, the director of this, the director of that, everything.

Clearly many women felt that the rest of the party machine was for the men.

'The women were being pushed back,' insisted a member of the women's national committee. 'We'd got too adventurous. They may even try to abolish the women's associations. The last few years have been very difficult because we've had no back-up. There was a bit of a rebellion, oh yes, but it failed – we're all too ladylike.'

'Things really developed under Angela Hooper and Janet Young,' recalled one of the politically ambitious members of the women's national committee. 'But they've slipped back, for instance the business of working parties and researched conferences. It was obvious that ministers came and hadn't bothered to read the documents and they just waffled. So they were stopped. But we should have expected them to take us seriously.'

After the 1984 conference the women complained about the performance of ministers who had not done their homework, but instead of being required to shape up they were relieved of the problem and the old format resumed. That was a defeat for the women and for modernisation. Emma Nicholson was regarded as being complicit in the defeat. She was seen by some as 'lighter-weight', an inexperienced appointment who would accommodate to the party leadership.

Not by politics alone

Emma Nicholson was appointed from outside the women's networks, in which she had not participated until her appointment. But that did not necessarily mean that in the longer term she would operate as an elegant contra against the radicals. Nicholson is a conservative feminist and is nothing if not enthusiastic. But things did change. The new conference format was abandoned, and it reverted to the ritual of resolutions and ministerial turns. Nicholson launched a recruitment drive and she launched a new campaign for women candidates – the campaign, of course, took the form of encouraging women to put themselves forward for the list. Selections were out of their hands. Regarded as an innocent by many of the stalwarts, she came up against the structural resistance to women's power in the party, which could not be overcome by women's will alone. 'She was an innocent, plus she had the right background, that's probably why Maggie put her there,' said one of her colleagues.

> She's in an impossible position. The party from Maggie down is not pro-women. She's not had a lot of support from the top, has she? She has tried to have an impact though, and Maggie wouldn't have wanted that. But she will have encountered barriers she's probably not met before, and which money and background just can't affect. Yes, she will have had access to the Prime Minister, like all the party vice-chairmen. She should have. But in practice what does that mean? Does it really mean promoting women? The answer is no. She hasn't had Maggie at the door with her saying, 'Come on, girls . . .'

Nicholson had her own innovations, however, which seemed initially to avoid challenge and to present to the party the acceptable face of modernisation.

Fringe meetings at the party conferences were about *successful* women. That meant that women's *struggles* were off their agenda, and it meant that the party was presented with the acceptable face of feminism – uncomplaining, smiling, smug even. Typical was the 1985 women's fringe meeting at the party conference about 'Women of Achievement'. A platform of successful ladies was presented to the female audience. 'The first essential to achievement is the will,' the actress Diana Sheridan told them: 'My proudest achievement is to have given birth to a future Conservative MP.' Angela Rumbold, MP said that to succeed in public life they'd need good health and stamina, 'because you're doing at least two jobs, and an ability to laugh at yourself, a supportive and loving family and you only get that if you deserve it'. Janet Young introduced a modest note of feminist caution. When she went into politics, she said, her children were three and five years old, and she was questioned about her personal arrangements. 'I felt it was not up to them to ask – these questions are not addressed to men.' It was, however, mostly merry quips and no anger.

Emma Nicholson, who is not afraid to be forthright when she disagrees with ministers on policies affecting women, is committed to the youth and success format. 'We're going younger and becoming more positive as a result. The response has been that people have said nice things. So presumably it must have made a little difference.' Nice rather than nasty ensured approval among the party managers if not always among the women. If women were to have a high profile in the party then ready-made success rather than the reparation of historic grievances was a surer route. One Parliamentary contender complained privately that this bore down heavily on women like herself, the main breadwinner in her household, responsible not only for keeping her job, but also for keeping her family and her political career on the road singlehandedly. Not surprisingly she was periodically seriously depressed, not just because the load was too heavy for any woman, but because there was no room in the Tory milieux to say so. She had to carry the load, and the knowledge of the load, alone.

The point was to get *modern* women, young and professional. But modernisation meant the audience rather than the form and content of the women's organisation. The younger women's conference in Solihull in 1985 didn't particularly talk about younger women. Its agenda wasn't job opportunities, parenthood and childcare, the law, control over fertility, men, or even women, although there was a heterodox argument over Victoria Gillick's campaign against teenage contraception and an inevitable bout of law and order: rape and child murder were invoked by a supporter of capital punishment while Anna McCurley, the irreverent Scottish MP, announced that she'd voted against capital punishment in the Commons and had opposed it ever since the death of a woman, Ruth Ellis. 'I recall the story of her last days and I got my feelings from that. It's not a deterrent and never was. In a humane society we must have other ways of coping.' A sister MP, Marion Roe, said she had voted for capital punishment because of growing violence on the picketlines and in the streets. 'Women are afraid to open the door because they might be mugged or raped.'

It was the old agenda, the old ministerial star turns. These were the 'Next' women; there were no jeans, but there weren't the home-knits or the eternal Jaeger either. The uniform insofar as there was one was the feminised executive suit, blouse and bow. They were very upset when the *Sunday Times* report carried pictures of the only two women wearing hats – real Tory ladies no longer wear hats – but even these weren't the hair-hiding felt hats, they were the cheeky pillboxes of the woman who dresses for a party conference as if it weren't a congregation but a cocktail party. It could have been argued that this was what moving into the mainstream meant – but in fact it largely meant that it wasn't about women at all. It was a kind of Americanisation without the politics – the United States' professional women take their rights very seriously. A new departure was the 'High Flyers' conference organised in 1986 for successful women – going for a new Yuppie image, and yet doggedly anachronistic: little debate and much piety from the platform. Norman Tebbit's speech, which was no doubt intended to encourage women to stand for Parliament, prompted little response during the conference itself but outside the silence erupted into furious dissent. 'It was the "come on girls you're not trying" routine, it's just an insult,' complained a Tory activist in middle management who had been searching in vain for Parliamentary selection. Some of the non-Tory women who had been invited were amazed by the acquiescent atmosphere – and some left after lunch. 'God, it was awful,' said a publishing managing director, one of the evacuees.

The modernisation was a chimera – it may have changed the *audience* but it didn't change the *agenda*. It reformed neither form nor content. In such an authoritarian party as the Conservative Party, the absence of an acceptable opportunity to challenge contained the whole exercise within an antique formula.

The annual women's conferences were still largely addressed by men. Perhaps that's because the format demanded Very Important Persons and they were all men, except, of course, for the one and only Most Important Person. I recall listening to one of her speeches to the women's conference and murmuring naïvely to another woman reporter that there was nothing in the speech about women. That was because it was a *political* speech, she parried. But the Young-Hooper era had raised expectations and encouraged women to have a sense of who they really were in the party. 'We are the party of the people,' Tessa Holroyd from Colne Valley told the 1985 women's conference. But the leaders had to come down and listen to the grassroots she said. Aspiring Parliamentary candidate Dr Elizabeth Cottrell reiterated the theme: women were the party's 'mouths, hands, feet'. Corinne Lovell from the New Forest complained that women were the poor souls who had to explain away the party's bungles on the doorstep. The only voice of outright feminist criticism came from Leah Hertz, who seemed to be the only woman wearing trousers, and who chided not only Emma Nicholson for her over-optimistic representation of the women's achievements, but the party for its failure to let women represent women. 'Who is this grassroots?' she wondered.

> It is appropriate to call on the government to call on more
> women to help women run the country. But not all
> Conservative women are satisfied with the role of women in
> the party as Emma is. Fifty-two per cent – they're women.
> We talk about one nation – women are part of this nation.

Transposing the Disraelian case for Conservative unification of all classes to embrace the divided sexes, she declared: 'Involve more women in the running of this nation – so that we're truly representative of one nation.'

Much of this was directed not only to the women themselves but to their benign patriarch, Lord Whitelaw, whose credentials established him as coming from impeccable government stock. His life, said the chairman, was Army, Parliament and a thorough knowledge of country life. No woman could compete with that. He flattered and caressed the speakers, including among them two

Parliamentary contenders: 'I've fought ten general elections and I'd not have liked to have either of those ladies, I'm very sorry for the men who'd meet them in the next elections,' he said, seductively. But he cut through the codes of the debate. 'Presentation cannot alone be the answer. I detect that bad presentation is a coded message that people don't much like the policy. The policies have to be soundly based. No amount of good presentation can paper over cracks and divisions in our own ranks.' It was as if he could say it but they couldn't. But, of course, what he did not do was encourage them to come out into the open, for that would have been unthinkable. Nor did he engage with the problem of women's power implied in some of the speeches and asserted by Leah Hertz.

By 1986 even coded dissent was not to be heard at the women's conference. The rigidity of the Tory conference format was revealed when Clwyd representative Heather Collins embarrassed many and thrilled even more when she complained that 'we have been brainwashed into believing we live in a multi-racial society, but do we also have to believe that everything Britain does should be put down like an ageing cat.' Transgressing Tory rules of respectable racism she warned that Asian girls were committing suicide because of parental intransigence and that Britain was 'committing ethnic suicide on the altar of the Race Relations Act'. It wasn't what the platform wanted to hear, and several black representatives in the hall shook their heads in disapproval; but none rose to counter-attack, or perhaps to risk the wrath of the majority. The conference could not accommodate an impromptu argument. Afterwards, during a break, Asian representative Zarina Ahmed from West Marling in the South-East, who is involved in welfare work among local Asian women, said, 'I think she had some wrong information – there are suicides in every country. I should have gone to speak but you've got to register yourself beforehand.'

Neither was there a women's agenda. Chancellor Nigel Lawson introduced a long-awaited discussion on personal taxation in the wake of his Green Paper, which he suggested ended discrimination against the married woman by proposing a transferable tax allowance. The debate was desultory; it was as if the women were hardly ready for this moment which had been so long coming.

Nicholson's confidence about her connection with the 'real world' – she was a single, working woman, appointed from outside the party structures – no doubt steeled her commitment to bringing in the 'new woman', primarily the working woman, even if her relative inexperience left her imprisoned within the old discourse. Nonetheless, her combativity over child benefit must have put paid to the notion that she was only the cipher for the party bosses. She has also defended her conviction that there should be parity for part-time working women in terms and conditions – which went entirely against the grain of Tory policy in the 1980s. During her reign, working parties on the Warnock Report on reproductive technology and on Victoria Gillick have held the liberal centre against the moral right. In policy terms, there was no retreat further to the right during the 1980s among the Tory women; in fact, they have moved with the mainstream among women in general.

Thatcherism came too late

The Hooper–Young format would probably – I think inevitably – have confirmed the party managers' worst fears that the women were getting uppity, that they were dissenters, perhaps even rebels with a cause of their own. That was because the format devolved research and consciousness-raising among the area activists, and on the longer term it could have generated a relatively autonomous agenda among the women. Even without it, it is arguable whether by the 1980s the rank and file women could be contained comfortably by the moral right. That is one of the reasons why any serious attempt to reverse the so-called permissive sexual legislation of the 1960s would have provoked contumely within the party. Thatcher may have brought the women's anti-sex and violence tradition into the fold, and yet Thatcherism came too late, it could not constrain women's straining ambitions, and it could no more provide a moral agenda for the modern Conservative women than its predecessor.

Increasingly, Tory women are offered identities and identifications which prohibit any singular form of femininity and which, therefore, challenge the Tory tendency to essentialise women, to define women by the domestic and the biological. The availability of competing ideologies is also reflected in the way many Conservative women I interviewed supported, for example, both abortion and Victoria Gillick's campaign against teenage contraception.

Women's experience is coded within the dominant ideologies of Conservatism. In the absence of a political prospectus designed by the women themselves – and it would necessarily be a dissenting programme, for at the very least, women's aspirations for political power have been thwarted within the Conservative Party rather more than in any of the other major political parties – women fitted themselves into the 'master' discourses. They buried themselves in borrowed causes.[6]

Law and order is the paradigm: it contains Tory women's stream of consciousness as the victims of men. Unlike the late nineteenth- and early twentieth-century feminist movements against the sexual abuse of women, whether represented by the social purists like Josephine Butler and the Tory Frances Power Cobbe, or the more radical Women's Freedom League, what is not, and has not been part of Conservative women's consciousness for the last fifty years, is the political reform of masculinity. Not surprisingly, perhaps, in the absence of a feminist ambience, Tory women have located their feminine grievances in the image of woman as a victim, not only of men but of the pathologies of nature: only men rape, but only mad men rape.

During the era of Thatcherism, women found their experience affirmed in some measure by another politics – by feminism. Whatever Tory Conservative women thought about feminism, the women's movement's impact on politics was to re-arrange the questions that women could ask of political parties so that women could begin to contemplate their own condition as citizens with unrequited rights and values.

The best party for women?

Many of the women with whom I talked did not know that the Conservative Party had tended to enjoy a bigger margin of support among women than the Labour Party. 'I'm surprised. I've no idea why women vote Conservative,' said farmer's wife Brenda Beaver rather typically.

Some did believe that the Tories were best for women. 'I always thought the Conservatives were better for women,' said Fiona Younger, a neighbouring farmer's wife.

'The Conservatives do most for women, they seem to have more women on the council and in Parliament. Women have a better chance in the Tory Party,' commented Birmingham shopworker, Carol McKurniss.

That was borne out for some others who felt, as a Midlands housewife put it, that 'the Conservative Party has put a woman up there at last. Margaret Thatcher has done most by being there and standing up to them.' Standing up to whom? 'Men!'

But the majority did not believe that either the Tories or anyone else were particularly good for women. 'Let's be honest, it's only in the last twenty years that women have managed to enter the male bastions in all parties,' said Wendy Mitchell, a London councillor and member of the party's women's national committee.

'None of them are very keen on women,' said Elsie Webb, a retired woman living in Northumbria.

'The Conservative Party hasn't done more for women, not even with Margaret Thatcher,' said Judy Worth, a Birmingham house-wife.

'The Conservatives have never done anything for women. None of the parties is any better. Women don't really matter to them. There's not a lot of difference, they never take women seriously. It always feels like women are being put down,' said Lucy Robson. 'There's things that women need, that women would have more feeling about than men. They should listen to women more.'

'Labour has done nothing for women. They don't have a place for women, they expect women to make the tea and do the leafletting, but the fun, the power, that's not for the women. And the Tories, they're just as bad,' said Lorna Walters, a Cumbrian civil servant.

A Northumbrian woman, re-training as a secretary, Eleanor Hartshorn, who was brought up as a Tory but is changing her mind, reckoned that 'Labour is probably best for women, though I don't know why. Labour benefits us, we were never so badly off under a Labour government. I'm very involved in things like raising money for Ethiopia and no party has stood out for that sort of thing.'

'Labour isn't attractive because it's so masculine. The men come over very male and macho and I think women would think that, despite its efforts to get women's committees,' said an active member of the Women's Institutes. 'The Conservative Party doesn't have rows, so it appears loyal, whereas Labour appears to be one series of punch-ups – though I'm beginning to feel that about the Tories, all those ghastly uncaring men. No party appeals to me as a woman.'

That Conservative women should see their party like this exposes the political void created by the subordination of women within Conservatism: the party *organises* women as women, and yet *disorganises* their political resistance and their potential power.

Given the strength of the Tories' roots among women, what

explains the apparent incoherence of Tory women's ideology, and their strategies as a subordinate sex? Gramsci was interested in exactly this dynamic: how conservative ideas embedded in common sense appear obvious and natural, and how they assimilate a real experience of power. When your view of the world is not 'critical and coherent' – and it can't be if you are disorganised and defeated – if your ideas are 'disjointed and episodic', then according to Gramsci you know yourself as 'a product of historical processes which have deposited in you an infinity of traces, without leaving an inventory'.[7] This kind of process makes Conservative women's common sense *ad hoc* and improvised, often below the threshold of consciousness, drawing both on patriarchal ideas, proto-feminist and even feminist ideas.

The language of common sense modifies the experience of powerlessness and reveals the quest for strength and survival in the face of defeat among susbordinate social groups. 'When you don't have the initiative in the struggle and the struggle itself eventually comes to be identified with a series of defeats, mechanical resistance becomes a tremendous force of moral resistance, of cohesion and of patient and obstinate perseverance.'[8] Conservative women do not have the initiative within their political universe, and yet they have their women's world, and this dominion is their secret life. It never comes out into the open, because in it, to paraphrase Janice Winship's descriptions of the ideology of femininity, they justify their lack of power as well as recognising it as such.[9] And within their world they share the sub-culture of the subordinate sex, which transcends the boundaries of class and political affiliation. Their politics manoeuvre 'within and against masculine hegemony'.[10]

Everyone acknowledges that women are the spine of the party, but what do they join the party for? What does the party do for them? For many Tory women, the party seems to be less about politics than a way of being *in* the social world. They are in the political party and yet out of politics. Why? Perhaps it is that the conventions of their proper place, the feminine role, prescribe their de-politicisation and express their alienation from politics. After all, it really has little to do with them, it is not *about* them. So, they are both *aligned and yet alienated*.

Hitherto the party has enabled them to let their alienation lie. But the last decade has made new demands of the women among the rank and file. In the 1970s and 1980s all the ideological movements of the party have come typically from the top. Thatcherism appeared to speak the language of the rank and file's common sense, but far from changing the balance of power between leaders and led, it centralised power within the party and it failed to redistribute power between men and women.

Women's relationship to the political agenda has been touched not only by Thatcherism (and Thatcher herself) but by feminism. Feminism may not describe the politics of Tory women, but Tory women more than most have a gendered politics, and these days that cannot exist entirely outside the frame of feminism. Thatcherism and feminism are two of the forces which have impacted on the lives of women in the 1970s and 1980s. Feminism inhabits the same household as femininity: it is about naming the contradictions of 'feminine' experience and it seeks to transform aspects of the experience of subordination into *feminist strength*.[11]

Conservative women's politics, however, are a tactical calculation of the limits of challenge. Their politics always carry a pessimistic estimate of the risk of calumny – after all, they know their enemy. But the Tory woman is no victim, she can often appear coy and yet controlling, evasive and yet strong. When she intervenes she covers her tracks. She feels she is the prisoner of fate. Her subversions are surreptitious, she rarely comes out into the open because she cannot risk the humiliation of defeat, and she already knows what that feels like.

In the aftermath of everyday defeat, which is part of the folk memory of the subordinate sex, 'a strong activity of the will is present even here, directly intervening in the "force of circumstance", but only implicitly, and in a veiled hand and, as it were, shamefaced manner'.[12] A key word for Gramsci is fatalism, which for him is 'nothing other than the clothing worn by real and active will when in a weak position'.[13] Fatalism is the frock the Tory woman wears.

Women are everywhere in a weak position and yet are not weak. Women are subordinate and yet are strong. That describes the Tory woman.

References to Conservative Party conferences are taken from reports in the Conservative Party Archive at the Bodleian Library, Oxford.

The Primrose League records, publications of the British Housewives League, the Selborne Papers and the Sandars Papers can also be found at the Bodleian Library.

The Catherine Marshall Papers are in the Carlisle Record Office.

Conservative Central Office papers are designated as CCO.

1 The Primrose League

1 Janet Robb, *The Primrose League 1883–1906*, New York 1968.
2 *Ibid.*, pp. 22–3.
3 M. Ostrogorski, *Democracy and the Organisation of Political Parties*, London 1902, p. 533.
4 Robert Blake, *The Conservative Party from Peel to Thatcher*, London 1985, p. 148.
5 *Ibid.*, p. 156.
6 *Ibid.*, p. 149.
7 *Ibid.*, p. 156.
8 *The Reminiscences of Lady Dorothy Nevill*, ed. Ralph Nevill, London 1906, pp. 285–6.
9 Ralph G. Martin, *Jennie, the Life of Lady Randolph Churchill: The Romantic Years 1845–1895*, London 1969, p. 172.
10 Nevill, *op. cit.*, p. 286.
11 Disraeli, *Sybil* (Penguin edition), London 1980, p. 165.
12 Mrs George Cornwallis West, *The Reminiscences of Lady Randolph Churchill*, London 1908, p. 98.
13 Martin, *op. cit.*, p. 173.
14 Cornwallis West, p. 124.
15 *Ibid.*, p. 124.
16 *Ibid.*, p. 124.
17 *Ibid.*, p. 125.
18 *Ibid.*, p. 128.
19 Ostrogorski, *op. cit.*, p. 558.
20 H. J. Hanham, *Elections and the Party Machine*, London 1959, p. xvii.
21 Martin Pugh, *The Making of Modern British Politics 1867–1939*, p. 15.
22 *Ibid.*, p. 15.
23 *Ibid.*, p. 50.
24 *Morning Post*, 25 May 1887.
25 Robb, *op. cit.*, p. 94.
26 Hanham, *op. cit.*, pp. 12–13.

27   *Ibid.*, p. 6.
28   Robb, *op. cit.*, p. 135.
29   *Ibid.*, p. 135.
30   Ostrogorski, *op. cit.*, p. 535.
31   Robb, *op. cit.* p. 50.
32   Ostrogorski, *op. cit.*, p. 534.
33   Robb, *op. cit.*, p. 50.
34   C. W. Radcliffe Cook, *Four Years in Parliament*, quoted in Ostrogorski, *op. cit.*, p. 543.
35   Ostrogorski, *op. cit.*, p. 533.
36   Cornwallis-West, *op. cit.*, p. 98.
37   Robb, *op. cit.*, p. 92.
38   *Ibid.*, pp. 120–1.
39   Frederick Willis, *101 Jubilee Road: A Book of London Yesterdays*, London 1948, p. 80.
40   Frances Power Cobbe, *Life of Frances Power Cobbe as Told by Herself*, London 1904, p. 610.
41   Lady Montagu, at the AGM of the Primrose League Grand Council, May 1888.

2   The Olde Worlde

1   Brian Harrison, *Separate Spheres*, London 1978, p. 115.
2   *Primrose League Gazette*, November 1909.
3   Constance Rover, *Women's Suffrage and Party Politics in Britain 1866–1914*, London 1967, p. 171.
4   Harrison, *op. cit.*, p. 128.
5   *Ibid.*, p. 128.
6   *Ibid.*, p. 128.
7   *Ibid.*, p. 129.
8   Rover, *op. cit.*, p. 172.
9   *Ibid.*, p. 172.
10   Rover, *op. cit.*, p. 173.
11   *Primrose League Gazette*, January 1912.
12   Harrison, *op. cit.*, p. 83.
13   Rover, *op. cit.*, p. 175.
14   Harrison, *op. cit.*, p. 82.
15   *Ibid.*, p. 84.
16   Charles H. Roberts, *The Radical Countess*, London 1962, p. 116.
17   *Ibid.*, p. 117.
18   George Dangerfield, *The Strange Death of Liberal England*, London 1983, p. 136.
19   Ann Toulmin, *Through the Decades, Women's Liberal Federation*, London 1986.
20   Dangerfield, *op. cit.*, p. 173.
21   *Primrose League Gazette*, March 1908.
22   *Primrose League Gazette*, November 1909.
23   Rover, *op. cit.*, pp. 108–10.
24   *Primrose League Gazette*, December 1910.
25   The Marchioness of Londonderry, *Retrospect*, London 1938, p. 105.
26   *Ibid.*, p. 105.
27   *Ibid.*, pp. 105–6.
28   *Ibid.*, p. 108.
29   *Ibid.*, p. 127.
30   Countess of Selborne's Papers 1912–18.
31   *Ibid.*
32   Maud, Countess of Selborne to Catherine Marshall, 7 February 1912.

33   Catherine Marshall Papers D/Mar/3/14.
34   *Letters of Constance Lytton*, edited and arranged by Betty Balfour, London 1925, p. 205.
35   *Ibid.*, p. 219.
36   *Ibid.*, p. 222.
37   *Ibid.*, p. 134.
38   *Ibid.*, p. 223.
39   *Ibid.*, p. 224.
40   Violet Markham, *Return Passage*, London 1935, p. 157.
41   *Ibid.*, p. 96.
42   *Ibid.*, p. 97.
43   *Ibid.*, p. 98.
44   *Ibid.*, p. 98.
45   Letter to John Sandars, Sandars Papers January–July 1906.
46   *Ibid.*
47   *Primrose League Gazette*, May 1910.
48   Norman Lewis, *Jackdaw Cake*, London 1985, pp. 45–6.
49   *Home and Politics* No. 4, 1920.
50   *Home and Politics* No. 7, 1921.
51   *Ibid.*
52   *Ibid.*
53   *Ibid.*, No. 6, 1921.
54   *Ibid.*, No. 43, 1924.
55   *Ibid.*, No. 55, 1925.
56   *Ibid.*
57   Bill Schwarz, 'The Language and Constitutionalism: Baldwinite Conservatism', in *Formations of Nation and People*, London 1984, p. 2.
58   *Ibid.*, p. 2.
59   *Home and Politics*, No. 14, 1922.
60   Schwarz, p. 2.
61   *Ibid.*, p. 16.
62   Sarah Boston, *Women Workers and the Trade Union Movement*, London 1980, pp. 126–32.
63   Londonderry, *op. cit.*, p. 110.
64   *The Popular View*, June 1921.
65   Boston, *op. cit.*, p. 132.
66   Barbara Taylor, '"The Men Are as Bad as Their Masters . . ." Socialism, Feminism and Sexual Antagonism in the London Tailoring Trade in the 1830s', Judith L. Newton, Mary P. Ryan and Judith R. Walkowitz (eds.), *Sex and Class in Women's History*, London 1983.
67   Lewis Minkin, *The Labour Party Conference*, Manchester 1980, p. 256.
68   Schwarz, *op. cit.*, p. 8.
69   *Home and Politics* No. 1, 1920.
70   *Ibid.*
71   *Home and Politics* No. 4, 1921.
72   *Home and Politics* No. 43, 1924.
73   *Ibid.*
74   *Home and Politics* No. 44, 1924.
75   *Home and Politics* No. 6, 1921.
76   *Home and Politics* No. 55, 1925.
77   Boston, *op. cit.*, pp. 155–6.
78   *Home and Politics* No. 42, 1924.
79   *Home and Politics* No. 62, 1926.

80   Anna Davin, 'Imperialism and Motherhood', *History Workshop Journal*, No. 5, 1978.
81   *Home and Politics* No. 43, 1924.
82   *Home and Politics* No. 49, 1925.
83   *Ibid.*
84   Margaret Llewellyn Davies, *Life As We Have Known It*, Co-operative Working Women (Virago edition), London 1977, p. xii.
85   *Ibid.*, p. 65.
86   *Ibid.*, p. xiv.
87   *Home and Politics*, No. 7, 1921.
88   Robert Blake, *The Conservative Party from Peel to Thatcher*, London 1985, p. 237.
89   *Ibid.*, p. 238.

3   The New World
1   Lewis Minkin, *The Labour Party Conference*, Manchester 1980, p. 256.
2   *Daily Worker*, 2 January 1947.
3   Denise Riley, *War in the Nursery*, London 1983, p. 133.
4   *Daily Worker*, 10 June 1947.
5   Riley, *op. cit.*, p. 130.
6   Sarah Boston, *Women Workers and the Trade Unions*, London 1980, p. 235.
7   *Ibid.*, p. 223.
8   *Ibid.*, p. 223.
9   *Daily Herald*, 12 June 1947.
10   *Daily Herald*, 13 June 1947.
11   *Daily Herald*, 6 June 1947.
12   *Housewives Today*, No. 1, April 1947.
13   *Ibid.*
14   *British Housewives League Newsletter*, No. 6, p. 11.
15   *Housewives Today*, No. 1.
16   Kenneth O. Morgan, *Labour in Power 1945–51*, Oxford 1984, p. 369.
17   Edith Summerskill, *A Woman's World*, London 1967, p. 91.
18   *Ibid.*, p. 91.
19   *Housewives Today*, No. 7, p. 9.
20   Michael Foot, *Aneurin Bevan 1945–60*, London 1975, p. 318.
21   *Ibid.*, p. 318.
22   *The Times*, 7 June 1947.
23   *Daily Worker*, 7 June 1947.
24   *Daily Herald*, 13 June 1947.
25   *The Times*, 7 June 1947.
26   *Daily Worker*, 7 June 1947.
27   *Ibid.*
28   *Daily Worker*, 9 June 1947.
29   *Daily Herald*, 8 September 1947.
30   *Daily Herald*, 12 September 1947.
31   *Housewives Today*, No. 7, 1948.
32   *Housewives Today*, No. 8, 1948.
33   *Housewives Today*, No. 14, 1950.
34   *Housewives Today*, Vol. II, No. 5, 1947.
35   Conservative Party Archive, CCO/3/2/39–49.
36   CCO 3/119–25.
37   CCO 3/2/39–48.
38   *Ibid.*
39   CCO 3/119–25.

40   David Butler, *The British General Election of 1951*, London 1952, p. 62.
41   Michael Foot, *op. cit.*, London 1975, p. 76.
42   *Ibid.*, p. 72.
43   *Ibid.*, p. 77.
44   *Ibid.*, p. 83.
45   *Onward*, May 1954.
46   *Onward*, July 1954.
47   *Onward*, September 1954.
48   Sarah Boston, *op. cit.*, pp. 260–1.
49   *Ibid.*, pp. 244–51.
50   *Onward*, July 1956.
51   *Onward*, July 1954.
52   *Onward*, November 1953.
53   *Onward*, December 1953.
54   *Onward*, July 1956.
55   Andrew Gamble, *The Conservative Nation*, London 1974, p. 81.
56   Michael Tracey and David Morrison, *Whitehouse*, London 1979, p. 24.
57   Mary Whitehouse, *Who Does She Think She Is?*, London 1971, pp. 35–6.
58   *Ibid.*, p. 39.
59   *Ibid.*, p. 44.
60   Andrew Gamble, *op. cit.*, p. 102.
61   Janice Winship, 'A Woman's World: "Woman" – an ideology of femininity', in Women's Studies Group, Birmingham Centre for Contemporary Cultural Studies (eds), *Women Take Issue*, London 1978, p. 133.
62   David Butler and Anthony King, *The British General Election of 1964*, London 1965, p. 7.
63   *Ibid.*, p. 55.
64   Anna Coote and Beatrix Campbell, *Sweet Freedom*, London 1982, p. 150.
65   David Butler and Dennis Kavannagh, *The British General Election of October 1974*, London 1975, p. 325.
66   Andrew Gamble, 'Thatcher and Conservative Politics', in Stuart Hall and Martin Jacques, eds., *The Politics of Thatcherism*, London 1985, p. 111.
67   David Butler and Dennis Kavannagh, *The British General Election of 1979*, London 1980, p. 326.
68   Conservative Central Office.
69   CCO, 21 May 1975.
70   Butler and Kavannagh, *op. cit.*, p. 326.
71   *Ibid.*, p. 57.
72   *Ibid.*, p. 35.

4 Patriarchal Polls

1   Robert Worcester, 'Where Are we Now?' in *Working Woman*, April 1985, p. 57.
2   David Butler and Donald Stokes, *Political Change in Britain: Forces Shaping Electoral Choice*, London 1969, p. 70.
3   Mark Abrams and Richard Rose, *Must Labour Lose?*, London 1960.
4   Butler and Stokes, *op. cit.*, p. 70.
5   Susan Bourque and Jean Grossholtz, 'Politics an unnatural practice: political science looks at female participation', in *Women and the Public Sphere*, ed. Michele Stanworth and Janet Siltanen, London 1984, p. 104.
6   Butler and Stokes, *op. cit.*, p. 70.
7   Abrams and Rose, *op. cit.*, p. 66.
8   *Ibid.*, p. 66.

9   Murray Goot and Elizabeth Reid, 'Women: if not apolitical then conservative', in Stanworth and Siltanen, *op. cit.*, p. 129.
10   *Ibid.*, p. 123.
11   Patrick Dunleavy and Christopher T. Husbands, *British Democracy at the Cross-roads*, London 1985, p. 127.
12   *Ibid.*, p. 129.
13   *Ibid.*, pp. 130–1.
14   *Ibid.*, pp. 128–9.
15   Anthony Heath, Roger Jowell and John Curtice, *How Britain Votes*, Oxford 1985, p. 23.
16   *Ibid.* pp. 21–2.
17   *Ibid.*, p. 22.
18   *New Statesman*, 9 November 1984.
19   Peter Kellner, *Observer*, 5 October 1986.
20   Sue Lees, *Losing Out*, London 1985, p. 10.
21   Evans Witt, 'What the Republicans Have Learned About Women', *Public Opinion*, October–November 1985.
22   *Ibid.*
23   John Ross, *Thatcher and Friends*, London 1983, p. 80.
24   Jill Hills, 'Britain', in Joni Lovenduski (ed), *The Politics of the Second Electorate*, London 1981, p. 16.
25   *Ibid.*, p. 138.

5   War and Peace

1   *Guardian*, 26 September 1986.
2   *Daily Telegraph*, 14 April 1986.
3   Peter Kellner, 'Revealed: How Sex Influences Politics', *New Statesman*, 9 November 1984.

6   The Fugitives

1   John Berger, *Ways of Seeing*, London 1972, p. 47.
2   *Ibid.*, p. 46.
3   *Daily Mail*, 9 December 1985.
4   Islington Crime Survey, 1986.
5   Janice Winship, 'A Woman's World: "Woman" – an ideology of femininity', in Women's Studies Group, Birmingham Centre for Cultural Studies (eds), *Women Take Issue*, London 1978, p. 134.
6   *Ibid.*, p. 134.

7   The Moral Crusade

1   Ann Oakley, *Housewife*, London 1976, p. 6.
2   Beatrix Campbell, interview with Baroness Platt, *City Limits* No. 106, 14–20 October 1983.
3   Patrick Jenkin, in Melanie Phillips, 'Maggie's Family Policy, A Plot Against Women?,' *Cosmopolitan*, May 1983.
4   Anna Davin, 'Imperialism and Motherhood', *History Workshop Journal* No. 5, Spring 1978.
5   Ros Franey, *Poor Law*, London 1983.
6   Quoted in Anna Coote and Beatrix Campbell, *Sweet Freedom*, London 1982, p. 97.
7   Margaret Thatcher, in *Woman's Own*, 6 December 1980.
8   Ian Gilmour, *Inside Right*, London 1978, p. 148.
9   *Ibid.*, p. 149.

10   Tom Fitzgerald, 'The New Right and the Family', in M. Londy, D. Boswell and J. Clarke (eds), *Social Policy and Social Welfare*, London 1983.

11   Roger Scruton, *The Meaning of Conservatism*, London 1980, p. 27.

12   *Ibid.*, p. 26.

13   Ferdinand Mount, *The Subversive Family*, London 1982, p. 162.

14   *Ibid.*, p. 163.

15   *Ibid.*, p. 161.

16   Barbara Taylor, *Eve and the New Jerusalem*, London 1983, p. 285.

17   Barbara Taylor, '"The Men Are as Bad as Their Masters" . . . Socialism, Feminism and Sexual Antagonism in the London Tailoring Trade in the Early 1830s', *Feminist Studies* Vol. 5 No. 1, 1979, p. 214.

18   Mount, pp. 173–4.

19   *Ibid.*, p. 175.

20   Sir Alfred Sherman, *The Times*, 21 June 1984.

21   Digby Anderson and Graham Dawson, 'Popular But Unrepresented: The Curious Case of the Normal Family', in Digby Anderson and Graham Dawson (eds), *Family Portraits*, London 1986, p. 14.

22   Mary Kenny, 'The Ideological Battle Over the Family', in Anderson and Dawson, *op. cit.*

23   Patricia Morgan, 'Feminist Attempts to Sack the Father: A Case of Unfair Dismissal?', in Anderson and Dawson, *op. cit.*, pp. 38–61.

24   Davin, *op. cit.*

25   Robert Chester, 'The Myth of the Disappearing Family' in Anderson and Dawson, *op. cit.*, pp. 19–29.

26   Tom Fitzgerald, *op. cit.*, p. 50.

27   *Child Care and Equal Opportunities: Some Policy Perspectives*, Equal Opportunities Commission, HMSO 1986.

28   *Daily Telegraph*, 14 November 1985.

29   Victoria Gillick, *Dear Mrs Gillick*, Basingstoke 1985, p. 7.

30   *Ibid.*, p. 8.

31   *Ibid.*, p. 220.

32   *Ibid.*, p. 220.

33   *Ibid.*, p. 108.

34   *Ibid.*, pp. 71–2.

35   *Ibid.*, p. 22.

36   *Ibid.*, p. 98.

37   *Ibid.*

38   *Ibid.*, p. 49.

39   Jacqueline Rose, *The Case of Peter Pan*, London 1984, p. 1.

40   *Ibid.*, p. 9.

41   *Ibid.*, p. 8.

42   Gillick, *op. cit.*, p. 33.

43   Wendy Hollway, 'Fitting Work', in Julian Henriques *et al* (eds), *Changing the Subject*, London 1984, p. 231.

44   Gillick, *op. cit.*, p. 97.

45   Shere Hite, *The Hite Report*, London 1977, p. 232.

46   Hite, *ibid.*, p. 384. See also Beatrix Campbell, 'Feminist Sexual Politics: Now You See It Now You Don't', *Feminist Review* No. 5, 1980; and in Mary Evans, *The Woman Question*, London 1982.

47   Rose, p. 16.

48   Judith Walkowitz, *Prostitution and Victorian Society*, Cambridge 1980, p. 256.

49   Gillick, *op. cit.*, p. 9.

50   Antonio Gramsci, *Selections from the Prison Notebooks*, London 1982, p. 321.

51   *Ibid.*, p. 324.
52   Linda Gordon and Ellen DuBois, 'Seeking Ecstasy on the Battlefield', in Carole Vance (ed.), *Pleasure and Danger*, London 1984, p. 32; also in *Feminist Review* No. 13, 1983.
53   Stuart Hall, Introduction to James Donald and Stuart Hall (eds) *Politics and Ideology*, London 1986, pp. ix–xx.
54   *Ibid.*.
55   Gillick, *op. cit.*, p. 8.
56   Hall, *op. cit.*, p. ix–xx.

8   Equal in the Sight of God

1   *Employment Gazette*, October 1985.
2   *The Fact About Women Is . . .*, Equal Opportunities Commission, London 1986.
3   *Hansard*, 20 July 1983.
4   Ann Wickham, 'Engendering Social Policy in the EEC', *m/f* No. 4, London 1980.
5   *Ibid.*
6   Wickham's paper was written before the extension of mothers' rights to men, thereby challenging notions of what it is to be a man.
7   For feminist debates on the family wage and collective bargaining, see Beatrix Campbell and Valerie Charlton, 'Work to Rule', in *No Turning Back*, London 1981; 'United We Fall', *Red Rag*, London 1979; Anne Phillips, *Hidden Hands*, London 1983.
8   House of Lords Committee on the EEC, *Leave for Family Reasons*, HMSO, February 1985.
9   Sally Holtermann, *The Costs of Implementing Parental Leave in Great Britain*, Equal Opportunities Commission, London 1986.
10 *Guardian*, 28 October 1986.
11 W. W. Daniels, *Maternity Rights: The Experience of Women*, Policy Studies Institute, London 1986.
12 *The Times*, 12 June 1985.
13 *Hansard*, 11 March 1985.
14 Juliet Mitchell, 'Women and Equality', in *Rights and Wrongs of Women*, London 1976.
15 Ivy Papps, *For Love or Money*, Institute of Economic Affairs, London 1980.
16 *Ibid.*
17 *Ibid.*
18 Roger Jowell and Sharon Witherspoon (eds.), *British Social Attitudes 1985*, Social and Community Planning, London 1985.

9   To Be or Not to Be a Woman

1   Stuart Hall, 'The Great Moving Right Show', in Stuart Hall and Martin Jacques (eds), *The Politics of Thatcherism*, London 1983, p. 19.
2   Margaret Thatcher, 21 May 1975, CCO.
3   Margaret Thatcher, 28 June 1975, CCO.
4   Hugo Young and Anne Sloman, *The Thatcher Phenomenon*, London 1986, pp. 67–8.
5   *Ibid.*, pp. 63–4.
6   Patrick Cosgrave, *Thatcher: The First Term*, London 1985, p. 5.
7   Margaret Thatcher, 4 July 1977, CCO.
8   *Woman's Own*, 6 December 1981.
9   Charlotte Brunsden, 'It is well known that by nature women are inclined to be

rather personal' in Women's Studies Group, Birmingham Centre for Cultural
Studies, *op. cit.*, pp. 18–35.
10 Jenny Junor, *Margaret Thatcher*, London 1984, p. 35.
11 Margaret Thatcher, quoted in Melanie Phillips, 'Maggie's Family Policy: A Plot
Against Women', *Cosmopolitan*, May 1983.
12 Junor, p. 40.
13 Junor, p. 3.
14 *Ibid.*
15 *Ibid.*
16 Margaret Thatcher, 5 June 1985, CCO.
17 Margaret Thatcher, 31 January 1976, CCO.
18 Cosgrave, *op. cit.*, p. 5.

10 **The Candidate**
1 Elisabeth Sturges-Jones and Susan Hewitt (eds.), *Women in Politics*, CCO,
London 1980.
2 David Butler and Donald Stokes, *The British General Election of 1983*, London
1984, p. 194.
3 *New Society*, 3 October 1986.

11 **Sex and Power**
1 Andrew Gamble, *The Conservative Nation*, London 1984, p. 13.
2 Wendy Hollway, 'Fitting Work', in Julian Henriques *et al*, *Changing the Subject*,
London 1984, pp. 232–3.
3 *Ibid.*, pp. 232–3.
4 *Ibid.*
5 *Ibid.*, p. 229.
6 Antonio Gramsci, *Selections from the Prison Notebooks*, London 1982,
pp. 336–7.
7 *Ibid.*, p. 324.
8 *Ibid.*, p. 336.
9 Janice Winship, 'A Woman's Word: "Woman" – an ideology of femininity' in
Women's Studies Group, Birmingham Centre for Cultural Studies, *op. cit.*,
p. 137.
10 *Ibid.*, p. 134.
11 *Ibid.*
12 Gramsci, *op. cit.*, p. 336.
13 *Ibid.*, p. 336.

Index